Dr Daniel Freeman is one of the UK's leading clinical psychologists. He is an MRC Senior Clinical Fellow at the Institute of Psychiatry, King's College London, and a consultant clinical psychologist in the South London and Maudsley NHS Foundation Trust. He was awarded the 2008 May Davidson prize by the British Psychological Society, which marks 'an outstanding contribution to the development of clinical psychology'.

Jason Freeman is a writer and editor in the areas of popular psychology and self-help.

Daniel and Jason are the authors of several psychology titles, including *Know Your Mind: Everyday Emotional and Psychological Problems and How to Overcome Them* (2009). Their work has appeared in various national newspapers and magazines, among them *The Times*, the *Guardian*, the *Independent* and *Psychologies*.

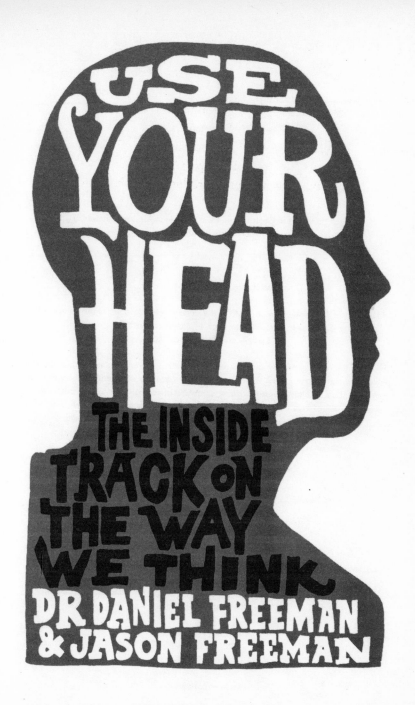

USE YOUR HEAD

THE INSIDE TRACK ON THE WAY WE THINK

DR DANIEL FREEMAN & JASON FREEMAN

JOHN MURRAY

First published in Great Britain in 2010 by John Murray (Publishers)
An Hachette UK Company

1

© Dr Daniel Freeman and Jason Freeman 2010

The right of Dr Daniel Freeman and Jason Freeman to be identified as the Authors of
the Work has been asserted by them in accordance with the Copyright,
Designs and Patents Act 1988.

A CIP catalogue record for this title is available from the British Library

ISBN 978-1-84854-324-9

Typeset in Sabon MT by Palimpsest Book Production Limited,
Falkirk, Stirlingshire

Printed and bound by Clays Ltd, St Ives plc

John Murray policy is to use papers that are natural, renewable and recyclable
products and made from wood grown in sustainable forests. The logging and
manufacturing processes are expected to conform to the environmental regulations
of the country of origin.

John Murray (Publishers)
338 Euston Road
London NW1 3BH

www.johnmurray.co.uk

To our parents, Gail and Laurence Freeman

CONTENTS

PREFACE

My soul is a hidden orchestra; I know not what instruments, what fiddle strings and harps, drums and tambours I sound and clash inside myself. All I hear is the symphony.
  – Fernando Pessoa (1888–1935)

Is anything we encounter in life more complex, unpredictable and at times plain baffling than human behaviour? Understanding the way in which our own mind works can be tricky enough. How much more obscure and confusing then can seem the behaviour of *other* people?

And yet these are not matters we can ignore: at almost every moment of the day, we are required to make judgements and decisions (sometimes subconsciously) about our own actions and feelings and those of others. What should I say? What do I really think? Did that guy look at me oddly? What should I wear today? Am I in the right job? Why is my memory so terrible? Are my feelings normal? Should I be concerned about my child's behaviour? Am I getting enough sleep? Should I offer to buy that person a drink? Why do I feel so low today? What should I do next?

A poignant irony is at play here: what we're most familiar with – ourselves and other people – is often what we understand the least. Why exactly do we think and feel and act in the ways that we do? Why do other people? And how *should* we behave? Most of us, much of the time, haven't a clue.

This book is an attempt to shed light on these puzzling and yet vitally important questions. It doesn't offer all the answers: many of the ways in which the human mind works remain opaque, despite many years of scientific study. But nor is the situation as hopeless as it may sometimes appear: it really is possible to make sense of much of human behaviour, and the key to this is the discipline dedicated to understanding the mind – psychology.

Use Your Head presents a distillation – and, we hope, an entertaining one – of the best and most up-to-date psychological research on human behaviour. So if you've ever wondered, for example, about the differences between men and women, how your personality influences your day-to-day life, what we can do to increase our happiness, why we're attracted to certain people and not others, the way the human brain functions, why we make the decisions we do, how our memory works (or doesn't work), or what's really going on when we experience emotions like happiness, sadness or fear – you'll find much of interest in the following chapters. We'll show you how to analyse both your own behaviour and that of the people around you, and we'll teach you to think like a psychologist without having to slog through a university degree course. If you do happen to be taking a psychology course, we're sure the book will still be of interest, providing accessible yet reliable summaries of the latest thinking on the key topics.

There's no need to read the book in strict sequential order. The chapters are designed to be self-contained, so, if a particular topic grabs you, feel free to start there and then dip in wherever you fancy. *Use Your Head* is intended to be a fun – as well as informative – read, so we've tried to keep the theory and jargon firmly under control. But if you'd like a brief overview of the various clinical and academic approaches that inform the book, and the key figures behind them, you'll find it in the final chapter: 'Theories, Theories, Theories'.

Finally, it's worth remembering that the human mind isn't simply a source of confusion, a riddle to be unravelled: it is also endlessly fascinating, enormously complex, and constantly surprising. Because of this, *Use Your Head* has been a hugely pleasurable book to write. And, for the same reason (if no other), we think it will be an enjoyable – and informative – book to read. If we've done any justice to the power, diversity and amazing sophistication of human psychology, it certainly should be.

ACKNOWLEDGEMENTS

We owe a huge debt of gratitude to Roland Philipps, Helen Hawksfield and Victoria Murray-Browne at John Murray, who commissioned *Use Your Head* and have played a pivotal role in shaping it into the book it is today. And very many thanks, as ever, to Zoë King at the Darley Anderson Agency, without whom the book would surely have never seen the light of day.

The Medical Research Council (MRC) and the Wellcome Trust fund Daniel's research programme on understanding and treating severe mental illness, and provide invaluable support for scientists. Life as a psychologist is also immeasurably enriched for him by the long-standing research collaboration with Philippa Garety, Elizabeth Kuipers, Paul Bebbington, David Fowler and Graham Dunn. The breadth of human behaviour that we review in this book brought back many memories of undergraduate psychology lectures – when Daniel was, he admits, not a model student – and therefore he'd very much like to thank the psychologists who had faith in him and all those who subsequently taught and inspired him.

This is a book by two brothers, but it couldn't have been written without the support of yet more family members. So Jason would like to thank Eleanor for stepping into the breach more often than anyone could reasonably expect, and Ethan, Evelyn and Jude for listening politely while their dad regaled them with endless 'fascinating' facts from the day's labours. He promises not to do it again (for a few weeks at least).

1. PERSONALITY

Where better to begin a chapter on personality than with the curious case of Leonard Zelig? Born to an impoverished Jewish family in New York at the beginning of the twentieth century, Zelig became legendary for his ability to change both his physical appearance and his personality to suit the social milieu in which he happened to find himself.

Thus the uneducated Zelig was able to engage in brilliant literary discussions with F. Scott Fitzgerald. Decidedly unathletic, he nevertheless played baseball for the New York Yankees. Able to adapt to the most diverse social circles, he was friendly with Al Capone, Charlie Chaplin, Josephine Baker, William Randolph Hearst, presidents Coolidge and Hoover, Pope Pius XI and even Adolf Hitler. Despite being entirely untrained, Zelig practised – briefly – as a doctor ('To the gentleman whose appendix I took out, I don't know what to say. If it's any consolation I may still have it somewhere around the house'). His extraordinary life so captivated the US in the 1920s and '30s that he was the subject of a song by Cole Porter ('You're the top, / You're Leonard Zelig'), unfortunately abandoned when the composer was unable to think of a rhyme for 'Zelig'. He was, however, eventually the subject of an Oscar-nominated feature film, *Zelig*, made by Woody Allen in 1983.

Whatever we have in mind when we use the term 'personality', it surely isn't Leonard Zelig's chameleonizing. Although the word's etymology suggests transience (*persona* being the Latin term for the character masks worn by ancient Greek and Roman actors), for us 'personality' denotes a relatively stable set of characteristics that helps determine the way we think, feel and behave. Knowing someone's personality, we generally assume, enables us to understand both why they've acted as they have and how they are likely to behave in the future. We may diverge from our personality in certain situations, but this is regarded as exceptional (hence the phrase 'acting out of character'). Compulsively switching between multiple personalities, Zelig in reality had none.

But how accurate is this popular view of personality? Are we really so predictable? Are there personality types? What causes our personality? Do women and men differ in their typical personalities? Does our personality alter as we grow older? Do animals possess personalities? We'll discover the answers to all these questions, and a few more besides, in the following pages.

Theories of personality have ancient roots. For several centuries arguably the most influential hypothesis was based on the idea that the human body contains four essential 'humours': black bile, yellow bile, phlegm and blood. This notion was taken up by the 'father of medicine', Hippocrates (born on the Greek island of Kos *c.*460 BC), who argued that all illnesses resulted from an imbalance of these essential substances. The ancient Greek philosopher Theophrastus (born *c.*371 BC), the Roman thinker and physician Galen (born AD 129) and others developed Hippocrates' medical theory of 'humorism' into an account of personality. Thus bad-tempered – or *choleric* – individuals were regarded as suffering from an excess of yellow bile; the predominance of black bile, on the other hand, made people *melancholic*. Lively, sociable and confident, a *sanguine* individual benefited from a surplus of blood, while too much phlegm typically resulted in a calm and easy-going (or *phlegmatic*) personality.

Humorism proved an astonishingly durable theory, its medical precepts remaining dominant among European doctors right up until the nineteenth century and its application to personality so pervasive that we continue to use its terminology today. Indeed, at least as far as personality is concerned, it is arguable that the first major challenge to the consensus came only with the theories of Sigmund Freud in the late nineteenth and early twentieth centuries.

For Freud, our personality is the product of our psychological development as infants and young children, and specifically the way in which we come to terms with our maturing sexual drives. Freud had much more to say about the problems that arise when this developmental process goes awry than he did about 'normal' personality – an emphasis that doubtless reflected his day-to-day work as a practising psychoanalyst. There's little evidence to support Freud's theory of personality, and so we won't attempt a full account here. Nevertheless, to give a flavour of what's involved, let's take a brief illustrative look at Freud's notion of the so-called 'anal stage'.

Beginning at around the age of eighteen months and continuing until they are three, Freud believed, children experience pleasure by retaining and expelling faeces. This is also the time when they are beginning to explore the world around them, and learning to recognize and negotiate the controls imposed by their parents. But what if for some reason a child becomes stuck at this developmental stage? Well, if they're 'anal-expulsive' they might become a disorganized, emotional, rebellious adult. If, however, they are 'anal-retentive' – a term of abuse still employed today, long after Freud's theory of personality has withered into obsolescence – their personality will be distinguished by excessive stubbornness, meanness and love of order.

*

By 1920 Freud had become a renowned psychoanalyst with a thriving practice in Vienna. One morning he received a visit from a young American named Gordon Allport. After several months teaching and travelling in Europe, Allport was about to return to Harvard to pursue a doctorate in psychology. Keen to break the ice with an anecdote he thought the great man might appreciate, he told Freud about a little boy he'd recently seen on a train who appeared to be afraid of dirt. The little boy was saying, 'I don't want to sit *there*! Don't let him sit near me, he's dirty!' Freud listened thoughtfully to the young man's story, and then asked, 'Was that little boy you?' Allport – flabbergasted – quickly changed the subject.

As it happened, Gordon Allport (1897–1967) went on to become one of the most prominent psychologists of the twentieth century and a hugely influential theorist of personality. (Indeed, he was the first person to teach a university course in personality, in 1924.) His contribution was to conceive of personality in terms of relatively stable character *traits*, and to investigate what those traits might be.

Allport recognized that we don't *always* behave in accordance with our dominant personality traits. We might be naturally gregarious, for example, but we're unlikely to start a conversation in the middle of an examination. We may like to keep our office tidy, but will draw the line at spending our leisure time tackling the chaos of our children's bedrooms. Nevertheless, these exceptions don't, by definition, invalidate the general truth of our personality: in most situations we are extrovert; on balance, we prefer to keep things well ordered. (The extent to which our behaviour is determined by the respective influences of our personality traits and the specific situation has been vigorously disputed by psychologists in what has been termed the 'person–situation controversy'. The best evidence indicates – perhaps unsurprisingly – that both factors are generally at work.)

Today, psychologists believe that there are five fundamental personality traits, known as the 'Big Five':

- **Extroversion** (people high in this trait are pleasure-seekers and thrill junkies)
- **Agreeableness** (the quality of being helpful, kind and sensitive to the needs of others)
- **Conscientiousness** (being hard-working, goal-oriented and self-disciplined)
- **Neuroticism** (the trait of the worriers: always alert for potential disaster)
- **Openness** (being curious, imaginative and unconventional)

We'll look in detail at each of these traits later in this chapter, for they provide a pretty effective means of gaining some insight into both your own behaviour and that of the people around you. And it's worth noting that, for a highly disputatious discipline such as psychology, there's an unusual degree of agreement that the Big Five represent the most useful and accurate way of understanding personality. Individuals are generally tested using specially designed questionnaires; the results are remarkably consistent, both when compared to ratings by close friends and family and to previous tests completed by the individual (implying that our personalities don't change a whole lot, at least in the short to medium term). In fact research suggests that the Big Five can be meaningfully applied to animals including horses, chimpanzees, cats, dogs, donkeys, pigs, and even guppies and octopuses. (As any pet-owner will attest, it's not only humans who have personalities.)

But it's worth remembering that these traits exist on a spectrum. We're not dealing with absolutes here, but rather with relative descriptions of people's personalities. No one, for example, is simply 'extrovert' or (its opposite) 'introverted' – it's better to think in terms of some people being high in extroversion and others low. Personality traits are 'dimensional', to use the jargon, and, because each of us can be positioned at any point on each of the Big Five, the number of possible permutations (and personalities) is infinite. If you'd prefer to put a figure on it, however, you could use the one calculated by the psychologist Daniel Nettle. Assuming ten distinct points on each of the five trait dimensions, this would mean there are 100,000 possible personalities.

This way of thinking about personality is much more nuanced than many older accounts, which tended to see individuals as simply representatives of one of a fixed number of 'types' (or stereotypes) – the jocular fat man, for example, or the gossip-mongering busybody; the virtuous maiden or the manly hero. Clearly, this was a pretty one-dimensional take on personality. But its traces can be detected in the belief, first put forward in the 1950s and prevalent until very recently, that there is a Type A personality, a noxious blend of extreme aggression, competitiveness, impatience and hostility. Type As, it was argued, are far more likely to suffer from heart disease than their flexible, easy-going and tolerant Type B opposites. In fact there is no evidence for the existence of Type A (or Type B): personality is much more complex than that. And what looked like a connection between personality and coronary heart disease turns out to be a link to one specific emotion: anger.

By now you may be wondering where you fit in with the Big Five. Well, here's your chance to find out, courtesy of the Newcastle Personality Assessor. Below are twelve descriptions of different thoughts or types of behaviour. All you have to do is indicate how characteristic each one is – generally speaking – for you, from 'Very uncharacteristic' to 'Very characteristic'.

	Very uncharacteristic	Moderately uncharacteristic	Neither uncharacteristic nor characteristic	Moderately characteristic	Very characteristic	Score
1. Starting a conversation with a stranger						
2. Making sure others are comfortable and happy.						
3. Creating an artwork, a piece of writing, or a piece of music.						
4. Preparing for things well in advance.						
5. Feeling blue or depressed.						
6. Planning parties or social events.						
7. Insulting people.						
8. Thinking about philosophical or spiritual questions.						
9. Letting things get into a mess.						
10. Feeling stressed or worried.						
11. Using difficult words.						
12. Sympathizing with others' feelings.						

When you've dealt with all twelve, it's time to work out your score.

For questions 7 and 9
Very uncharacteristic = **1**
Moderately uncharacteristic = **2**
Neither uncharacteristic nor characteristic = **3**
Moderately characteristic = **4**
Very characteristic = **5**

For all questions except 7 and 9
Very uncharacteristic = **5**
Moderately uncharacteristic = **4**
Neither uncharacteristic nor characteristic = **3**
Moderately characteristic = **2**
Very characteristic = **1**

To arrive at your extroversion total, add together your scores for questions 1 and 6. For neuroticism, it's questions 5 and 10; for conscientiousness, questions 4 and 9; for agreeableness, questions 2, 7 and 12; and for openness, questions 3, 8 and 11.

Now you have a score for each of the Big Five, what do they mean? The table below will give you an indication of how you rate compared to the population as a whole, but bear in mind that there are no right answers when it comes to personality. Everyone's personality has its strengths and weaknesses; none is intrinsically 'better' than another.

Personality dimension	Low	Low-medium	Medium-high	High
Extroversion	2-4	5-6	7-8	9-10
Neuroticism	2-4	5-6	7-8	9-10
Conscientiousness	2-4	5-6	7-8	9-10
Agreeableness (women)	3-11	12-13	14	15
Agreeableness (men)	3-9	10-11	12-13	14-15
Openness	3-8	9-10	11-12	13-15

What kind of personality does it take to climb Everest? This intriguing question was the subject of a research study published in 2003 by the psychologists Sean Egan and Robert Stelmack. They interviewed thirty-nine climbers who were gathered at Everest Base Camp, acclimatizing before their assault on the mountain. Egan and Stelmack found that the climbers had relatively low levels of neuroticism (this is probably not a major surprise: on the whole, anxious people are not well suited to tackling hazardous mountains). They also discovered that the climbers had significantly higher *extroversion* scores than most non-mountaineering folk.

We're all familiar with the term 'extrovert'. It describes a person at ease in the company of others: sociable, outgoing and fun-loving. In terms of the Big Five, high levels of extroversion also characterize someone who prefers life lived in the fast lane – full of adventure, thrills and risk (hence the interest in climbing the highest mountain on Earth). Extroverts are 'sensation-seekers'; they're ambitious, aggressive and action-oriented. Someone low on extroversion will, by definition, score highly on introversion, meaning that they are relatively restrained, even-tempered and able to find satisfaction in relatively peaceful, perhaps solitary, pursuits.

Incidentally – and contrary to received wisdom – introverts aren't necessarily shy. Shyness is essentially anxiety about how we're perceived by others; as such, it's really a feature of neuroticism. Introverts may well enjoy the company of others; they're just able to get along better without it than extroverts for most of the time.

Professional athletes tend to exhibit high levels of extroversion – in fact there's some evidence to suggest that the better the athlete, the more extroverted they are. So too do actors, successful business leaders and many workaholics (or at least those who spend so many hours in the office because they love their work and miss the stimulus when they're away from it, rather than those who work long hours because they fear the consequences if they don't).

As with each of the Big Five personality traits, scientists have attempted to find a biological explanation for extroversion. Hans Eysenck (1916–97) argued that a person's level of extroversion was determined by the responsiveness of their nervous system (which in turn was determined by their genetic make-up). And indeed there's some evidence to suggest that people high in extroversion possess relatively insensitive physiologies, which results in them seeking out strong sensory stimulation, whether that be a game of tennis, a party or an assault on a gigantic mountain. Those low in extroversion (and high in introversion), on the other hand, require much less stimulation and hence prefer quieter pursuits.

More recently, it's been suggested that the brains of people who score highly on extroversion are especially sensitive to the neurotransmitter dopamine, which is released when the senses detect potentially pleasurable rewards in the environment. Thus we can think of extroverts as people who are particularly alert to the potential rewards of life, whether in their career, their relationships and sexual life, or their leisure activities. Not only are they alert to those rewards, they are also extraordinarily energetic and determined in their pursuit of them. Given this, it is probably unwise to attempt to stand between an extrovert and a good time.

All personality traits are equal, but one appears decidedly less equal than others. People high in *neuroticism* are prone to moodiness, depression, anxiety, hypochondria, headaches, insomnia, worry, low self-esteem, insecurity, relationship problems and work dissatisfaction. This is because neuroticism is defined by acute sensitivity to the negative – or potentially negative – aspects of existence, be they events, thoughts or feelings. (This sensitivity seems to have its roots in the way that the brain functions – you can read more about this in Chapter 8, on fear and anxiety.) Even when things are going well, disaster seems to lurk just around the corner for someone who is highly neurotic: every silver lining is dwarfed by a whopping black cloud.

If we were to show you a distressing film, we could predict the strength of your reaction simply by knowing how neurotic you are. The higher your neuroticism score, the more upset you'd be. At the opposite end of the spectrum, people low in neuroticism are easy-going, calm and self-confident. Life's problems just don't seem to make as much of an impression on them.

If one were able to choose a personality trait to be rich in, it's unlikely to be neuroticism. And yet neuroticism has its uses. Being preternaturally vigilant for possible risk is miserable and exhausting, but it does at least mean that you're less likely to put yourself in dangerous situations. (Everest mountaineers aren't simply high in extroversion: they're also low on neuroticism.) There also seems to be a link between neuroticism and artistic achievement. No one knows why this should be the case, though perhaps being alert to the disappointments and dissatisfactions of life serves as a particularly effective spur to self-expression: people content with the status quo may feel less inclined to change it by making something new.

Can personality make a difference to how long we live? It appears that it can. For example, people high in extroversion, being natural risk-takers, are more likely to die in accidents. They also tend to drink and smoke more than others – perhaps because they socialize more frequently; perhaps because they're particularly receptive to the buzz that alcohol and tobacco can provide. Those high in *conscientiousness*, on the other hand, seem to have a significantly better chance of surviving into a ripe old age. For example, one study that followed a large group of US children for seventy years found that kids who were rated high in conscientiousness by their parents and teachers lived longer than their peers: in any given year the conscientious individuals were around 30 per cent less likely to die.

This is because very conscientious people are careful, self-disciplined and goal-oriented. As such, they're more likely than weaker-willed mortals to take regular exercise, eat healthily, avoid overindulgence in cigarettes and alcohol, and visit the doctor if they suspect a problem may be looming. If they do fall ill, the chances are they'll be pretty good at following the recommended treatment regime.

Because very conscientious people are typically well-organized, ambitious, efficient, punctual and hard-working folk, it may not be much fun working alongside them (unless of course you are similarly inclined, or can persuade them to take on some – or indeed all – of your workload). It's likely to be especially galling if you happen to be low on conscientiousness, in which case you're probably rather disorganized, aimless, lazy, unreliable, impulsive and weak-willed (though doubtless charming and attractive in your own way). Predictably, research shows that conscientiousness is the prime personality-related predictor of job success (though many other factors play a part – being conscientious certainly doesn't guarantee a glittering career). Interestingly, though we may not want our colleagues to be especially conscientious, it turns out to be the trait we value most highly in our politicians. (Insert your own ironic comment here.)

Of course, like all the Big Five personality traits, being highly conscientious has its drawbacks as well as its obvious benefits. For getting things done, there's nothing better to have in your personality locker. But conscientiousness can also bring with it a stressful perfectionism and a remorseless drive to succeed. Switching off can seem awfully difficult. Fun and relaxation will probably drift towards the bottom of your meticulously maintained to-do list. To rework the old joke: you may or may not live a lot longer if you're exceptionally conscientious, but it'll certainly feel like it.

*

Take a few moments to think about the personalities of your family, friends and colleagues. Do the men you know differ from the women, generally speaking? Could our personality, in other words, be partly a reflection of our gender?

When scientists have looked into this issue, they have found that women and men are generally pretty similar in their personalities – such differences as may exist between individual men and women are generally not a result of their gender. But a couple of gender-related differences do exist. First, women are more prone to depression than men – a fact that suggests they are also higher in neuroticism. (Remember, though, that we're talking about very general, high-level patterns here: individuals may – and very frequently do – diverge significantly from these abstractions.) The other difference between the sexes is that women tend to score more highly than men for a personality trait called *agreeableness*.

'Too right', you may be thinking – especially if you're a woman. But, in the context of the Big Five, agreeableness has a particular meaning, denoting the quality possessed by someone who is trusting, helpful, kind and, above all, sensitive to the needs and concerns of the people around them. A person low in agreeableness, on the other hand, will be self-centred, suspicious and uncooperative, and certainly won't lose any sleep worrying about other people's feelings. (Extremely low agreeableness is one of the hallmarks of psychopathy.)

Actors tend to score highly for agreeableness – a finding doubtless explained by the fact that they need to be able to understand and empathize with the characters they are portraying. The picture is rather different, however, for business executives. For example, a study of more than 3,700 European and US managers found that the more agreeable an individual was, the less successful they were (as measured by salary, career progression and the closeness of their relationship with the company's CEO). This may be because the business world often values characteristics that are antipathetic to agreeableness (for example, ruthlessness, scepticism and self-reliance). Or perhaps executives high in agreeableness are simply less concerned with personal advancement, because they're more people-focused.

Exactly why women are generally more agreeable than men is a matter of debate. Some experts have argued that it stems from women's relative lack of the hormone testosterone; when women are given this hormone, their behaviour – and their agreeableness score – changes accordingly. Whether or not this biological explanation is correct, social and cultural factors surely play a major part. Women, even today, tend to be what social scientists call 'nurturers': raising children, attending to the needs of others, and generally acting as the focal point of families. This is not a role well suited to those who find it difficult to understand and get along with other people. What you need for it is empathy, sensitivity, the ability to build relationships. What you need, in short, is agreeableness.

Here's a personal question: how do you feel about poetry? Do you read it – or perhaps write it? What about art: are you a regular visitor to your local gallery? Do you like to draw or paint? And how important is music in your life: are you constantly in search of new and inspiring sounds? Do you play an instrument, or even write music?

If you've answered yes to any of these questions (and the likelihood is that if you've done so for one you'll have done so for almost all the others), you're probably rich in the fifth of the Big Five personality traits: *openness*. Research into the Big Five has tended to focus on extroversion and neuroticism (indeed, these were the two central traits in Hans Eysenck's theory of personality), and openness is probably the one that's received the least attention. Sometimes confused with intelligence, openness is really a measure of our willingness to expose ourselves to new experiences. Thus someone who scores highly for openness is curious, unconventional, creative, imaginative and broad-minded. They're almost certainly dedicated followers of the arts and other cultural activities – and quite probably practitioners too.

'I'm no art critic, but I know what I hate,' remarked *The Simpsons*' malevolent oligarch, Montgomery H. Burns – an individual whose tally for openness would, as they say in cricket, scarcely trouble the scorers. Naturally, it would be unfair to tar all of us who aren't especially blessed with openness with the Monty Burns brush. But what we can say is that at the bottom end of the openness spectrum people are narrow-minded, conventional and uncreative. Most of us, of course (as with each of the personality traits), fall somewhere in the middle.

Whom should we thank – or blame – for our personality? Are we shy because of the way our parents raised us, or sociable because of our genes? Is our personality the product of our cumulative life experiences? Do we simply adapt to the circumstances in which we find ourselves? Is it correct that our personality is (at least in part) the result of whether we happened to be the first-born child in the family, or the last, or somewhere in between? Does it matter which season – or even month – we were born in?

Well, we can begin by ruling out a couple of theories. Despite the claims of astrology, there's no clear evidence that the date of our birth has any bearing on our personality. Some psychologists have argued that the *season* during which we are born can have an influence, but the case is very far from proved. Similarly, although some scientists have claimed that birth order can affect personality, on balance the evidence would suggest that this is unlikely. Firstborns are not – as the popular stereotype would have it – more likely to be reliable, conscientious and conventional; younger children are no more likely to be rebellious mavericks than their elder siblings. It's natural that people should characterize their siblings in this way when asked to look back on their childhood – an older brother or sister may well seem more staid and grown-up to a younger child, who in turn is likely to appear unruly and irresponsible to their older sibling. But these impressions don't shed light on our sibling's personality: they are too distorted by our relative ages for that. (Very recent research suggests that things may be different in families with six or more siblings, though as yet we have only one study of such large families.)

Having dismissed these theories, where does that leave us? Well, it leaves us with the two perennial candidates in the search for explanations of psychological phenomena: biology (essentially our genes) and environment. Quite how much of a role each has in the formation of personality is a hotly contested issue. Some scientists argue that personality is essentially a product of the way in which our nervous system works – which in turn derives from our genetic inheritance. (By way of an example of this way of thinking, have a look back at the paragraphs above on extroversion, and especially the notion that people high in this trait have relatively unresponsive nervous systems.) Others claim a much more significant role for environmental factors – in other words, our accumulated mass of life experiences, and especially (but not exclusively) those in childhood and adolescence.

In truth, any attempt to arrive at a definitive allocation of responsibility between genes and environment is probably futile. The neurobiologist Steven Hyman has put it nicely: 'In the dance of life, genes and environment are absolutely inextricable partners.' That said, the current best guess is that genes account for something like 40–50 per cent of variation in personality. As ever in discussions of heritability, we need to remember that this statistic does *not* mean that 40–50 per cent of a person's personality is necessarily the result of their genes. What it signifies is that 40–50 per cent of the differences in personality *across the population* are likely to be genetic in origin. The remainder is the product of our environment.

Exactly how the environment affects our personality is not well understood at present, but experts studying the personalities of siblings have come to a remarkable conclusion: our upbringing affects our personality, for sure, but what's critical is the distinctive, personal way in which we each respond to our early experiences. This is why two identical twins, who share the same genes and who have been brought up together, can nevertheless differ in personality. This may come as some small comfort to anxious parents.

Are you crippled by your conscientiousness, exhausted by your extroversion, nauseated by your neuroticism? Would you like to change aspects of your personality?

If you would, there's both good news and bad. The bad news is that our personalities, by definition, are relatively stable. They don't tend to change much, at least by the time we've reached adulthood. (There's some evidence to suggest that our person-ality is more fluid in the formative years of childhood and adolescence.) Studies have shown, for example, that people perform similarly in personality tests taken several years apart.

However – and this is the good news for anyone dissatisfied with their personality – things are not set in stone. Dramatic transformations in personality are unlikely – if you're hugely extrovert at age twenty-five, you're likely still to be relatively high in extroversion at age forty. Nevertheless, as we grow older our personality does seem to alter: we tend to score more highly for agreeableness and conscientiousness, and our ratings for neuroticism, extroversion and openness significantly decrease.

Scientists generally explain this as a reflection of our growing maturity as the restless, exploratory, insecure young adult striving to find their way in the world grows up into a (relatively) self-assured thirty-something, comfortable with their career and family responsibilities. (Remember, these are generalizations, albeit generalizations based on large amounts of statistical data: they don't tell us anything very much about individuals.) Interestingly, however, a number of recent studies have suggested that many of these personality changes continue into our forties, fifties and even sixties.

Exactly why our personality develops in this fashion is a matter of debate. Experts who believe that personality is principally the product of our neurobiological make-up and genetic inheritance tend to argue that these age-related shifts are all part of the innate package. They may also be sceptical about the amount of change that's possible (after all, there's nothing we can do to alter our genes, or the responsiveness of our neurological system). However, those who emphasize the role of our life experiences in the formation of personality will point to these same factors to account for personality change – and are likely to be much more bullish about the extent to which our personality can develop as we go through life.

Human personality is an infinitely varied, minutely nuanced phenomenon. Given this limitless diversity, is it meaningful to talk in terms of 'normal' personalities? Perhaps more importantly, is there such a thing as an *abnormal* personality? Can one's personality be so eccentric that it amounts to a form of mental illness?

As you might imagine, this is a contentious area. Certain people do indeed have very peculiar personalities, but some experts would argue that this doesn't betoken any sinister pathology; instead, these individuals simply occupy the extreme ends of the personality spectrum. This, however, is not the view taken by mainstream psychiatry, which has identified ten *personality disorders*. These disorders are defined by consistently odd and unpredictable behaviour – generally beginning as far back as childhood – which causes real problems for the person concerned and their family, friends and colleagues. They generally affect around 1–3 per cent of the population. (Incidentally, it's worth mentioning that these disorders aren't conceptualized in terms of the Big Five personality traits, as they relate to a very different theoretical background. That said, some attempts have been made recently to integrate the two frameworks.)

Here are the ten personality disorders, as described in the psychiatric handbooks. They are classified into three groups, beginning with the so-called *odd-eccentric*:

- **Paranoid personality disorder** – as the name implies, people with this disorder are extremely distrustful of other people and imagine themselves as constantly the subject of threats.
- **Schizoid personality disorder** – individuals with this are regarded as cold and unemotional loners; this disorder is believed by some experts to be related to autism.
- **Schizotypal personality disorder** – characterized by odd beliefs (for example, in extraterrestrials or their own special powers); rambling, incoherent speech; and difficulties forming relationships. Schizotypal personality disorder is closely linked to schizophrenia.

The *dramatic-emotional* disorders are:

- **Antisocial personality disorder (APD)** – people with this disorder (they're usually men) are wildly rebellious, deceitful, violent, impulsive and careless about both their own safety and that of others.
- **Borderline personality disorder (BPD)** – more often seen in women than in men. People with BPD are emotionally fragile, very unsure of themselves and their identity, and fearful of abandonment. Drug abuse, self-harm and suicidal thoughts are common.

- **Narcissistic personality disorder** – individuals have an exaggerated sense of their own importance. Needing constant reassurance and admiration, they will manipulate and exploit other people in order to get it.
- **Histrionic personality disorder** – characterized by dramatic, emotional behaviour designed to ensure that the person remains the centre of attention.

Finally, we have the *anxious/fearful* disorders:

- **Avoidant personality disorder** – struggling with rock-bottom self-esteem, and fearful that their supposed inadequacies will be exposed or ridiculed by other people, the individual with this disorder tries desperately to avoid social situations.
- **Dependent personality disorder** – people with this disorder feel they can't cope with life on their own; instead, they rely on others to make decisions and organize their time.
- **Obsessive–compulsive personality disorder (OCPD)** is characterized by an obsessive, perfectionist devotion to order and routine.

2.INTELLIGENCE

I think, therefore I am.
  – René Descartes (1596–1650)

Imagine that you have recently become a parent. Congratulations! Your offspring is a gorgeous infant – happy, healthy and blessed with the kind of angelic features that cause even the least broody adult to coo with pleasure. Although you do not know it yet, she also has an IQ (or intelligence quotient) well above the norm.

Intelligence is of course a much-prized attribute. Given the choice, it's probable that most parents would prefer their child to be bright rather than not. But how much of a difference does an above-average IQ really make? What bearing does it have on the kind of life our children will grow up to lead?

In fact intelligence – or at least the kind of intelligence measured by IQ tests – is arguably the most reliable index we have of how well individuals will fare in life. Take education, for example: a substantial body of research carried out over many years indicates that children with higher IQs are generally more successful at school exams than those with lower IQ test scores. And they stay longer in the education system, being more likely to attend university and other forms of higher education.

People with higher IQs tend to be more successful at work. That's why IQ tests are seen by many business-studies experts as the best way of selecting staff. Indeed, it's been suggested that *not* using some form of mental-ability test in recruitment could cost organizations around 20 per cent in lost productivity. (These tests are most effective at predicting a person's likely performance when the job is a relatively complex one.)

It's not simply employers who benefit, of course. The brighter you are, the more you're likely to earn. One study of more than 7,000 US adults even put a figure on it: each extra IQ point was associated with an additional $202 to $616 in annual salary (that's around £120 to £370). And IQ seems to have a clear impact on class mobility. For example, one research study analysed the life histories – and IQ scores – of more than 11,000 people all born in the UK in the week of 3–9 March 1958, and found a marked relation between their results in the intelligence tests they'd taken at age eleven and their social class (as defined by the jobs they were doing) at age forty-two. Put at its simplest, those who did very well in the tests were likely to have moved up in class, and those who'd fared poorly were likely to have slid downwards – regardless of the social background they came from.

But IQ isn't simply associated with material advantages. The higher your IQ, the longer you're likely to live. No one knows why, though several theories have been floated. Perhaps cleverer people have a better understanding of how to live healthily; maybe they're quicker to detect possible problems and seek medical help; it's even been suggested that the genetic factors that can influence health may also help determine our intelligence – in other words, smarter people are just 'fitter' all round.

Part of the explanation for this association between health and IQ may stem from the fact that bright children are more likely to be vegetarian (a vegetarian diet being linked to lower heart disease and lower obesity rates). A study of over 8,000 people published in the *British Medical Journal* found that those who were vegetarian at age thirty had scored around five points higher than average in intelligence tests they had sat at the age of ten. And your bright-as-a-button new baby isn't just likely to be a vegetarian: research carried out at Edinburgh University revealed that children who'd performed well at intelligence tests were more likely to turn into liberal, broad-minded adults – regardless of their social class.

IQ exerts a powerful influence on our development, but we're a very long way from simple determinism. Even for those areas where the correlation with IQ is strongest (such as educational success), innumerable other factors also play a part. Being born with an IQ of 135 or more (the top 1 per cent of scores) guarantees neither educational success nor a glittering career, nor a long and healthy life. But it certainly seems to help.

Is IQ truly a measure of intelligence, though? Well, the answer to that question depends on whom you ask, because, despite more than a hundred years of scientific research and debate, the nature of intelligence – indeed, even the *definition* of intelligence – remains hotly contested. The so-called 'psychometric' approach represented by IQ tests has come to dominate, but even so we still lack a durable consensus about what intelligence is, let alone how to measure it, why some people are brighter than others, whether one can permanently improve one's level of intelligence – and a whole host of other crucial questions.

Part of the problem is that intelligence appears to be culturally relative. When a number of Western experts were canvassed in the 1980s, the attributes they most strongly associated with intelligence were abstract reasoning, problem-solving and the ability to learn. In many African and Asian societies, however, intelligence is much more socially oriented, designating (at least in part) the qualities that help a community to function harmoniously. Among the Chinese people of Taiwan, intelligence is regarded as including both the capacity to empathize with others and the ability to understand oneself. Even within the same city, conceptions of intelligence may vary widely. A study of attitudes in San Jose, California, for instance, found that the Latino population emphasized social skills; for white and Asian people in the city, on the other hand, intelligence meant the kind of reasoning (or *cognitive*) skills measured by IQ tests.

So it's clear that there are many different versions of intelligence out there. This is reflected in the theories of a number of psychologists who take issue with the notion that intelligence can be captured meaningfully in a two-hour IQ test. Howard Gardner, for example, has proposed that there are multiple, unrelated, intelligences – including (but not confined to) the musical, the bodily kinaesthetic (facilitating complex movements) and the interpersonal, in addition to the logical and verbal intelligences highlighted by IQ tests. Daniel Goleman hit the bestseller charts in 1995 with *Emotional Intelligence: Why it Can Matter More than IQ*. (Goleman didn't invent the concept of emotional intelligence, though he certainly popularized it.) In Goleman's view, we're all born with a distinct form of intelligence that helps us understand and manage both our own emotions and those of the people around us.

It's fair to say – albeit at the risk of understatement – that neither Gardner nor Goleman has won over most experts. That said, there is a general acknowledgement that measuring IQ doesn't tell the whole story about intelligence. If it did, how would one explain the fact that many people display a range of mathematical skills when grocery shopping that they are quite unable to replicate in a formal test? Or the study of workers in a milk-processing plant which found that intelligence-test scores had no bearing on how efficiently the staff were able to fill packing cases (a task that drew on some quite sophisticated logical and mathematical thinking)?

Psychometric assessments are predicated on the idea that you can measure general, all-round intelligence. But of course, though many people tend to perform pretty similarly in all parts of the test, lots of us are much better at some kinds of intellectual task than others. Some people, for instance, struggle with mathematical problems but excel at linguistic ones; others are wonderfully imaginative and creative, and yet woeful at logical thinking. The most extreme examples of this phenomenon are the feats of so-called 'idiot savants' – individuals with autism and general learning difficulties who are nevertheless extraordinarily gifted at very particular activities. For example, idiot savants with apparently limited mathematical skills are astonishingly successful at the very complex task of identifying prime numbers. Indeed, one pair of twins with no understanding of multiplication or division was nonetheless able to swap ten-figure prime numbers after just a few minutes of thought. Their IQs, however, were less than 70 – well below average.

What does the name Alfred Binet mean to you? If your answer is 'Nothing', don't worry: you're in good company. Binet is virtually unknown these days, at least in English-speaking nations. This is ironic, because his work continues to influence the fate of millions of people around the world.

Alfred Binet was born in Nice in 1857, later moving to Paris with his mother when his parents separated. Initially Binet seemed destined for a career as a lawyer, but he was drawn to the fledgling discipline of psychology, eventually securing a post as a researcher at the Salpêtrière Hospital in Paris. This was a shrewd move: thanks to the work of the neurologist Jean-Martin Charcot (1825–93), the Salpêtrière had become a legendary centre for the treatment of mental illness. In 1894, and despite no formal academic or clinical training, Binet became head of the Laboratory of Experimental Psychology at the Sorbonne.

In 1904 Binet was asked by the Parisian authorities to devise a test that would help identify children in need of special education. It was a logical choice, since Binet had by then established himself as an expert on child development – a specialism first inspired, it's said, by observing his two young daughters as they tackled various puzzles and games. The result was the Binet–Simon scale, drawn up with the assistance of Théodore Simon and first published in 1905. It comprised around thirty tasks of increasing difficulty, including pointing to specified parts of the body, defining words, and repeating sequences of numbers. (The latter two tasks still crop up in modern intelligence tests.) Children were graded by measuring their performance against what an average child of the same age could be expected to achieve.

Binet later developed the concept of *mental age*, derived from the various age-related test-score averages. Thus, if the average score for a fourteen-year-old was 100, anyone achieving that score would be duly classed as having a mental age of fourteen. (Clearly, if the child in question was twelve, their mental age would be higher than their actual chronological age. A sixteen-year-old scoring 100 would receive a less positive categorization.) Binet, however, was not responsible for the term 'intelligence quotient'. That honour goes to the German psychologist Wilhelm Stern, who introduced it in *The Psychological Methods of Testing Intelligence*, published in 1914.

The Binet–Simon scale was the first scientific intelligence test, and it provided the blueprint for IQ tests for many decades to come. In fact so influential has the scale proved that the journal *Science* included it among the twenty most significant discoveries of the twentieth century.

Even the most vociferous advocate of psychometric testing would probably concede that intelligence takes many forms. But one variety in particular has pretty much eclipsed the others, certainly in the scientific community. Indeed, so complete is its dominance that it is often seen as intelligence itself, rather than as simply a variant. That type of intelligence is commonly known to scientists by an initial: *g*.

To trace the origins of the concept we must go all the way back to the nineteenth century, and specifically to the ground-breaking work of Francis Galton (1822–1910), a cousin of Charles Darwin and the first person to think scientifically about intelligence. Intelligence, in Galton's view, was an index of the speed and efficiency of one's nervous system. Rather than being the product of hard work and virtuous living (as much contemporary rhetoric alleged), intelligence was an inherited characteristic. To reinforce his argument, in 1869 Galton published *Hereditary Genius*, which traced the lineage of nearly a thousand eminent men and asserted that an astonishing one-third of them boasted similarly eminent antecedents, thus demonstrating the heritability of intelligence. (As it turns out, Galton was probably right: intelligence is, to a significant degree, genetically determined. His methods in *Hereditary Genius*, however, were idiosyncratic to say the least.) Significantly, Galton also believed that intelligence could be tested, though his own efforts in this area were a failure.

Galton nevertheless set out a revolutionary idea of intelligence: biologically determined, hereditary, unitary (there are no multiple intelligences in Galton's model) and testable. This idea was developed by Charles Spearman, a former British army officer who had made a somewhat unlikely career switch to psychology, spending virtually his entire career at University College London.

In 1904 Spearman decided to test the intelligence of twenty-four children in his local village school. This was a major undertaking, given that the first scientific intelligence test was still a year away. Spearman went about it by collating the views of teachers and classmates, and by conducting various sensory tests (measuring, for example, a child's ability to judge the weight of an object, or variations in light).

When he analysed the data – and especially when he looked at it in the context of his discovery, in separate studies, that children who performed well in certain academic subjects were likely to do just as well in others – Spearman concluded that we are each born with an inherited *general intelligence* that explains our performance on a wide variety of tasks. By the 1920s, general intelligence had become g, which Spearman likened to mental 'energy' or 'power'. Somewhat dishearteningly, at least for those of us who'd like the cogs to turn faster from time to time, Spearman believed there was little that could be done to boost one's allocation of *g*: 'a person can no more be trained to have it in higher degree than he can be trained to be taller'.

Spearman's theories are now more than a hundred years old. Details have been challenged and reworked by succeeding generations of scholars, but the essential tenets continue to exert an extraordinarily powerful influence on modern views of intelligence. As a fifty-strong panel of experts put it in 1994 'Intelligence is a *very general mental capability* [our emphasis] that ... involves the ability to reason, plan, solve problems, think abstractly, comprehend complex ideas, learn quickly and learn from experience.'

Crucially, this general – albeit multifaceted – intelligence lends itself pretty well to testing, and specifically by means of IQ tests. (In fact it's plausible that one of the principal reasons why this version of intelligence has achieved such prominence is precisely its measurability.) Moreover, there's no getting away from the fact that IQ test results seem to be of real practical value. Indeed, for many key areas of life – such as education and employment – no other data can provide such a reliable indicator of success.

If you were to take an IQ test tomorrow, what could you expect to encounter? There are numerous tests on the market, but the one most often used by professionals is the Wechsler Adult Intelligence Scale (or WAIS). This is made up of thirteen separate tests, which you'd work through with one-to-one guidance from a trained test administrator. Each of the thirteen tests consists of a series of questions of increasing difficulty, and it generally takes around a couple of hours to complete them all.

Each test contributes towards a picture of your capability in one of four broad areas:

- **Verbal comprehension** – for instance, you would be asked what particular words mean, or what two words have in common. Also falling into this category are questions testing your general knowledge and your ability to understand common sayings.
- **Perceptual organization** – you would, for example, be shown a sequence of shapes and be asked to select the next in the series (this is called matrix reasoning). In the picture completion part of the test, the aim is to spot the missing element in one of a set of images.
- **Working memory.** What are you like at mental arithmetic? How successfully can you memorize and repeat out loud a sequence of numbers and/or letters – first forwards and then backwards?
- **Processing speed** – this part of the WAIS measures how quickly you can reason. So, unlike in the other tests, whose questions you can answer at your own pace, here the aim is to recognize and decode the maximum number of symbols you can in a set time.

These four areas each represent a particular aspect of our intelligence, and you might find that you do better in one than in the others. However, in keeping with the theory of general intelligence – and acknowledging that there are many individual exceptions – people tend to perform similarly in each of the four areas. A high score in one is usually a pretty good predictor of high scores in the other three.

But what *is* a high score on an IQ test? The first thing to bear in mind is that such tests don't provide an absolute measure of intelligence. What they offer instead is an indication of where you rank in relation to people of a similar age. Moreover, the experts who construct IQ tests seek to ensure that the scores of the population will form a *bell curve* when plotted on a graph. What this means in essence is that a very small percentage of people will achieve a very low or very high score, with most people scoring somewhere in the middle. Average intelligence is equated with a score of 90–109. Approximately 50 per cent of people taking intelligence tests fall into this category. Anything above 109 ranks as 'superior' intelligence, and if you can make it to 130 you'll be classified as 'gifted' (only around 2 per cent of people attain 130 or better). To qualify as an IQ genius, you'll need a score of at least 140 (a feat achieved by just 0.4 per cent of those who take the tests).

Why are some people more intelligent than others? Or, to be more accurate, why are some people better at intelligence tests? Is it perhaps something to do with the nature of their brains? That certainly seems a plausible theory – the brain is, after all, the organ responsible for our thought processes. But the precise characteristics of the intelligent brain have proved difficult to specify, not least because, until the recent advent of fMRI (functional magnetic resonance imaging) technology, scientists had been unable properly to observe a brain in action.

What we know now, however, is that people with higher IQs tend to have bigger brains. This was actually a theory proposed many years before scientists had the means to verify it. For example, in *The Descent of Man*, first published in 1871, Darwin wrote, 'As the various mental faculties gradually developed themselves the brain would almost certainly become larger. No one, I presume, doubts that the large proportion which the size of man's brain bears to his body, compared to the same proportion in the gorilla or orang, is closely connected with his higher mental powers.'

When researchers analysed all the relevant studies conducted up to 1999 – there had been eleven, covering 432 people – they discovered that the average correlation between brain size and IQ was around 0.4. (A correlation is a statistical way of expressing the relationship between two factors, with 0 being the minimum and 1 the maximum. So, for example, a correlation of 0 between brain size and IQ would mean that there was no connection between the two; a correlation of 1 would indicate that IQ was solely determined by brain size. A correlation of 0.4 is classed as moderately large.)

To which remarkable fact the obvious question is: why? How exactly does brain size influence our intelligence? Unfortunately, no one knows. It is, as scientists are wont somewhat wistfully to put these things, an area in need of future research.

There seems also to be a correlation between IQ and the speed with which individuals can process visual information. The way researchers commonly test this is to sit someone in front of a computer screen upon which will flash one of two simple shapes:

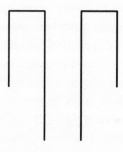

The person taking the test simply has to tell the tester which of these shapes they saw – in essence, whether the longer line was on the left or the right. Their task is made harder by the fact that, immediately after the image has vanished, a shape that looks rather similar but that has lines of equal length flashes on screen. The shapes are shown hundreds of times, though the duration of their appearance on screen varies.

It turns out that people who do well on IQ tests also tend to perform rather better at these perception tests than people with lower IQ ratings (the correlation is again around 0.4). But quite where this information gets us isn't clear. Is the ability to quickly and accurately recognize visual information a cause of intelligence, or merely a symptom? Are we intelligent *because* our brains are capable of such feats? Or is visual perception simply another task intelligent people happen to be good at? It's another topic for future research.

Let's return to your super-intelligent baby, who has been sleeping contentedly throughout the preceding discussion but is now wide awake and hungry for intellectual stimulation. Where, you may wonder, does her intelligence come from? Is she intelligent because of her genetic inheritance (for which you may legitimately claim half the credit), or because of the way you are bringing her up? Is it nature or nurture?

Well, genes certainly play an important role in determining intelligence. Take any large group of people and you'll find a wide range of intelligence levels. Scientists estimate that on average approximately 50 per cent of that variation is attributable to genes. (Note that this *heritability* statistic doesn't necessarily tell us a great deal about the causes of intelligence per se: what it speaks to are the differences between people. Imagine, for example, that you have an IQ of 130 and I have an IQ of 110. Half of that twenty-point difference is likely to be the result of our varying genetic make-up; the remainder of the difference may be the result of other factors entirely.)

The other 50 per cent of variation in levels of intelligence is due to environment – the people we spend time with, the places where we live, the events we experience. But the ratio of genes to environment tends to change throughout our lives – and in a rather unexpected way. One might expect genes to be most influential when we're young: as we get older, and acquire more experience of life, it would seem logical for environmental factors to grow increasingly significant. In fact the reverse seems to be true. The heritability of intelligence is around 20 per cent when we're babies, 40 per cent in childhood, and about 60 per cent during adulthood. Our environment seems to have *less* effect on us as we age, not more. Why this should be is as yet unknown.

There's a bigger surprise lurking in the gene–environment data. Many parents go to great lengths to foster their child's intelligence. This is not surprising, given the prevalence of the belief that a child's upbringing is critical to its intellectual development. Indeed, it's easy for parents to feel guilty if they're not constantly reading to their little ones, ferrying them from music lesson to French tutorial to ballet class, and generally laying before them a wondrous array of uplifting and enlightening cultural experiences. But, though family upbringing is important, its influence on children's intelligence is rather more indirect than most parents realize.

Imagine a family with two children, both girls, one a year older than the other. The sisters live in the same house; they attend the same schools; their parents strive to raise them in the same way. The upbringing these children receive is what scientists call their *shared* environment. Now, these factors will certainly have a bearing on the sisters' intelligence, but what's important is not so much the experiences themselves but each child's response to them. Both attend swimming and ballet lessons, but only one enjoys them. Both spend a good deal of time with their father, but one gets along with him a great deal better than the other. Both are taught by their parents to value education, but in the case of one of the girls the message seems to fall on deaf ears. It's the *non-shared* environment that counts: the experiences that are personal to each of us alone.

How do we know this? Much of the evidence comes from studies of twins. Consider, for example, the case of identical twins separated at birth and placed with different adoptive families. (Clearly this isn't an everyday occurrence; nevertheless, it does happen, and it has been studied by behavioural geneticists.) Each twin is brought up with adoptive siblings. Yet, despite sharing the same family environment throughout their childhood, when tested as adults each twin and its adoptive siblings have utterly different IQs. There is, however, a significant correlation between the score of one twin and that of the other – despite the fact that they have never met – and between the scores of the twins and their birth parents. (There's no correlation between the IQ scores of the twins and their adoptive parents.) The influence of our genes on our intelligence is thus clear. Most of the rest of the differences between us arise, as we've seen, from the accumulation of personal experiences known as the non-shared environment.

Your clever baby has been dealt some useful cards. All being well, she'll excel at school, thrive at university, enjoy a career that's both stimulating and financially rewarding, and live a longer, healthier life than her less intelligent peers. But what will happen to that intelligence as she moves into middle and then old age? Will it hold up, or perhaps even increase in power? Will it gradually decline?

There's no way of knowing. Many people perform less well at intelligence tests as they grow older, but age seems to make no difference for others, and some actually improve their overall score. Ageing is inescapable: the deterioration of our intelligence is not.

That said, when experts have looked at this issue a broad trend emerges. Older people often score less highly than younger people – and than their younger selves – on those parts of the IQ test that measure abstract or spatial reasoning, especially when this is tested under pressure (for example, in a timed exercise). In fact this kind of intelligence tends to wane from our mid-twenties onwards. On the other hand, age doesn't generally affect our performance in tests that involve our verbal skills, or that draw on acquired knowledge.

What can you do to ensure that your mind stays sharp as you grow older? Quite a lot, as it happens:

- **Look after your physical health.** Chronic illness (cardiovascular disease, for example) can often bring with it a decline in cognitive powers.
- **Aim to make your life as intellectually stimulating and enjoyable as possible.** Perhaps take up a hobby, or learn a new language or skill. Make time for family and friends.
- **Be open-minded about change, and embrace new experiences.**
- **Exercise your brain, and especially your abstract or spatial reasoning capabilities** (these are the mental skills that usually take the biggest hit as we age). Chess, crosswords, Sudoku and other puzzles will all help. For a really thorough mental workout, challenge yourself against the clock.

A couple of additional factors may be more difficult to arrange. The higher your social class, for example, the less likely it is that age will adversely affect your intelligence. And if your partner is intelligent, that will help you too.

One intriguing phenomenon in the world of intelligence studies is that people today – regardless of age – appear to be significantly brighter than previous generations. When the political scientist James Flynn analysed IQ scores in the US during the period 1932–78, he found that the average American in 1978 scored a whopping fourteen points more than their peer in the 1930s. And when Flynn looked at data from other countries the story was remarkably similar. In the UK, for instance, the average score in 1942 was 73; by 1992 it had risen to 100.

The 'Flynn effect' has been puzzling scientists for more than two decades, and a credible explanation still eludes us. Some experts believe that we are genuinely becoming more intelligent

– perhaps through such factors as better nutrition. After all, average height has increased, so why not average IQ? Others, including James Flynn himself, argue that we've simply learned how to perform better at intelligence assessments, possibly because elements in children's television programmes, books and computer games resemble aspects of the tests. While relatively small IQ gains are perhaps plausible, the sort of intellectual renaissance suggested by Flynn's data seems unlikely. Are today's schoolchildren really more gifted than those of previous generations? Does our society reflect this dramatic upsurge in brain power? Anecdotal evidence on both counts would tend to suggest not.

Scientists have argued about the nature of intelligence for more than a century, but generally without troubling wider public consciousness. In 1994, however, all that changed with the publication of *The Bell Curve*, written by the Harvard psychologist Richard Herrnstein and the conservative political scientist Charles Murray. *The Bell Curve* advanced many controversial arguments, but none more so than its attempt to explain why different ethnic groups in the US tend to perform differently in intelligence tests.

It had long been observed that African-Americans scored, on average, around fifteen IQ points less than their white compatriots. (Hispanic Americans tend to score somewhere between the two groups.) Herrnstein and Murray suggested that some of this difference might be the result of genetic factors. Predictably, the implication that African-Americans were innately less intelligent than whites caused a furore.

Is there any evidence to support such a theory? None at all. Unsurprisingly, Herrnstein and Murray's suggestion has therefore been roundly rejected by the scientific community. How then to account for the very real differences in IQ score between white and black Americans? The answer is that we simply do not know.

Some experts have speculated that the variation is a reflection of socioeconomic factors. African-Americans tend to be less well off than whites, and poverty probably doesn't offer the optimal conditions for intellectual development. But the data on intelligence tells the same story even after socioeconomic differences have been taken into account.

Others have suggested that intelligence tests are culturally biased, since they require knowledge that is not equally available to whites and blacks. When whites and African-Americans are given tests of their abstract, logical reasoning – that's to say, mental tasks that do not rely on prior knowledge – it's argued that the differences between the two groups vanish. In an extension of this argument, some experts have highlighted the fact that IQ tests measure only one version of intelligence, a version which they believe favours white (and Asian) Americans. (The American Psychological Association, incidentally, denies that intelligence tests discriminate against African-Americans.)

The affair of *The Bell Curve* served to remind intelligence experts of a crucial truth: we cannot hope to understand differences *between* groups simply by applying what we've learned about differences between individuals *within* a group. For example, we know that around half of the variation in IQ scores within a given group stems from genetic differences – but this tells us nothing about the contribution of genes to variations between groups. Whatever lies behind the variation in IQ scores of white and black Americans, we're going to have to try a completely new set of strategies to find it.

3. REASONING AND DECISION-MAKING

'Therefore you don't have a single answer to your questions?'
'Adso, if I did I would teach theology in Paris.'
'In Paris do they always have the true answer?'
'Never,' William said, 'but they are very sure of their errors.'
'And you,' I said with childish impertinence, 'never commit errors?'
'Often,' he answered. 'But instead of conceiving only one, I imagine many, so I become the slave of none.'
– Umberto Eco, The Name of the Rose (1980)

Here's a brain-teaser for you. Which of the following conclusions (a–e) follows logically from these two premises?

Premise 1: Some of my wishes are fulfilled.

Premise 2: Some of my wishes are small.

Therefore:
a. All small wishes are fulfilled.
b. Some fulfilled wishes are not small.
c. No valid conclusion is possible.
d. Some small wishes are fulfilled.
e. Some fulfilled wishes are small.

If you struggled with this exercise, don't be downhearted: very many people do likewise. This is because finding the correct solution requires a command of logic – and logic, for most of us, is not a strong point. (The answer, by the way, is c. We think.)

This may seem a little surprising. We are, after all, wont to point to the power of our brains as the main reason behind humanity's rapid rise to dominance of the planet. But, as we'll see in this chapter, as a rule human beings don't think very logically. We don't generally consider all the options before making a decision. We're often terrible at working out what's best for us, and even worse at acting on that knowledge. We aren't, in other words, nearly as *rational* as we might like to believe.

But we shouldn't be too hard on ourselves. Truly rational thinking in all situations is neither possible for the human brain, formidable though it is, nor desirable. Imagine, for example, that you were to apply the rules of logical decision-making to a game of chess, carefully weighing every option before you made a move. As Ken Manktelow has pointed out, there are around 30^{80} possible moves in a chess game. This means that there are fewer particles in the universe than choices in a game of chess. Clearly, a truly rational decision is beyond even the most formidably intelligent person. And even if they could compute the options, the game would then probably last a lifetime.

Chess, of course, is an especially complex game. But real life is often even more complicated. After all, other people are involved. While we may have to wait a few minutes to discover whether our chess move is a wise one, in real life we may never know whether we took the right option. In any case, what does 'right' mean exactly? The rules of life, such as they are, can seem bafflingly elusive. And of course we are constantly faced with decisions, from the very small to the dauntingly large: what to eat, how to dress, whom to date, which career to opt for, how to react to a colleague's remark, whether to have children, and so on and so on.

But, though human beings aren't always terribly good at thinking rationally, we must nevertheless be doing something right. Life can be messy, certainly, but most of us manage to negotiate it pretty well. Our decisions may not be entirely logical, but generally speaking they do the job. We seem to have what the Nobel Prize-winning economist and psychologist Herbert Simon (1916–2001) termed 'bounded rationality'. Instead of trying to arrive at the best possible decision in a given situation – and how long would that take? – we opt for the 'good enough'. (Simon coined the ugly but apt neologism 'satisficing' to describe this process.)

Another way of understanding how we reason is to think of humans as possessing two types of rationality. One is the kind of logical, analytic thinking we apply to mathematical and statistical calculations, abstract problems and moral deliberations. It means slow and usually pretty hard work. The other is the one we use most of the time: it's fast, easy and intuitive, and makes use of all sorts of short cuts, hunches and rules of thumb. How these short cuts – or *reasoning heuristics* – work was the subject of pioneering research by the psychologists Daniel Kahneman (1934–) and Amos Tversky (1937–96). In 2002 Kahneman was awarded a Nobel Prize for his contribution; had he lived, Tversky would doubtless have shared the prize.

Heuristics are generally very effective. But they can also lead us into all kinds of reasoning errors (or *biases*), and it's these that we focus on in the remainder of this chapter.

How much housework do you do? More than your partner? Well, you may be right, but research shows that people are prone to overestimate their own efforts and underestimate those of their other half. It seems to be much easier to recall the occasions when we cleaned the toilet or vacuumed the stairs than it is to remember the times when someone else did.

What's at work here is the *availability heuristic*. Our judgement of how frequently something occurs, or how likely it is to happen in the future, is hugely influenced by how easily we can remember or imagine it. In many situations the availability heuristic can be a reliable guide. After all, events that happen a lot are probably going to be easier to recall than those that are very unusual. But it can also skew our thinking, as it may when we assess our own contribution to the housework.

The problem is exacerbated by our tendency to focus on events that really stir our emotions. This is why people asked to estimate the relative prevalence of various causes of death typically over-estimate the likelihood of being murdered and underestimate the risk of, for example, dying as a result of diabetes. It's also why we tend to see air travel as more dangerous than making a trip by car, though the opposite is true. The emotional impact – or *stickiness* to use Malcolm Gladwell's term – is so great that mere facts make little impression.

How many people do you think were attacked or killed by sharks in 2008? According to the Florida Museum of Natural History, 2008 saw fifty-nine shark attacks – worldwide – four of which ended in a fatality. Grim though these statistics are, it's worth noting how few deaths there were. And 2008 wasn't exceptional: since records began, in 1990, the fatality count has never exceeded eleven, with most years getting nowhere near that figure. In the US alone, twenty-three people were killed by dogs in 2008. As for the number of sharks 'harvested' each year by fishing boats, the figures are disputed, but it seems to be somewhere between 26 and 73 million. Sharks clearly have a lot more to fear from humans than do humans from sharks.

And yet is there any animal on the planet that inspires more terror in the popular imagination than sharks? It's this terror that, for example, sends bathers fleeing, panic-stricken, from the sea in Cornwall at the first sighting of an entirely harmless basking shark. Why is our view of sharks so distorted, even in countries like the UK where there has never been a fatal attack? Part of the explanation is surely that in newspapers and on TV, in novels and – most famously – in movies, the shark functions as an icon of dread. Through the stories we tell, sharks have become the stuff of our nightmares. Thanks to the availability heuristic, this means we utterly misjudge the risk that sharks pose. And if you're inclined to doubt it, think back to your first dip in the sea after watching *Jaws*.

You're a very busy person, and this week is particularly hectic – so much so that you ask a friend to buy your lottery ticket for you. When they hand it over, you see that the seven numbers they have chosen are 1, 2, 3, 4, 5, 6 and 7. (Perhaps their life is just as busy as yours.) You are not amused, and have to resist the temptation to throw the ticket away there and then.

Most people do not choose consecutive numbers in a lottery, just as they don't generally pick numbers that have won recently. But they should: the probability of those numbers coming up is just the same as for any others, and, if the numbers *are* selected, the share of the prize will probably be greater because fewer other people will have plumped for them.

Why don't we do the logical thing when we pick our lottery numbers? Part of the explanation is that we aren't comfortable with the notion of randomness. We see connections and patterns where there are none. We assume, for example, that what happens in this week's lottery draw must be related in some way to what happened last week (it isn't), or that the future performance of stock markets can be reliably predicted from past performance (it can't). And then there's our tendency to base our judgement of the likelihood of a given situation or event on what we imagine to be normal or typical in such instances, a reasoning bias that's known as the *representativeness heuristic*. So a string of consecutive numbers in a lottery draw seems absolutely atypical, though it fact it is no more atypical than any other combination of randomly selected numbers.

Using representativeness as a criterion for a decision is certainly easy and quick – and actually, like all these heuristics, it's often reasonable. For instance, scheduling your wedding for July on the basis that the weather is likely to be better makes sense: we normally experience more sunshine in the summer. But this heuristic can lead to problems. What we *should* do, according to the eighteenth-century British mathematician and church minister the Reverend Thomas Bayes, is to make our judgements using two pieces of information: the specifics of the individual case and – this is the especially tricky part – an accurate idea of a given event's frequency or probability (this latter being called *base-rate information*).

Most of us, most of the time, aren't especially good at factoring in either of these pieces of information. Imagine, for instance, that you spot a shaven-headed teenager gazing at an immaculate 1960s sports car parked in your street. Many of us might suspect that the teenager is up to no good. But not only would we be failing to judge the case on its own merits – there's no evidence, after all, that the young man intends anything illegal – we'd also be ignoring the base-rate information: many men, of all ages, will stop to admire a vintage car, and most shaven-headed teenagers – despite the impression one might get from a cursory glance at the newspapers – are not criminals.

If you want to win an argument, or come out tops in a negoti-ation, there's a simple but highly effective trick: make sure you state your position before the other guy does. By doing so, you'll be setting the agenda for the ensuing discussion.

Why this works is down to something called the *anchoring-and-adjustment heuristic*: your opening statement anchors the discussion, and, though both parties may move on from this initial position, the subsequent movement – or adjustment – will be limited. (Research on this heuristic has focused on negoti-ations involving figures – a price, for example – though it seems plausible for it also to play a part in more abstract discussions.) Generally we're completely unaware of what's going on, which of course makes the heuristic especially powerful.

(Actually, you don't need two people for this particular

reasoning bias to occur: any time we need to make an estimate of something, we're unduly influenced by the first figure we think of, no matter how inaccurate it is. We come up with a number – say, for how much we want for our house, or how often it's reasonable for us to walk the dog – and then find reasons to justify it.)

The anchoring-and-adjustment heuristic was nicely demonstrated in a study carried out by Adam Galinsky and Thomas Mussweiler. They asked pairs of MBA students to participate in a number of role-play exercises in which one of the pair took the part of a buyer and the other that of a seller. In one of the exercises, for example, the 'buyer' was the chief financial officer of a pharmaceutical manufacturer in need of a new factory; the 'seller' represented a company that had decided to phase out the product line made at a particular plant and thus was looking to dispense with that facility. In another, the seller was a director of personnel bargaining with a prospective new employee (the buyer) about the size of bonus he or she would receive upon joining the company.

The picture that emerged from these exercises was striking: whoever made the first offer, regardless of whether it was the buyer or the seller, ultimately triumphed. Thus the final price for the pharmaceutical factory was much lower when the buyer had been the first to make an offer than when the seller had begun the conversation. The new employee pocketed a handsome bonus when the discussion started with their request, but agreed to a much reduced figure when the director of personnel had opened the negotiations. It's the first offer that counts: the other party, no matter what their aims or intentions were before the discussion began, will simply – helplessly perhaps – adjust to the anchor.

Actually, there's a way to beat the anchoring-and-adjustment heuristic, but it doesn't come naturally to most of us. Rather than unconsciously acquiescing to the other person's opening position, what you need to do is actively challenge it. That means consciously searching for reasons not to accept that first statement or offer. The participants in Galinsky and Mussweiler's study did this by, for example, repeatedly reminding themselves of what they wanted from the negotiations, or by trying to identify the minimum that the other person would accept before they walked away. And when they put these strategies into practice, sure enough the power of the opening statement was nullified and the negotiation swung their way.

What does the name Reginald Dwight mean to you? How about Maria Kalogeropoulos? Or Frances Gumm? Not a lot, we'd guess. In fact these are the real names of Elton John, Maria Callas and Judy Garland.

We may scoff at the tendency for entertainers to swap their birth name for something more agreeable, but it's more than mere vanity. Names really do seem to affect the way we perceive people. Research has shown that work produced by individuals with less pleasing names is generally assumed to be inferior. Elton John, we're sure, makes better records than Reginald Dwight would ever have done.

This is just one example of the way in which our emotions influence our reasoning, a phenomenon the psychologist Paul Slovic has named the *affect heuristic* ('affect' being a technical term for a feeling or emotion). What we should do – at least according to the precepts of formal rationality – is make a cool, objective appraisal of a given situation, analysing all the available evidence, before coming to a decision. In practice, and though we're frequently unaware of it, how we *feel* about that situation often determines how we *think* about it.

Advertising and public-relations professionals, of course, have long exploited the affect heuristic. This is why, for example, car commercials seem always to show young, attractive, carefree motorists driving along deserted roads, often against the backdrop of a spectacular natural environment, rather than fuming in an urban traffic jam; why the death of civilians in a military operation is termed 'collateral damage'; and why so many of the groceries in our shops are labelled 'natural', 'new' or 'improved'. The aim is not to convey information, but to induce positive feelings. And positive feelings, as these professionals know very well, can play a big part in our decision-making – though we may subsequently spend much time constructing a rational justification for our emotional preference.

Clearly, then, our feelings can distort our judgement – sometimes with disastrous effects. As most of us know from bitter experience, rationality is often routed by the mere prospect of pleasure (however fleeting or illusory). We become risk-takers: eating or drinking more than is healthy, smoking or taking recreational drugs, indulging in reckless sexual behaviour, or driving faster than we know is wise. But, though we should be alert to the influence of our emotions, we shouldn't automatically dismiss it. Without our emotions guiding our thinking, we'd cope much less well in the world than we actually do. They are, after all, our early warning system, kicking in well before the rational part of our brain and drawing on our accumulated experience to alert us to possible danger and to potential reward. Indeed, the neurologist Antonio Damasio has argued that emotions are an integral part of what we call 'thoughts'. We don't need to sit down and work through the pros and cons of eating a rotten piece of food, or approaching a barking dog, or curling up for a nap after an exhausting day: our emotions will guide us well enough.

Say we were to propose a gamble in which you stood a 50 per cent chance of losing £100 and a 50 per cent chance of winning £200, and then after your first attempt we gave you the chance to play again. Would you go for it?

If you would, you'd be in the minority. Even though over the course of the two gambles you could expect to finish up better off, around two-thirds of people tested in psychological experiments opted out. Why? Well, for most of us the prospect of losing money is a much more compelling motivator than the chance of gaining some cash. It's so powerful, in fact, that it can mean that, as in this example, we don't act rationally. (Given the greater probability of winning cash than of losing it, the logical thing to do is to accept the gamble.) To use the jargon, we are *loss-aversive*.

So awful do most of us find the idea of losing money that we're often reluctant to admit that we've done so. This is one of the reasons why people often stay to the end of a film they're not enjoying. If I stick it out, we reason, I'll have had my money's worth. In truth, of course, all we've done is squander a couple of hours. This kind of thinking is known as the *sunk-cost effect*, and it can mean that we're quite prepared to throw good money after bad. Thus we keep paying that monthly direct debit to the gym even though we can hardly remember the last time we stepped on the running machine or lifted a weight. Cancelling the payments wouldn't simply mean that one more New Year's resolution had petered out: it would feel like an admission that all the money paid had been wasted. (Actually, of course, cancelling the payments and thus cutting our losses is the rational thing to do.)

We're loss-averse, certainly, but how we respond to a given situation is often heavily influenced by the way in which that situation is described. (Psychologists call this a *framing effect*.) You can see this at work in an experiment in which engineers were asked to assess a funding application for a project that was already over budget and behind schedule. The first group of engineers was told, 'Of the projects undertaken by this team, thirty of the last fifty have been successful'; the second group learned that 'Of the projects undertaken by this team, twenty of the last fifty have been unsuccessful.' The information the two groups were given was thus identical, but it was framed in very different ways. This had a significant influence on the decision-makers' willingness to commit further funds to the project. The second group, whose information had focused on previous unsuccessful projects, was much less ready to commit further funds and much more concerned with minimizing losses.

A new confectionery shop opened recently on our high street. Much to our initial delight, it is crammed from floor to ceiling with a dizzying array of chocolates from around the world, almost none of which we have seen elsewhere and all of which seem to cry out to be sampled. In comparison to this palace of wonders, the existing local chocolate shop could hardly compete. And yet a strange thing has happened: over time we have gravitated back to the old shop. The number of products it sells is much more limited, but the range is perfectly adequate and indeed much more manageable than that of the new shop, where we feel bamboozled by choice.

This anecdote seems counterintuitive, because it has become almost axiomatic in Western cultures that choice is inherently good – and the more choice the better. Hence the extraordinary proliferation of product lines in everything from cooking oil to cars. And yet, although no choice at all is rarely preferable, research indicates that we're much more comfortable making a decision when our options are limited. For example, one experiment, conducted by the psychologists Sheena Iyengar and Mark Lepper, first offered shoppers at an upmarket Californian grocery store the opportunity to taste six speciality jams and then, the following week, a range of twenty-four. The wider variety certainly brought more people to the tasting booth, but they didn't sample any more jams than the folk who'd visited the week before. Moreover, it was the shoppers who'd been presented with the six-sample range who were most likely actually to buy a jar (30 per cent of them, as opposed to 4 per cent of the others). The sheer quantity of jams on offer in the twenty-four-sample range seemed to inhibit shoppers' decision-making: in almost every case, they simply walked away from the tasting table empty-handed.

Selecting which jar of jam to buy is a trivial decision, of course, but Iyengar and Lepper's findings have been replicated in many other studies. Choosing from a wide variety of options can be more exciting – at least initially – than picking from a limited range, but also much more frustrating, and ultimately unsatisfying. Why? Perhaps it's because as the options multiply it becomes increasingly difficult to know whether our decision will be the right one (this has been called 'choice overload'). The higher the stakes – our career rather than jam, perhaps, or our children's school rather than sweets – the more fraught that choice becomes.

Some experts have argued that personality can play a part in this. Certain people are 'satisficers', comfortable picking the first option that appeals to them. Others are 'maximizers', carefully pondering each alternative, but then plagued with doubt as to whether the decision they've made is the right one. Whether there can ever be a wrong decision when it comes to chocolate is, however, surely a moot point.

In 1983 the psychologists John Darley and P. H. Gross showed two groups of people a videotape of a child sitting a school test. The first group was told that the child came from a well-off family; the second was told that the child's background was deprived. When the two groups were asked to judge how well the child was doing in the test, the first concluded that she was doing better than average and the second that she was doing worse. What seemed to be happening was that the groups were making assumptions about the level of academic ability one can expect from children of particular social backgrounds – and then reading those assumptions into what they saw on the video.

Darley and Gross's experiment generated a pointed example of what psychologists call the *belief confirmation bias*: we're much more comfortable with our existing opinions than we are with information that challenges those preconceptions. This bias can be useful – imagine having to consider the plausibility of every single proposition – but it can also skew our perception of the world around us. Like the people in Darley and Gross's study, we're prone to employ stereotypes. We tend to attach excessive importance to information that appears to confirm our prior beliefs and to dismiss anything that doesn't. Rather than exploring alternative interpretations, we prefer to stick with what we (think we) know.

There's nothing new, of course, about the belief confirmation bias except its name. The phenomenon was noted, for example, by the English philosopher and scientist Francis Bacon in his *New Organon* of 1620:

> The human understanding when it has once adopted an opinion ... draws all things else to support and agree with it. And though there be a greater number and weight of instances to be found on the other side, yet these it either neglects and despises, or else by some distinction sets aside and rejects, in order that by this great and pernicious pre-determination the authority of its former conclusions may remain inviolate.

The most notable experimental demonstration of this bias was carried out in 1960 by the British psychologist Peter Wason. In what Wason called the 2–4–6 task, the participant must decide what rule links these three numbers. They do this by suggesting their own sets of three numbers, and each time they do so the researcher lets them know whether or not their set fits the rule. Most people instantly decide the rule is 'numbers increasing by two' and spend their time trying to prove this assumption by suggesting triplets like 6–8–10 or 68–70–72. In keeping with the belief conformation bias, they don't test their assumption by trying alternative theories. The upshot of this strategy is that they discover they're mistaken only when they tell the researcher what they've decided the rule is. Because the rule isn't 'numbers increasing by two': it's 'any increasing numbers'.

Just as we tend to be uncritically accepting of our own opinions and beliefs, we're often overly disdainful of other people's views – unless, of course, they happen to agree with ours.

This *disconfirmation bias* was famously observed in an experiment carried out in the late 1970s. The researchers gathered together two groups of people: one in favour of the death penalty and one staunchly opposed to it. The groups were asked to read two analyses of the merits of capital punishment; one of the studies concluded that the death penalty was effective, the other that it was ineffective. Did exposing the groups to an alternative viewpoint change their minds? Not a jot. In fact it merely intensified their existing beliefs: both groups ended the experiment even more convinced of the correctness of their view than they had been initially. They'd read both studies, for sure, but only the one that supported their views had seemed convincing.

What's going on here is a little more complex than meets the eye. Because we don't simply ignore views we don't like: as a study undertaken by Kari Edwards and Edward Smith demonstrated, we actively seek to undermine them. Edwards and Smith asked undergraduates at the University of Michigan to assess a number of arguments relating to issues such as whether it's ever appropriate to strike a child, whether employers should be obliged to hire people from minority groups, and whether gay or lesbian couples should be permitted to adopt children. The researchers stressed that what they were interested in was not whether a participant agreed with a particular argument, but rather how strong they found it.

This crucial point, however, seemed to fall on deaf ears: the propositions that the students found strongest were the ones they agreed with. Conversely, the arguments the students spent *longest* evaluating were those they opposed. Now that might sound promising, but actually this extra time wasn't spent judiciously considering the merits of an alternative viewpoint. Far from it. All the additional effort went into refuting that viewpoint. And the more strongly the students felt about an issue, the more reasons they found to dispute an opposing argument. More reasons, but not better reasons: in fact most were thinly veiled restatements of an objection the person had already made. But then, as we all know, it's hard to think analytically when emotions are high.

As you'll have gathered by now, human beings aren't always expert decision-makers. (Or at least we are not when we think about the process: as Herbert Simon wrote, referring to our intuitive powers of reasoning, 'We cannot, of course, rule out the possibility than the unconscious is a better decision-maker than the conscious.') Ironically, one judgement we tend to be especially poor at is assessing whether or not our decisions have been sound ones. This is because we often find it difficult accurately to recall a decision. Thanks to something called *hindsight bias*, our memory is heavily influenced by our knowledge of how things turned out. Not only does the event seem to have been inevitable, we often feel – erroneously – that we predicted it in the first place. Imagine, for example, that you and a friend go on a camping holiday. If it's a success, you'll probably congratulate yourself for suggesting the trip: *I was right!* If, on the other hand, it rains constantly and you're forced to head home early, what you're more likely to recall are your doubts when your friend first mentioned the possibility: *I was right!*

But we aren't merely overconfident about decisions we've made in the past: we tend to be equally bullish about those we'll make in the future. Indeed, most of us, for much of the time, are quite astoundingly confident about our abilities in almost every area of life, overrating our own prospects and underestimating those of everyone else. Take intellectual or academic ability, for example. It's well known that people usually believe their general knowledge is better than it really is. And when, in another piece of research, students were asked to rate their performance in a number of academic tests, the majority believed that they'd performed better than average (only the highest achievers underestimated their level of attainment).

We can see the same tendency at work in the business world. When, for example, 3,000 new business owners were asked to assess their chances of success, 81 per cent believed they'd make a go of it. When they were asked to rate the chances of a similar business run by someone else, their estimate was lower, at 59 per cent. In fact only a third of new businesses last longer than four years.

Incidentally, it appears that men are typically more over-confident than women. One fascinating study looked at the performance of both sexes in the stockbroking sector. The more confident a broker is, the more often they'll engage in the inherently risky business of trading shares. When the researchers analysed 35,000 broker accounts, they discovered that men completed 45 per cent more trades than women. Yet the men's estimation of their own abilities proved to be misplaced: the women traded less often, but they enjoyed greater success.

Related to this overconfidence is a striking optimism about life in general. (This isn't necessarily a bad thing, by the way: there's a strong correlation between optimism and happiness.) For example, who do you think is more likely to be involved in a serious car crash – you or the average person? Most people asked this sort of question choose the other fellow. What about the probability of surviving into a happy and healthy old age? This time, people usually back their own chances. Positive events, we tend to assume, are more likely to happen to us than to other people. They, on the other hand, are first in line for the bad stuff.

This chapter may have given the impression that human beings are fundamentally irrational, our reasoning contorted by such a profusion of biases that thinking straight is virtually impossible. But things aren't so bad. For a start, many people are adept at highly sophisticated abstract thought: indeed, it's hard to think of a technology whose development hasn't necessitated this kind of skill. And almost all of us are capable of this kind of reasoning on occasion, albeit at a less elevated level – remember those maths exams you did at school, for example? More importantly, although our thought processes tend to be quick and intuitive rather than methodically rational, they're usually perfectly adequate. Life is too short, and too complex, for us to proceed in any other fashion. The way we reason usually can't give us the best possible decision, but what it does generally provide – and fast – is a *good enough* one.

That said, because our reasoning isn't exhaustively logical, it's prone to errors – as we've seen. Can we do anything to minimize such problems? Yes, we can. The first step is one you've already taken (assuming, that is, you've read the previous ten pages and haven't skipped straight to the end of the chapter): becoming aware of the biases that often affect our thinking. After all, you can't deal with something unless you know it's there. The second step is to try to compensate for these biases. How you do that will depend in part on the specifics of the situation, but there are some sound general principles you can apply:

- **Don't neglect the base rate.** Remember, when you're trying to work out how likely something is, it's wise to follow the advice of the Reverend Bayes. Judge each case on its merits, but in the context of what you know about how probable that event is in general. That horse is fast, for sure, but how often has it actually won?

- **Consider the alternatives.** We generally make judgements quickly, and often with our emotions rather than our intellect in the driving seat. This is fine for trivial decisions, but less prudent when more is at stake. So take the time to think through a range of options, weighing up the evidence, and assessing the prospective pros and cons.

- **Challenge your preconceptions.** Most of us are pretty set in our ways. We have our opinions, our habitual ways of responding to situations, and we don't like changing them. But every so often these preconceptions need a shake-up. How you do this is by consciously challenging them: again, mull over the evidence for and against, and do the same for any alternative viewpoints you can think of.

4. MEMORY

When I first heard about the explosion I was sitting in my freshman dorm room with my roommate and we were watching TV. It came on a news flash and we were both totally shocked. I was really upset and I went upstairs to talk to a friend of mine and then I called my parents.

Can you recall where you were on 28 January 1986 when the space shuttle *Challenger* disintegrated over the Atlantic? What about 11 September 2001? Or the day in 1990 when Nelson Mandela walked free after twenty-seven years in prison? Like most people, you probably have a very clear memory of what you were doing when you first heard the news of these momentous events. Indeed, our recollections of such historic incidents tend to be so vivid and persistent, even dozens of years later, that they are known as 'flashbulb memories'. But, though these may feel like some of the strongest memories we possess, they are often much less reliable than we assume.

How do we know? After all, a personal memory, almost by definition, is inordinately difficult to verify. Well, the short quote at the top of this page is taken from a recollection of the *Challenger* disaster written by an undergraduate at Emory University in Atlanta, Georgia, almost three years after the event. And here's an account written by the same student the day after *Challenger* was lost:

I was in my religion class and some people walked in and
started talking about [it]. I didn't know any of the details
except that it had exploded and the schoolteacher's students
had all been watching which I thought was so sad. Then after
class I went to my room and watched the TV program talking
about it and I got all the details from that.

The accounts aren't entirely different from each other – the
student remembered that she'd heard the news while at the
university rather than, say, at the dentist or at her family home.
She recalled having watched coverage of the event on television.
The discrepancies, however, are far more striking than the
similarities. And yet, until she was shown her original account,
the student was sure that her 1988 memory was totally accurate.

This was typical of the forty-three other Emory undergraduates surveyed by Ulric Neisser and Nicole Harsch. By 1988
and 1989, precisely none of the students was able to remember
exactly how they'd learned about the disaster, and, although
a few were relatively close, many were way off. In fact three-
quarters of the students couldn't even remember having been
asked in 1986 to record their experiences of the event.

Though it seems counterintuitive, the fact that an event
provokes a deep emotional reaction within us is no guarantee
that we will remember it accurately. And equally irrelevant is
the degree of confidence we have in our recollections: Neisser
and Harsch found no correlation between the certainty with
which the students regarded their memories and the accuracy of
them. Indeed, most were flabbergasted to see just how little their
original accounts had in common with their later memories. As
one of the students exclaimed, 'Whoa! That's totally different
from how I remember it!'

On a scale from one to ten, how would you rate your everyday
memory? Many people – and particularly once they're closer to

forty than thirty – tend to feel that their memory isn't as good as they'd like it to be. It's true that there's usually a gradual deterioration as we get into middle age and beyond. But, even so, your memory is almost certainly better than you think, not least because we often have an unrealistic belief in the accuracy of everyone else's powers of recollection. It's easy to feel that you're the scatty one in the office when you mislay something important, but, as we saw in the previous section, forgetting is normal.

Moreover, despite the habit of describing memory as if it is a single faculty ('My memory is terrible'/'I have a pretty good memory'), most of us are better at remembering some kinds of information than others. We may be able to recall in some detail the topics we discussed with our friend over dinner, for example, and yet not have a clue about how they were dressed. Or we may possess an encyclopedic memory for films we've seen, but struggle to put a name to a face. Memory, it seems, is diverse rather than unitary, complex rather than straightforward. As Fanny Price remarks in Jane Austen's *Mansfield Park* (1814):

> If any one faculty of our nature may be called more wonderful than the rest, I do think it is memory ... The memory is sometimes so retentive, so serviceable, so obedient; at others, so bewildered and so weak; and at others again, so tyrannic, so beyond control! We are, to be sure, a miracle every way; but our powers of recollecting and forgetting do seem peculiarly past finding out.

But the situation isn't quite as hopeless as all that. There's much about memory that remains a mystery, for sure, but the three main processes have been identified:

- **Encoding** – how we register an event in our memory
- **Storage** – where our memories are deposited
- **Retrieval** – how we bring a memory into consciousness

You can read about encoding on pages 70–2, and about retrieval on pages 72–4. But first let's look at the three main types of memory storage: sensory, short-term and long-term.

What do you see if you wave a lit cigarette in circles at night-time? What you see, of course, is a continuous bright-orange ring as the multiple retinal images of the burning tobacco merge into one. This phenomenon – known as persistence of vision – is an illustration of *sensory memory*.

Sensory memory has more in common with perception than it does with what we normally think of as memory. Each sense produces a copy of whatever stimulus it detects (in the example we've just given, it's the image of the cigarette), and stores it until more information is registered. In the case of hearing (so-called echoic memory), that might be a couple of seconds later; for vision (iconic memory), it's usually no more than half a second.

The second form of memory is *short-term* – also known as *working* memory, because completing virtually any task becomes impossible without it. Working memory is very limited in the amount of information it can store, but this is sufficient to allow you to retain the beginning of this sentence in order to make sense of the end, or to remember what someone has said long enough to reply. In the view of Alan Baddeley, the guru of memory research, working memory has three distinct components. The *phonological loop* handles verbal information; visual and spatial data are processed by the *visuo-spatial sketchpad*; and the *central executive* co-ordinates the whole process.

How much information can our short-term memory cope with? In 1956 the psychologist George Miller famously confessed, 'My problem is that I have been persecuted by an integer. For seven years this number has followed me around, has intruded in my most private data, and has assaulted me from the pages of our most public journals ... Either there really is something unusual about the number or else I am suffering from delusions of persecution.'

The integer that Miller believed was stalking him was the 'magical number seven' – plus or minus two. He realized that most people given a list of numbers or one-syllable words are able to recall just seven of them (this is known as memory span). And for virtually all sensory stimuli our ability to discriminate between individual instances – for example, musical notes, tastes, the size of objects, the volume of sounds, brightness, colours – fails once we have more than seven (plus or minus two) to compare. It seems that our working memory simply cannot retain the necessary information. As Miller wrote, 'There seems to be some limitation built into us either by learning or by the design of our nervous systems.'

Now, imagine that you're visiting your local pub and ask for a glass of red wine. 'Sure,' says the bartender, 'which would you like?' So of course you ask, 'What do you have?' 'Well,' answers the bartender, 'we have Rioja, Chinon, Merlot, Chianti, Pinot Noir, Bordeaux, Malbec, Shiraz, Beaujolais, Tempranillo, Côtes du Rhône, Sangiovese, Petit Verdot ... ' By this point in the torrent of names you're utterly lost. 'I think I'll go for the Rioja,' you answer – partly because you like it, but principally because it's one of the few names you're sure you can remember being paraded before you.

You've managed to choose a wine, but that choice has been heavily influenced by what's known as the *primacy effect*: the tendency for us to remember items at the beginning of a list rather than those that follow. Apart, that is, from the items at the very end of a sequence: those we can usually recall pretty well too, which isn't surprising since they're the last thing we hear and thus need to be stored in our working memory for the least amount of time. This is called the *recency effect*. And it explains why you may also have been tempted by the Sangiovese or the Petit Verdot, but have absolutely no idea which wines were mentioned in the middle of that long and bewildering recital.

How long must a memory last for it to qualify *as* a memory?

As we've just seen, strictly speaking it can be as little as half a second. But this seems very far short of what most of us think of as memory, just a fleeting impression rather than an enduring recollection – almost, in fact, the antithesis of memory.

There is, however, a form of memory that fits the common-sense view: *long-term memory*. Long-term memory seems to rely on different areas of the brain from short-term and sensory memory. But even long-term memories can be rather briefer than we may imagine. In fact anything we remember for more than about a minute is classified as a long-term memory. Clearly, sixty seconds is a pretty short passage of time, but research has shown that these very recent memories behave much like older memories.

Until the 1960s, scientists generally regarded memory as a relatively undifferentiated system. We know now that there are several different forms of long-term memory, not to mention the sensory and short-term varieties. That the earlier view changed was due in no small part to the efforts of the psychologist Endel Tulving, who was born in Estonia in 1927 but emigrated to Canada in his early twenties. Tulving apparently stumbled into memory research. When he was appointed to his first teaching post, at the University of Toronto in 1956, he intended to carry on with his studies of visual perception. But there was no budget for the necessary equipment. At that time Tulving knew absolutely nothing about memory, except that the research materials – principally pens and paper – were likely to be extremely cheap.

There are three main types of long-term memory. The first is *procedural*, a form of automatic memory for how to perform certain tasks – riding a bike or driving a car, for example. Once learned, procedural memories are very hard to shake. Even patients with severe amnesia who have forgotten many of their past memories can normally exercise these sorts of skill, though they may be quite unable to recall having done so in the past.

Procedural memory is *implicit*: we don't have to try to remember how to perform these tasks; the information just appears when we need it. The other two types of long-term memory, on the other hand, are *explicit* (sometimes called *declarative*), meaning that conscious effort is required to produce them:

- **Semantic memory** comprises information about the world – for example, that the capital of the United Kingdom is London, or indeed what the words 'United Kingdom' and 'London' mean – that we can't remember learning: we just seem to know it.
- **Episodic memories** are memories of experiences.

Tulving believes that episodic memory represents a pinnacle of the developmental, and evolutionary, process (procedural memory being the most basic form of long-term memory). Only humans, he argues, possess episodic memory. And, even in humans, episodic memory is the last to develop – in Tulving's view it usually appears at around the age of four. Unable to recall past experiences clearly, or truly imagine the future, young children instead live in the moment. On the other hand, it's episodic memory that is the first to deteriorate as we age.

*

Right now, I'm wondering. Have I done or said anything amiss? You see, at this moment everything looks clear to me, but what happened just before? That's what worries me. It's like waking from a dream; I just don't remember.

In the 1950s doctors in the US began experimenting with a new technique to treat severe epilepsy. One of the patients to undergo this treatment, which involved surgically excising parts of the brain, was a twenty-seven-year-old man subsequently known (in order to protect his privacy) as H.M. On his death in 2008, at the age of eighty-two, the *New York Times* called H.M. – now revealed as Henry Gustav Molaison – 'the most important patient in the history of brain science'.

Following the operation in 1953 in Hartford, Connecticut, H.M.'s epilepsy improved. But the effects of the surgery were unfortunately much more profound than this. H.M. was utterly – and, as it turned out, permanently – unable to form new memories (a condition known as *anteriograde amnesia*). He could recall details of his life before his operation, and he hadn't forgotten how to speak or read or write. He could learn practical skills, meaning that his procedural memory was intact (though he had no recollection of how he had acquired such new knowledge). H.M.'s short-term memory was also unaffected: for example, he was quite capable of carrying on a conversation or reading an article in the newspaper (remember that if our short-term memory isn't functioning properly such basic tasks become extremely difficult).

But H.M.'s long-term memory was so damaged that, even several years after his surgery, he would get lost if he strayed more than a couple of blocks from his home. He was unsure about his age, and had to guess what year it was. He couldn't remember what he'd had for breakfast that morning, the dramatic item he'd just heard on the news, or who had come to visit him a few minutes earlier. He was unable to work, or to live independently. Until the age of fifty-four he lived with his family, and then with a relative; thereafter he was cared for in a nursing home in Connecticut.

At the time, many experts doubted whether H.M.'s memory impairment was the direct result of his surgery. They believed that the faculty of memory was distributed throughout the brain, and that therefore the removal of specific parts could not cause such catastrophic effects. But this view was conclusively overturned by a British-born psychologist named Brenda Milner, who was based at the Montreal Neurological Institute. Milner travelled from Canada to meet H.M. many times over the years, 'yet every time I walked in the room it was like we'd never met'.

After much testing, Milner was able to pinpoint the cause of H.M.'s plight – and simultaneously transform our understanding of the neurological basis of memory. Among the parts of H.M.'s brain that had been excised was the hippocampus, a small structure situated in the limbic system (a region located in the subcortex, which sits above the brain stem, at the top of the spinal cord, and below the cerebral cortex), and taking its name from the ancient Greek term for 'sea horse', which it is said to resemble in shape. Milner demonstrated that the hippocampus plays a crucial role in the formation of new memories – and it seems that the more you use it, the bigger it grows. For example, London black-cab drivers, who require an exceptionally comprehensive knowledge of the city's streets, tend to have a relatively large hippocampus. Conversely, the hippocampus in people with Alzheimer's disease – whose memory is of course progressively damaged by their illness – shrinks dramatically. And without his hippocampus it was as if H.M. had been unmoored from normal temporality and cast adrift in a vast and bewildering eternal present.

*

As soon as I had recognized the taste of the piece of madeleine dipped in lime-blossom tea that my aunt used to give me ... immediately the old grey house on the street, where her bedroom was, came like a stage-set to attach itself to the little wing opening on to the garden that had been built for my parents ... and with the house the town, from morning to night and in all weathers, the Square, where they sent me before lunch, the streets where I went to do errands, the paths we took if the weather was fine ...
  – **Marcel Proust**, *The Way by Swann's* (1913)

We've looked at how our memories are stored; now we'll explore how we retrieve them. Let's start by asking you to write down the names of the twenty-one prime ministers that have governed the UK between 1900 and 2009. How many can you think of?

Suppose we were to offer you the initial letters of their names in chronological order of their first period in office (running from left to right, with the initials of the earliest prime minister in the top left):

M of S	AB	HC-B	HA	DLG	ABL
SB	RM	NC	WC	CA	AE
HM	AD-H	HW	EH	JC	MT
JM	TB	GB			

How many can you recall? Probably more than you managed first time around.

Now, how many of the following names do you recognize?

Marquess of Salisbury	Arthur Balfour	Henry Campell-Bannerman
Herbert Asquith	David Lloyd George	Andrew Bonar Law
Stanley Baldwin	Ramsay MacDonald	Neville Chamberlain
Winston Churchill	Clement Atlee	Anthony Eden
Harold Macmillan	Alec Douglas-Home	Harold Wilson
Edward Heath	James Callaghan	Margaret Thatcher
John Major	Tony Blair	Gordon Brown

Almost certainly you'll know more of these names than you were able to produce either from the top of your head or by using the clue of their initials.

This brain-teaser illustrates three of the main ways in which we retrieve our memories. Your first attempt at remembering the names of the prime ministers was an example of what's known as *free recall*. When we gave you the initials, you were then able to engage in *cued recall*. This is the kind of remembering experienced by the narrator in Proust's *In Search of Lost*

Time when he dips the madeleine into his tisane. (Our memory for tastes and smells is actually remarkably resilient, perhaps because we encounter relatively few of them during the course of our lives.) And, just as in Proust's novel, if you can manage to pull one detail from the lime-blossom tea, others often follow (this is called *content addressability*). Finally, knowing the names when you saw them is an example of *recognition*.

Generally speaking, recognition is easier than cued recall, which in turn is easier than free recall. More straightforward still are the kind of memories that come to us automatically, such as for procedural tasks like riding a bike. The memories we can produce through free recall constitute merely the tip of a very much larger iceberg.

We're also much more likely to recall something when we're back where we first experienced it. This was demonstrated in a classic experiment carried out by Alan Baddeley and Duncan Godden. While they were about three metres under water, sixteen divers were played a tape recorded list of thirty-six words and asked to memorize them. Once back on land, they were asked to listen to, and memorize, an alternative set of words.

Baddeley and Godden then tested the divers, both under water and on land, to see how many of the words they could remember. They found that the divers performed better when they were back where they'd learned the particular lists. So words heard under water were most accurately recalled when under water; those learned on land were best remembered on land. The divers' memories, in other words, were *context-dependent*.

Without checking your wallet, can you remember who is pictured on the reverse of a £5 note (that's to say, the side that doesn't feature a profile of the Queen's head)?

Perhaps you know who it is: we did not. And how frustrating it is to realize that one cannot remember a major feature of an object that one has seen hundreds, perhaps even thousands, of times. (The answer – at least for notes currently issued by the Bank of England rather than the Scottish or Northern Irish banks – is Elizabeth Fry, the nineteenth-century campaigner for prison reform.) One might think that recalling something one sees frequently would be relatively easy, but in fact people tend to find it extremely difficult, perhaps because of its very mundanity. As the Victorian psychologist J. M. Cattell noted, most of us 'cannot state much better what the weather was a week ago than what it will be a week hence'.

If we are so poor at remembering everyday objects and events, do we fare any better when it comes to recalling very dramatic or significant incidents? Yes and no. We're certainly unlikely to forget our wedding day, the night our home was burgled, or our child's first day at school, for example. Indeed, the more unusual an experience is, the greater the likelihood that we will remember it. But, as we saw when we discussed 'flashbulb' memories on p. 56, these recollections are often neither particularly accurate nor especially detailed. Does this matter? When you consider how important eyewitness testimony is to the outcome of many trials, the fallibility of human memory becomes very significant indeed.

No one has done more to develop our understanding of this crucial issue than Elizabeth Loftus, currently based at the University of California, Irvine, and rated the most eminent female psychologist of the twentieth century by the American Psychological Association. In a series of classic studies, Loftus and her colleagues demonstrated just how vulnerable witnesses are to leading questions. For example, a videotape of a car crash was shown to several groups of people. When members of one group were asked, 'How fast were the cars going when they collided with each other?', their average response was 31.8 miles per hour (51.2 kilometres per hour). A different group were asked, 'How fast were the cars going when they smashed into each other?' These participants reckoned the cars were travelling a full nine miles per hour faster, at 40.8 miles per hour (65.6 kilometres per hour). Each group's estimate of the cars' speed was heavily influenced by the particular verb used in the question.

Similarly, when the questioners mentioned a stop sign, many of the participants remembered seeing it – even though no such sign had appeared in the video. Asking 'Did you see the broken headlight?' was much more likely to elicit an affirmative from participants than the more tentative 'Did you see a broken headlight?' And groups who'd heard the incident described as a 'smash' were far more inclined to agree that they'd seen broken glass than those for whom the accident had been described in less loaded terminology (again, there was no broken glass).

Bear in mind that Loftus's experiments were carried out in a psychological laboratory. If people are so suggestible in a lab, one can only imagine how they are likely to perform in the intensely stressful atmosphere of a courtroom. Moreover, many eyewitnesses manage just a fleeting glimpse of an incident – it's not something they were expecting, after all. And where a weapon was used in a crime, it's often this feature of the incident that – for understandable reasons – drew most of their attention. (This tendency is known as *weapon focus*.)

This is not to suggest that eyewitness accounts are inherently unreliable – indeed, some studies show that people are often very good at remembering aspects of an incident that they see very clearly and face on. What they tend to be less proficient at is recalling peripheral details (a face seen in profile, for example, or an accomplice standing off to one side). And sometimes, of course, it's these peripheral elements that are most important to the outcome of a case.

Let's flip the coin of memory and take an excursion to the dark side. Because there's no memory without forgetting, just as there's no Dr Jekyll without Mr Hyde, no Batman without the Joker, and no Harry Potter without Lord Voldemort.

We may be overdramatizing the situation somewhat: after all, forgetting is perfectly normal. (Indeed, for many of us it's actually remembering something that can seem like the anomaly.) But there's no doubting the joy that our memories can bring us, nor how frustrating – and sometimes frankly distressing – it is to sense that a memory has disappeared for good. Our memories are integral to our sense of self: without them we can feel diminished, even bereft.

The process of forgetting is usually quite straightforward. It happens fastest during the first twenty minutes after an incident has been committed to long-term memory, then gradually slows down over the next twenty-four hours before finally levelling out to a fairly constant (and small) rate. What you're left with then is likely to remain with you for as long as the memory lasts.

This so-called 'forgetting curve' was discovered by the first person to undertake a properly scientific study of memory, the German philosopher Hermann Ebbinghaus (1850–1909). Ebbinghaus was a rather remarkable individual, not least in the dedication he brought to his research. Rather than conducting his experiments on a range of volunteers (as is standard in psychological research), Ebbinghaus himself memorized hundreds of items, day after day, and then tested his ability to recall them, sometimes at hourly intervals.

Some memories are especially resistant to forgetting – particularly procedural information (how to type, for instance, or what to do with a toothbrush and a tube of toothpaste). Most vulnerable, on the other hand, are episodic memories – that's to say, conscious recollections of specific information and experiences. These memories are vulnerable to *interference* from other similar memories. This can be *proactive*, in which our efforts to remember something new – for example, how to tune the radio in your recently purchased car – are sabotaged by the memory of how we used to do it, or *retroactive*, whereby an old memory is endangered by the creation of a new one – for instance, learning your current phone number may make it much more difficult to recall your previous one.

Why do we forget? Scientists don't really know. For Sigmund Freud, forgetting was the product of a psychological force he named repression, which drives unacceptable thoughts (primarily sexual in character) from consciousness. There's little evidence to support this view, however. Much forgetting seems to be 'cue-dependent': the information is there in our memory, but we're unable to find the trigger that will bring it to light. (Some experts have argued – without producing much evidence, it's fair to say – that nothing ever really vanishes from memory: it's all there somewhere, were we only able to locate it.) Maybe our memories die out if they're not retrieved sufficiently often. Or perhaps we shed them in order to make room for new memories. This latter view would be something like the Homer Simpson theory of memory: 'Every time I learn something new, it pushes some old stuff out of my brain. Remember when I took that home wine-making course, and I forgot how to drive?'

What can you do to strengthen your memory? Well, it's primarily a matter of improving the way you organize and store the material – in other words, how you *encode* your memories. There are several ways to do this:

Pay attention. The more we focus on something, the more likely we are to remember it. Cut out distractions and really concentrate on whatever it is you want to memorize.

Make it memorable. If you don't want information to disappear into the mists, you need to make it as memorable as possible. An effective way to do this is to link the item you want to remember to something you already know, and preferably to yourself (since nothing is more fascinating and memorable). So if you meet someone at a party, say, you've more chance of remembering their name if you also register the fact that your partner knows their sister.

Try associating the item with an image, preferably one as amusing and distinctive as possible. (These images are called *visual mnemonics*.) Exaggeration often works well. If someone is very tall, for example, you might visualize their head scraping the ceiling. Memorizing a list of items is easier if you weave them into story. The more entertaining the story, and the more of your senses it involves, the better. So conjure up the way something looks, sounds, feels and even smells.

There are many established visual mnemonic systems – one that goes back to the ancient Greeks is structured around the rooms of a house. Imagine a route through your home – from front door to hallway to kitchen to bathroom and so on. Once you have this route clear in your mind, you can use the various points in it as pegs on which to hang other information.

Rehearse. The more often you recall a memory, the more readily you'll be able to remember it in the future.

Chunk. Research shows that we find it easier to remember complicated information if we break it down into manageable chunks (seven items is normally seen as the maximum for each chunk). For example, it's easier to remember a multi-digit telephone number if you split it up into smaller units.

Use verbal mnemonics. This is a tried-and-tested technique in which a memorable rhyme or phrase helps you recall otherwise unrelated pieces of information. 'Richard Of York Gave Battle In Vain', for example, is a traditional device for remembering the colours of the rainbow, and we like 'On Old Olympia's Towering Top A Finn And German Vault And Hop', a mnemonic used by medical students to help them memorize the names of the cranial nerves.

Learn it perfectly. Remembering something properly is much easier if we learn it perfectly in the first place. Once uncertainty or error creeps in, it's difficult to shake off. So if you're trying to memorize a set of directions, for example, take the time to really concentrate on the information. Make sure you can repeat it back to yourself without mistakes. Check you can still remember the directions perfectly after an hour or so, and then test yourself again on the following days (this is an example of rehearsal).

If you're revising for an exam, or have a lot of new information to memorize, it's best to break down your work into short periods of around half an hour, interspersed with regular brief breaks. And make sure you can remember the information without needing a clue or hint (what you're after is recall, not recognition).

To aid retrieval of your memories:

Use cues and context. If you can improve the encoding of your memories, you'll find it much easier to recall information when you need it. But you can also help yourself by using reminders, or *cues* – for example, putting an egg carton on the passenger seat of your car so you remember to buy eggs when you're out, or leaving items you need to take to the post office on the doormat so you can't miss them when you leave.

As we've seen, our memories are hugely context-dependent. We're more likely to remember something if we can re-create the situation in which we first experienced it. So if you're struggling to remember what your friend told you in the pub last night, visualize the scene in as much detail as possible.

Write it down. Diaries, calendars, to-do lists, shopping lists, notes to yourself – most of us use at least some of these to help our overburdened memories. And there are many more of these memory aids. The traditional knot in the handkerchief, writing on your hand, a wristwatch or mobile-phone alarm, for example, are all great ways of reminding yourself to do something.

*

If you want to win friends, make it a point to remember them. If you remember my name, you pay me a subtle compliment; you indicate that I have made an impression on you. Remember my name and you add to my feeling of importance.

This astute advice is taken from Dale Carnegie's classic *How to Win Friends and Influence People*, first published in 1936 and still, some 15 million copies later, as popular as ever.

How good are you at remembering names? What about faces? And how do you get on when faced with the ultimate challenge: putting the correct name to a face?

If you struggle with any of these skills, you're certainly not alone. And it doesn't necessarily mean that your memory as a whole is poor. For example, there's often little or no correlation between someone's memory for faces and their ability to recall verbal information, such as names. Indeed, some experts have speculated that our ability to perceive and remember faces may rely on a specific (though as yet unidentified) system in the brain. In support of this idea that we process facial information differently from other visual data, research has shown that it's comparatively easy to deduce what a building looks like when we see a photo of it upside down, but much harder to identify and read the expression of an inverted face. And patients afflicted with the neurological disorder prosopagnosia (of which the most famous sufferer was Oliver Sack's 'Dr P.' of *The Man Who Mistook His Wife for a Hat*) are often able to identify inanimate objects successfully, but cannot recognize faces.

If your memory for names and faces isn't what you'd like it to be, try these techniques:

When you meet someone for the first time, pay close attention to the way they look. Make a mental note of any distinctive feature – the colour of their eyes, or the shape of their nose, for instance.

Try to imagine the person's character: do they seem intelligent, trustworthy or friendly, for example? The more information you can associate with someone (that's to say, the more richly you can 'encode' your memory), the better the chances of you recalling them when the need arises.

Pay attention to the sound of the person's name. This sounds obvious, but it's easy to be distracted in social situations, especially if we're a bit shy or nervous.

Ask the person to say their name again – even if you've heard it perfectly well. No one will mind repeating this information, and with luck it'll save you the embarrassment of having to confess some time later that you've no idea what they're called.

Use the person's name when you're saying goodbye.

Remind yourself of the person's name, and check that you can visualize their face. Do this a few minutes after you've met them, a few hours later (on your way home, for instance), and then the following day. If you want to retain your memories, rehearse them as often as possible.

Use the techniques we mention above – developing an amusing visual reminder or story, for example – to make names and faces as memorable (because richly encoded) as possible.

5. SEEING AND HEARING

Sometimes the things that seem the simplest in life turn out to be the most complicated. Take this very moment, for example. There you are, reading this book, effortlessly transforming a sequence of small black shapes into meaningful units of information. Wherever you happen to be, when you lift your gaze from the page an extraordinarily diverse scene awaits, full of colours and shapes and sizes. Pause to listen and you'll discover an equally rich array of sounds – perhaps the hum of conversation from people nearby, the growl of a car as it makes its way down the street, or simply the rise and fall of your own breathing. And what scents can you smell? What do the objects around you feel like – your desk or chair, the clothes that you wear?

All day long, and largely subconsciously, we receive and process sensory information. Despite the apparent ease with which we accomplish this task, it's a truly mind-boggling achievement; indeed, vision alone utilizes one-third of the human brain.

We use this sensory information to *perceive* our environment, which really amounts to building our knowledge of the world around us. As you might imagine, this isn't a trivial matter: that knowledge helps determine our chances of survival and success. An animal that can't see or hear well, for example, probably won't last long. The consequences for a modern human are unlikely to be as stark, but life will almost certainly become much more challenging. Navigating the amazing world of sensation and perception in a single chapter is a daunting assignment. To make it just a little more practicable, we focus on the two most critical areas: seeing and hearing.

Whichever of our senses we're using, the essential process is the same. What we're doing is detecting sources of energy in our environment and then converting the information obtained into a form that our brain can use. (This conversion process is known as *transduction*.) In the case of vision, that energy is in the form of light. Ancient Greek philosophers believed that we emit light from our eyes to illuminate the world around us. Now we know that light is really electromagnetic radiation produced by the sun. Much of this radiation we can't see, for very good reasons. Take ultraviolet (UV) light, for instance. This is the stuff that causes sunburn and most cases of skin cancer. It's so damaging that our eyes filter it out; if they didn't, it would probably destroy them. And yet many animals – such as birds and insects – do possess UV vision. Since their lifespan is so much shorter than that of the average human, presumably there simply isn't enough time for UV radiation to cause problems.

Light travels fast – around 300,000 kilometres per second – and it travels in straight lines, which means that it's comparatively easy for the brain to work out where it's coming from (unlike sound waves, for example). When the rays of light illuminating, say, a chair strike your eye, they are focused by the lens to form an image on the *retina*, a layer of cells deep within the eyeball. The retina connects to the optic nerve, along which information passes to the areas of the brain devoted to visual processing. (Actually, the retina is regarded as part of the brain – indeed, it's the only part of the brain that can be observed directly while its owner is still alive.)

The retina contains millions of light-sensitive cells (or *photoreceptors*) called rods and cones. The rods help us see black, white and grey; the cones register colour. Humans – or almost all humans – have a more diverse range of cones than other mammals, meaning that we're able to detect a greater number of colours. Bulls, for example, do not see a red rag as red. (One theory suggests that primates developed colour vision in order to help them spot fruit in the massed foliage of the forest.) People who are colour-blind, however, generally lack the type of cone that allows us to distinguish between red and green. Those who suffer from 'true' colour blindness have no cones at all.

Rods and cones don't only differ in their handling of colours: they also vary in their responsiveness to brightness. In good light, the cones do most of the work. They're gathered around the centre of the retina, in an area called the fovea. This is why we need to focus our attention on something in order to see it well. The much more numerous rods – there are around 120 million of them, as opposed to just 7 million cones – are spread out around the edges of the retina, so we tend to use them for peripheral vision. The rods are a thousand times more sensitive to brightness than the cones, meaning that they're just what we need to see in poor light. Nocturnal animals have an even smaller proportion of cones than diurnal creatures such as humans; bats and deep-sea fish, which spend their entire lives in darkness, have no cones at all. The rods in our eyes take a while to warm up, however, because light depletes their stock of a chemical called rhodopsin. So when we first walk into a dark room we can't see anything at all. But, as the rhodopsin is regenerated (a process that takes half an hour to complete), our vision improves and objects that just a few minutes ago were invisible beneath a blanket of darkness are gradually revealed to us.

The footage has to be seen to be believed.* An elderly man, completely blind, his vision extinguished by two strokes, makes

------

*You can watch the video at
http://www.nytimes.com/2008/12/23/health/23blin.html?_r=1.

his way gingerly down a corridor littered with obstacles (boxes, a tripod, a waste-paper basket, a pack of A4 paper). Following a couple of paces behind him is a researcher, poised to come to the rescue if the man should trip on any of the obstructions. But the blind man needs no such help: to the delight and amazement of the researcher, he negotiates the obstacle course perfectly.

How is this possible? How can a person who is totally blind navigate with the skill of someone with perfect sight? The answer lies in the remarkable way in which the brain deals with visual information. Photoreceptor cells (the rods and cones) in the retina transform light into a kind of energy that the brain can process – electrical signals that make their way along the optic nerve. You can detect the point at which the optic nerve joins your retina because there are no photoreceptors there, creating a blind spot. To do so, cover your left eye and focus on the circle below while gently moving your head backwards and forwards. Eventually the cross will disappear into your blind spot. Then focus your gaze, with only your left eye open, on the cross. As you move your head to around twenty to thirty centimetres away, the circle will vanish.

Eventually, and after progressive winnowing has left only the essential data, information passed along the optic nerve arrives in a region at the back of the brain known as the *occipital lobes*. It's here, in the visual cortices, that we make sense of the raw sensory information captured by our eyes. This is a conscious process – albeit one that generally seems to happen automatically. We're not aware of thinking 'I want to look at that bookcase'; nevertheless, we deliberately focus our gaze in that direction. One of the first scientists to discover the central role played by the occipital lobes was the Japanese army physician Tatsuji Inouye. Charged with assessing the level of blindness of soldiers wounded in the Russo-Japanese war (1904–5), Inouye invented a device to pinpoint exactly where a bullet had penetrated (and exited) the skull and thus which areas of the brain the gunshot had damaged.

But there's another, unconscious, kind of visual processing going on in our brains that bypasses the occipital lobes in favour of the more primitive mid-brain region. This unconscious processing is as rapid and instinctual as a reflex – for example, letting us know which way our face is pointing, or when we're near a boundary of some sort, or when the expression on someone's face is threatening. It's this system of visual processing that enabled the blind man to walk down a cluttered corridor without so much as brushing against any of the objects in his path, a phenomenon termed *blindsight*. His visual cortices had been destroyed by the strokes he had suffered, but the other parts of his brain – and his eyes – were intact. Though he was completely unable to see, his subconscious blindsight nevertheless guided him safely home.

One New Year's Eve some years ago, a colleague was making the long journey home after spending Christmas with friends. It was around nine o'clock at night. He had been driving for several hours, and was exhausted. The roads were eerily deserted. As he emerged from a long dark stretch of woodland, he suddenly realized that the sky to his right was aglow, lit up as though the fields below were aflame. In the centre of this extraordinary scene, looming low over the countryside, was the moon. Or at least he *presumed* it was the moon – what else could it be? But our colleague had never seen anything like it: a vast orange disc dominating the sky. Indeed, so strange did the moon appear that it seemed to him almost supernatural.

In fact our colleague had experienced a particularly dramatic example of what's known as the moon illusion, in which the moon appears – misleadingly – to be larger when near the horizon than when it's higher in the sky. The eye isn't fooled: the image of the moon on our retina is exactly the same size regardless of where it happens to be in the sky. But for some reason the brain seems to disregard this information. That reason has been the subject of conjecture as far back as the fourth century BC, and we still don't have a definitive explanation.

Theories abound, but one possibility is that the brain infers from the moon's position on the horizon that it is further away than it really is. Normally, the brain perceives the size of an object by assessing its retinal image in the context of how far away that object is (remember that one of the advantages of light travelling in straight lines is that it makes it possible for the eye to compute with great accuracy the distance of objects illuminated by that light). This is how we know that the book a few metres away on our bookshelf is of roughly similar size to the book on our desk, even though the retinal image of the latter is larger than that of the former. Generally speaking, objects on the horizon – an aeroplane, perhaps, or a cloud – are further away than those same objects when directly overhead, and the images they cast on our retina will therefore be smaller. By this logic, the moon on the horizon should be smaller too – and yet the retinal image is the same size as when the moon is high in the sky. If objects A and B appear to be the same size, and yet B is further away, B must in reality be larger than A. Mistaking the distance of the moon on the horizon, the brain thereby mistakes its size too.

Perhaps, however, it's not so much the moon itself that lies at the heart of this illusion, but the objects – or lack of them –

around it. As we look across the horizon towards the low moon, we're likely to see houses, trees, electricity pylons. In relation to these objects, the moon inevitably seems gigantic. When the moon is high in the night sky, however, we have nothing to compare it to, and thus no reason to assume that it's any larger than it really is.

An unwritten law: whenever you're running late, the first train to leave the station will always be the one directly adjacent to the one you're sitting on. This is an especially painful experience because for several happy seconds it appears that it is *your* train that is moving and not the other one. In fact, of course, you are the victim of an optical illusion.

What causes this illusion tells us much about how we perceive movement. Take a look around the room where you are right now. You'll probably turn your head; your eyes will certainly be moving, consciously and unconsciously (our eyes make several automatic movements – or *saccades* – per second in order to focus on various aspects of a scene). The image of the room on your retina will shift, but, because it initiated your movements, your brain knows that it's not the room that's in motion: it's your head. Now imagine that you are gazing out of the window of a speeding train, watching the countryside recede into the distance. Because the retinal image is moving even after the brain has allowed for the motions of your eyes, the brain detects movement. But how does the brain decide whether it's you that's in motion or the countryside? Well, other sensory information – for example, the noise and vibration of the train – provides vital clues. And the fact that all the objects you see are travelling in the same direction at the same time also suggests that it's you that is moving and not the countryside. But making this judgement in the station when it's the train adjacent to our own that's pulling away is much trickier. The fact that there's no obvious noise or sense of movement isn't much of a guide, since trains generally start pretty gradually. And when we look out of the window, what we see is the whole image sliding steadily – and coherently – out of view, which is exactly what it would look like if *our* train were moving. It's the difficulty of deciding what's moving – you or the train opposite – that accounts for the illusion.

Vision is a specialist business. And not only does it require a specific organ (the eye) and dedicated areas of the brain (the occipital lobes), there's a huge degree of specialization *within* both the eye and the brain. Individual cells in the retina, and neurons (cells dedicated to the processing of sensory data) in the optic nerve and the occipital lobe, are receptive to particular types of stimuli – for example, colours, brightness, shapes and movement. It's this specialization that accounts for optical tricks like the 'waterfall illusion' described by Robert Adams in 1834 following a visit to the Falls of Foyer in Scotland.

Adams noticed that if he stared at the waterfall for about a minute, and then looked at some nearby rocks, the rocks appeared to be moving upwards slightly. This happened because the brain gets used to the movement of the water, and the neurons that are especially receptive to downward motion become progressively less active. Now the brain perceives the characteristics of an object by comparing the activity of groups of neurons. For example, to judge in which direction the water is moving at the Falls of Foyer, it assesses the activity not simply of the neurons dedicated to perceiving downward motion, but also of those specializing in upward motion. The downward-motion neurons are exceptionally busy, while the upward neurons are relatively quiet (though not completely inactive), and thus the brain correctly perceives the direction of the water's flow. But when we transfer our gaze to the rocks, the balance is temporarily skewed. The upward-motion neurons are still pretty quiet, appropriately enough, but the downward-motion neurons – fatigued by so long staring at the waterfall – are even quieter, not even reaching the relatively low rate of activity triggered in response to a stationary object. Thus until they recover – which takes a few seconds – the rocks seem to be moving upwards.

This process of adaptation isn't confined to vision incidentally: it occurs across the senses. Think how much hotter your bath water feels if you've just held your hand under cold water, for example.

Today, psychology is an extraordinarily diverse discipline, with one current textbook listing no fewer than twenty-six separate areas of specialization. But it began with the study of perception – that's to say, how we turn the mass of raw material gathered by our senses into meaningful information about the world around us. This was what Wilhelm Wundt was trying to fathom when he established the first psychological laboratory, at the University of Leipzig in 1879, and in so doing inaugurated psychology as a scientific enterprise. Over the following 130 or so years, psychology has – unsurprisingly – adopted various approaches to the study of perception, and particularly vision, and here's a very quick overview of three of the most important. At the heart of them all is the question of how direct and innate perception is. Do our senses tell us pretty much all we need to know, or must our brain substantially interpret their data? To what extent is perception a learned skill rather than an instinctive, inborn, faculty?

For the Gestalt school, which flourished in Germany in the early twentieth century, the ability to make sense of groups of sensory stimuli, and specifically to perceive them as representing a distinct shape or pattern (Gestalt means 'form' in German), is largely innate. The object we perceive is more than simply the sum of its parts. Thus we see four lines of roughly equal length set at right angles to one another as a square, even when the lines aren't touching:

Gestalt theories were hugely influential, though they've been criticized for merely describing – rather than explaining – our ability to perceive coherent shapes and patterns.

The idea that perception is largely innate is shared by the so-called *nativist* theorists, of whom the most well-known was the American psychologist James Gibson (1904–79). Gibson argued that perception is largely direct. Our senses simply pick up information about the visual world and pass it up to the brain for it to act accordingly. According to Gibson, perception is a pretty passive affair – but that's fine, because the data the eye receives is generally sufficient: the brain doesn't need to go to any great lengths to make sense of it.

At the opposite end of the theoretical spectrum stand the *constructivists*, whose approach is nicely summed up in this quotation from Richard Gregory's ground-breaking *Eye and Brain*, first published in 1966: 'Visual and other perception is intelligent decision-making ... sensory signals are not adequate for direct or certain perceptions; so intelligent guesswork is needed for seeing objects ... perceptions are predictive, never entirely certain, *hypotheses* of what may be out there.' Seeing the world means applying learned knowledge to the data picked up by our senses: instead of passively receiving an image of the world, we actively construct a representation. Rather than Gibson's 'bottom-up' perception, with sensory data simply being passed on to the brain, Gregory argues for a 'top-down' process in which the higher regions of the brain constantly revise and interpret the information they receive from the senses.

And who, you may be wondering, has prevailed in the battle between the nativists and the constructivists? Well, the current consensus is that both accounts are useful. Gibson's theories are more applicable to very immediate, intuitive forms of perception, while Gregory's account provides a more plausible explanation of what happens when things are more complex.

What must it feel like, after years of blindness, finally to experience vision?

The psychologist Richard Gregory met S.B. in 1959. S.B. had been blind since he was a baby, but at the age of fifty-two he underwent a successful corneal graft. Within a few days his sight was sufficiently restored for him to walk about the hospital securely and to tell the time by looking at the clock on the wall. He was, predictably, delighted. But over the following months, though his vision continued to improve, the happiness he had always imagined would follow should he ever regain his sight did not materialize.

After his operation the world seemed to become both duller and more terrifying for S.B. While blind, he'd been fearless when crossing roads alone. Now that he could see, he was petrified even when accompanied by friends. What struck him most forcefully about his surroundings was how drab and disappointing they were. He liked the light to be bright and colours to be vivid, and was upset when they weren't. Imperfections in paintwork or wood troubled him. As his depression deepened, he would spend his evenings in darkness, not bothering to switch on the light. (Contrary to what one might expect, this kind of reaction isn't uncommon among people whose sight has been restored after a long period of blindness.)

Surprisingly – but tellingly – S.B. rarely seemed surprised by what he saw. Rather than revealing a wondrous new world, his sight merely presented him with a drabber, diminished version of what he had already come to know via his sense of touch. Even objects he had not previously touched did not appear to excite him. On a trip to London Zoo, for example, he instantly recognized an elephant, remarking that it looked much as he had imagined (presumably by extrapolating from the domestic animals he had petted). So important did his tactile sense remain to S.B.'s experience of the world that for a long time he seemed to see only those features of an object that he had previously been able to touch. (When S.B. sketched London buses, for example, his drawings initially included details – such as spokes in the wheels – that came not from a real bus but from his experience of touching other wheels.) In fact S.B. sometimes preferred touch to sight as a means of identifying objects. Shown a lathe, for instance, he was completely at a loss until allowed to touch it. 'Now that I've felt it', he explained, 'I can see.'

Our senses are highly specialized, with each one dedicated to collecting a particular type of information about our environment. But at bottom they all have the same essential function: the detection of energy. In the case of hearing, that energy is in the form of sound waves, which are basically vibrating air molecules.

Sound waves involve changes in air pressure. The greater the change – known as the *amplitude* of the wave – the louder the sound. Volume is generally measured in decibels (in tribute to the inventor of the telephone, Alexander Graham Bell). A chat with a friend will generally clock in at around 60 dB. A clap of thunder overhead will register about 120 dB. Anything above 140 dB can cause damage to our hearing.

The pitch of a given noise – that is, how high or low it seems to us – is determined by how rapidly the sound wave is vibrating. This is called its *frequency*, and is measured in hertz. Most people can hear sounds ranging from 20 to 16,000 hertz; some animals can pick up much higher frequencies, which explains why Fido will respond to a dog whistle that's inaudible to his owner.

The fleshy outer part of our ear is called the *pinna*, and its job is to channel the sound waves in towards the *eardrum*, a thin membrane that extends across the ear canal. When the sound waves strike the eardrum the membrane vibrates. These vibrations are transmitted to three minute bones called the *ossicles*, which in turn pass them on to the *cochlea*, which lies deep within the inner ear. The cochlea is around ten millimetres in diameter; it's shaped rather like a snail shell, and consists of a number of bony cavities filled with fluid. When the sound waves arrive in the cochlea, they cause the fluid to ripple, and these movements are picked up by around 4,000 *hair cells* (so called because of their long, thin shape), where the information is converted into electrical form for transmission along the acoustic nerve to the brain.

Unlike light, sound waves don't travel in straight lines. For humans, this is both good and bad news. The good news is that it means we can detect sound even when we can't see its source. On the other hand, it can be tricky to pinpoint exactly where a sound is coming from. Unlike many other mammals, we can't move our ears in the direction of a noise, but we do have a couple of tricks up our sleeve. Fortunately for our purposes, sound moves much less quickly than light (around 300 metres per second, as opposed to 300,000 kilometres per second). You can detect this variation in speeds in real life: imagine you're walking in the countryside, for example, and spot a farmer in the distance hammering in a fence post: the sound will be out of sync with what you see. Light waves bring you the sight of the hammer striking the post, but the resultant sound trails in appreciably later.

If sound travelled as fast as light, however, the task of ascertaining its source would become a great deal harder. As it is, the internal structure of the pinna helps us estimate the height of the object making the sound, and working out the direction from which a sound emanates is made possible by the arrangement of our ears, which are typically around fourteen centimetres apart. A noise made to our left will reach that ear about 700 microseconds before it reaches the right ear. Obviously, things are rarely so clear-cut: sounds come at us from all directions. But the brain can detect intervals as small as ten microseconds, allowing it to make a pretty good guess at where a noise has originated.

How proficient are you at learning foreign languages? Do you thrive on the challenge of making yourself understood abroad, or find yourself resorting to mumbled snippets from phrasebooks? Well, it just so happens that your talent – or lack of it – may be a consequence of the size of your brain.

Actually, that's not quite accurate. It's not how large your brain is in total that matters: what counts is the size of a particular region called Heschl's gyrus – and specifically its left-hand side.

Heschl's gyrus is part of the cerebral cortex, which handles most of the higher-level processing. It's believed to play a central role in processing the pitch of sounds – and in fact Heschl's gyrus has been found to be larger in musicians than in non-musicians. Speech, on the other hand, is normally handled by different, albeit related, regions of the brain. And yet there's a clear association between the size of the left-hand part of Heschl's gyrus and our ability to learn foreign languages. How so? What does a region of the brain specializing in pitch have to do with language learning?

The answer is that, unlike in English, in most languages the pitch of a word is of critical importance, often determining which meaning a given word has in a particular context. Thus the more attuned to nuances of pitch we are, the easier we'll find it to grasp a new language.

Of course, pitch is just one aspect of the range of sounds the brain must process. It carries out this processing in the temporal lobes (of which Heschl's gyrus is just one small part). Say, for example, you are woken late one night by the frenzied barking of your next-door neighbour's dog. As we've seen, the sound waves are picked up by your outer ear (or pinna) and are eventually channelled through to the cochlea, where they're converted into electrical signals suitable for use by the brain. From the cochlea, these signals travel along the 50,000 fibres that make up the auditory nerve before reaching the temporal lobes. Here the signals are gathered together and then interpreted, partly by comparing them to our memory of previous sounds (thus you know that the noise emanates from a dog and not, for instance, a Wurlitzer).

The temporal lobes also draw on information from other areas of the brain – including, as you glare angrily out of the window in the direction of your neighbour's garden, visual data from the occipital lobes – to understand the sound in context. Once the temporal lobes have completed their work of interpretation, the information is passed on to the frontal lobes, which will make a decision on any necessary action – in this case, whether or not to telephone your neighbour and, if you do, with what degree of politeness.

What links the avant-garde composer Olivier Messiaen, the novelist Vladimir Nabokov, the modernist painter Wassily Kandinsky, jazz great Duke Ellington, the contemporary artist David Hockney, Nobel Prize-winning physicist Richard Feynman and electronic musician Richard D. James, better known as Aphex Twin?

The answer is that they are or were all synaesthetes. A synaesthete is someone for whom one type of sensation (for example, seeing a word or hearing a particular noise) automatically triggers another very different sensory experience (such as the image of a colour or a scent).

Synaesthesia is much more widespread than you might think:

in fact it's reckoned that as many as one in every twenty-three people may experience it. It tends to be especially prevalent among creative people, perhaps because synaesthesia is an inherently metaphorical way of experiencing the world, forging highly imaginative links between otherwise disparate phenomena.

Synaesthesia can take many diverse forms, but the most common are the tendency to see individual letters and numbers as coloured ('7' might for example be experienced as yellow, or 'a' as red) and that of associating a particular day of the week with a specific colour (Tuesdays might be blue, for instance). In so-called sound ➤ colour synaesthesia, certain types of sound spark the appearance of colours and shapes, and each noise is likely to have its own distinct shape, with a consistent colour, brightness and direction of movement. (One synaesthete describes music as generating 'oscilloscope configurations – lines moving in colour, often metallic with height, width and, most importantly, depth'.) Much less common is lexical ➤ gustatory synaesthesia, in which particular words (or parts of words) trigger specific tastes in the mouth. Generally the tastes are those of foods familiar from childhood.

Synaesthesia often runs in families, so genes may play a part in determining whether or not a person develops the condition. However, we still don't really know what's happening in the brain during a synaesthetic experience. Probably the best current bet is that synaesthesia is the result of neurological 'cross-wiring', in which information flows between regions of the brain that normally process particular types of sensory experience separately, though exactly how and why this happens remains a mystery. But though synaesthesia is an abnormality, at least in statistical terms, it is certainly not a psychological disorder. People with the condition don't seem to find it problematic or distressing: indeed, far from being a curse or a disability, synaesthesia is typically experienced as a rare and precious gift.

*

You may have guessed it already, but if you're older than, say, twenty-five you're already over the hill – at least in terms of perceptual ability, which generally peaks in our late teens and early twenties.

During the first year of our lives, our vision and hearing improve dramatically, partly through the physical development of our eyes and ears and partly because of changes in our brain. But this development starts from a pretty modest baseline. For example, newborns can see only vague shadowy shapes, and only at very short distances. Even at six months of age a baby's vision is five times worse than that of the average ninety-year-old. In fact a child's sight doesn't attain adult levels until age four or five.

From our mid-twenties onward, however, perceptual capability steadily declines, and particularly when we're elderly. By the time we reach the grand old age of ninety, for example, our hearing will typically have lost around sixty decibels of sensitivity (loss of anything over about twenty-five decibels indicates a hearing impairment, so there's no getting away from the size of the deterioration).

This remorseless decline is due to two types of change. The first is ageing of the sensory organs themselves. For instance, the lens of the eye gradually becomes less flexible, and the retina deteriorates; the eardrum loses elasticity, and the hair cells in the cochlea – responsible for converting sound into electrical impulses for the brain to process – decrease in both number and efficiency. The second factor is the change in the weight of our brain. This grows significantly in childhood, reaching its maximum level at around age twenty. Yet it shrinks by about 9 per cent between the ages of twenty and eighty – not, as used to be thought, because of a decline in the number of brain cells, but rather because of the loss of a fatty substance called myelin, which helps facilitate the transmission of signals between various parts of the brain. Loss of myelin is thought to impair both our perceptual and our cognitive functioning.

Age clearly accounts for some variations in perceptual ability between individuals, but what about sex? Contrary to some popular wisdom, there's actually little difference between women and men in this respect. When perceptual skills are tested – for example, sensitivity to touch or taste, or the ability to discriminate between sounds – women tend to perform better than men, but generally the disparity is pretty small. Moreover, the variation between individuals of a particular sex is usually much more significant than the variation between the sexes as a whole, meaning that, though women on average slightly outperform men, it's quite likely that an individual man may score more highly than a particular woman. However, one task at which men consistently do better than women is 'mental rotation', which involves imagining how a given shape will look from various angles – though again individual women may well outperform individual men.

One heartening finding from the research on perceptual differences is that practice can make a difference. Like almost any skill, it's possible to improve our hearing or vision or sense of smell by working at it. Trained musicians, for example, are more adept at discerning timbre (the particular tonal quality of a musical instrument or voice) than non-musicians. In comparison to non-artists, trained painters find it easier to overcome the normal human tendency to see objects as we imagine them to be rather than as they actually appear from a given perspective. Part of the explanation for these enhanced perceptual abilities may be natural talent, but practice is likely to play a part too. After all, any trained professional will have spent countless hours honing their skills, and several studies have shown that most people will improve at a perceptual task if they repeat it sufficiently.

6. MOTIVATION

Your motivation? Your motivation is your pay packet on Friday.
Now get on with it.
  − Noël Coward (1899–1973)

The Seven Hidden Secrets of Motivation, *100 Ways to Motivate Yourself*, *The Tao of Motivation*, *Great Motivation Secrets of Great Leaders*, *Get Motivated!* − our thirst for books on motivation seems unquenchable. Indeed, a search on Amazon turns up more than 360,000 of the things. So if it's money that drives you, perhaps writing a guide to motivation is the answer.

Most of these books, however, focus on achievement − how to get things done − and specifically on success in the workplace. This is a pretty narrow view of motivation. The word has its origins in the Latin verb *movere* ('to move'), and it refers to the causes that lie behind our behaviour: the factors that *move* us to action. And that means *all* our behaviour, whether it be eating and drinking, sex and relationships, or work. Everything we do, without exception, has a motive, no matter how unconscious or inconsequential.

The really tricky task is defining such motives. What drives people to behave in the (often baffling) ways that they do? Why, for example, does one person work all hours in order to succeed in their career, when another is content to devote their life to raising children or to a cherished hobby? What motivates the person who leaves their home every morning at six to run for an hour in the park? How do they differ from their partner, who simply turns over for another hour's sleep? Why does one person collect sexual partners as if they were rare stamps, while another remains happily monogamous? And, most significantly, how is it that one of the authors of this book can never resist a biscuit and the other always can?

Philosophers, scientists, artists – all manner of thinkers have had a go at explaining motivation. Their answers, predictably, have varied wildly. Sigmund Freud, for example, believed that human behaviour was principally the consequence of an individual's unconscious sexual drives. The English philosopher Thomas Hobbes (1588–1679) argued that behaviour is motivated by the desire to maximize our pleasure and minimize pain (an approach also known as *hedonism*). Charles Darwin, on the other hand, looked to evolutionary history to explain the way in which animals (including humans) act, with the ultimate goal being the continued survival of our species.

Arguably the most influential psychological theory of motivation was proposed by Abraham Maslow. Maslow was born in 1908 in Brooklyn, New York, the eldest child of Jewish immigrants from Russia. Though his parents were keen for him to become a lawyer, he gave up his legal degree in favour of psychology, initially specializing in human sexuality. Indeed, his expertise in this field was later to bring an invitation from Alfred Kinsey to collaborate with him on his celebrated studies of American sexual behaviour – an invitation withdrawn after Maslow published critical comments on Kinsey's work.

Maslow believed that psychology and Freudian psychoanalysis, with their focus on psychological and emotional problems, were both too preoccupied with the negative aspects of existence. In contrast, he sought an explanation of human behaviour that emphasized positive, life-affirming instincts. The result was Maslow's hierarchy of needs, an all-embracing theory of human motivation. At the bottom of the hierarchy are our physiological needs – for oxygen, food, drink, sleep and sex, for example. One level above these is our need for safety and security, both physical and psychological. Then come our needs for love and self-esteem and, at the next level, for knowledge. Near the apex of the hierarchy lies our aesthetic need for beauty and order, and at the pinnacle is the drive for what Maslow called 'self-actualization'. We tend to address our basic, biological, requirements first and then work our way up the hierarchy to the quasi-spiritual needs at the top.

Self-actualization is a somewhat slippery concept, though in essence it's about fulfilling one's potential, whatever that may be. Maslow wrote, 'A musician must make music, an artist must paint, a poet must write, if he is to be ultimately at peace with himself. What a man can be, he must be.' Maslow's choice of personal pronoun here should not be taken to signify that women cannot attain self-actualization, but the concept is nevertheless a fairly exclusive one. Although Maslow believed that all humans have this need, in his opinion only a small proportion (around 2 per cent in fact) actually manage to fulfil it. If you *can* make it that far, you'll be in elevated company: among Maslow's select band of successful self-actualizers were Abraham Lincoln, Eleanor Roosevelt, Walt Whitman, Ludwig van Beethoven and Albert Einstein.

One of the appealing features of Maslow's picture of human motivation is its roundedness. Our behaviour isn't driven by a single fundamental cause, as many earlier theorists had argued: instead, it's the product of a variety of factors, some physiological, some psychological, some spiritual. And Maslow's is an immensely optimistic take on the human condition. We are not simply at the mercy of primal or biological urges, he argues: instead, innate in all of us is the need for love, beauty and self-affirmation. (Indeed, Maslow was one of the founders – with Carl Rogers – of humanistic psychology, an approach which put at centre stage the drive for individual fulfilment. You can read more about humanistic psychology on pp. 289–90.)

Yet Maslow's hierarchy has received a fair amount of criticism in recent years, often focusing on the vagueness of the notion of self-actualization and on the argument that everyone possesses the 'higher' needs. (You certainly can't rely on what people tell researchers: if you could, theatres and opera houses would be full and the ratings for reality TV shows and soaps would plummet.) But if Maslow's set of basic motives is flawed, what are the alternatives?

Identifying motivation is a peculiarly difficult assignment. After all, it can be tough enough to fathom your own behaviour, let alone to understand the motives of someone else. One strategy is simply to ask people what drives them (though, as we've just seen, this isn't a foolproof method). Steven Reiss, a psychologist at Ohio State University, surveyed more than 2,500 people of various ages, backgrounds and occupations. From these conversations, Reiss produced a list of 'sixteen basic desires':

- power
- curiosity
- independence
- status
- social contact
- vengeance
- honour (defined as loyalty to the values of family and community)
- idealism (the desire to improve society)
- physical exercise
- romance (or sex)
- family (the desire to raise children)
- order (resulting in organizing behaviour)
- eating
- acceptance (the desire for approval from other people)
- tranquillity
- saving (the desire to collect objects and to be frugal)

These basic desires are what psychologists call 'intrinsic' motives. That's to say, we act upon them not for any ulterior motive, but *for their own sake.* For example, no additional incentive is necessary for us to accept a promotion at work: the gratification of our desire for status is reward in itself. By contrast, an 'extrinsic' – or 'instrumental' – motive can always be traced back to an intrinsic one. Thus we may attend a party because we feel we don't have anything better to do that evening, or to catch up with friends, when what really drives our decision is the thought that we might meet an attractive partner there (intrinsic motive: romance).

It's these sixteen intrinsic motives that, in Reiss's view, underlie all human behaviour, though each person will respond to them in their own individual fashion. (Some of us have a very moderate desire for physical exercise, for example; others are particularly driven by the need for power.) It's worth remembering that, in compiling this list, Reiss isn't simply following in the footsteps of Maslow. The path stretches much further back than that. Aristotle, for instance, argued that there are twelve basic motives: confidence, pleasure, saving, magnificence, honour, ambition, patience, sincerity, conversation, social contact, modesty and righteousness. Descartes halved the number of basic drives, proposing that the six were wonder, love, hatred, desire, joy and sadness.

If you have a few moments, try recalling some of the things you've done this week. Which of the sixteen basic desires can you trace them back to?

We began writing this section as noon approached. Painfully, we typed out a couple of paragraphs and then, dismayed by the awkwardness of the sentences, deleted them. We slowly rewrote the paragraphs, and then immediately deleted them again. At this point we gave in to hunger and headed off for lunch. Suitably refreshed, we returned to our labours and found that the words, miraculously, were flowing once more. (If, having read these sentences, you doubt it, remember that all things are relative.)

As everyone knows, hunger rarely helps us get things done – unless, of course, the thing is eating, when it's usually a very effective inducement indeed. The desire to eat is clearly one of the most basic motivations in human beings – in fact it's hard to think of many that are more fundamental, given that without eating we will certainly die. But how exactly does it function? Do we simply eat when we get hungry? According to the theory of *homeostasis*, that's exactly what happens.

The concept was developed by Walter Cannon (1871–1945), a professor of physiology at Harvard Medical School. Cannon built on work by the French physiologist Claude Bernard (1813-78), who had realized that the human body is adept at maintaining its internal condition – for example, its temperature, water content, or blood pressure – despite changes in the world around it. Cannon argued that the body is able to detect when certain critical internal thresholds are passed, and to act to correct such abnormalities. It's analogous to a domestic central-heating system: when the room temperature dips below a specified level, a thermostat triggers ignition of the boiler, and hot water is supplied to the radiators. Once the required temperature has been reached, the thermostat reading causes the boiler to cut out. In the case of food, the body monitors the amount of glucose and other nutrients in the system. When this amount dwindles to a potentially problematic level, hunger pangs are generated, stimulating us to eat and thereby to restore our stock of nutrients. When we've taken in sufficient nourishment, our hunger passes and we stop eating.

This model of basic physiological motivation has proved immensely influential. In a sort of biological determinism, it sees key aspects of human behaviour ('homeostatic drives') as the result of carefully balanced and finely calibrated internal mechanisms, often involving a part of the brain called the hypo-thalamus. In fact things aren't so simple. Homeostasis certainly plays a part in driving certain fundamental human behaviours, but it doesn't explain them totally – or at least not in the case of hunger.

For example, being hungry isn't always enough to cause us to eat (as anyone on a diet will testify). Equally, we frequently eat when we aren't hungry. In fact our food intake is heavily influenced by social factors: we eat at set times of the day, for instance, and we're likely to eat more when we're dining with other people. As to the idea that we stop eating when we're no longer hungry – if only! (Because digestion takes hours rather than minutes, whether or not nutrient levels have reached appropriate levels can't have much of an influence on whether we continue to eat.) The homeostatic account also omits any mention of pleasure: after all, we often eat simply because we enjoy it. Pleasure acts as an *incentive*, and we swiftly learn that we can access that pleasure by eating particular foods. Interestingly, we tend to derive more pleasure from a meal containing various food types, which reflects the fact that humans require diverse sources of nutrients. Eat something pleasant for long enough and your enjoyment will decrease, prompting you to try something else. Now, where did those biscuits go?

'Pleasure', wrote Oscar Wilde, 'is the only thing to live for.' That may be something of an exaggeration, but there's no doubting how powerful a motivational force the prospect of pleasure can be. Sometimes there's just nothing that can compete with it: temptation is impossible to resist.

Perhaps this isn't surprising: we're neurologically 'hard-wired' to be especially receptive to pleasurable sensations. This makes evolutionary sense: an animal that is able to derive pleasure from advantageous behaviour is much more likely to thrive than one that cannot. The 'pleasure centre' of the human brain is believed to be the *nucleus accumbens*; it's part of the subcortex, the region below the outer layer of the brain. The nucleus accumbens produces pleasure by releasing the neurochemical dopamine during essential activities, such as eating or having sex (as well as during other, less essential and even harmful, activities, as we'll see in a moment). Thanks to its interaction with the memory systems in the brain, the nucleus accumbens helps us to associate this pleasure with those activities and thus want to repeat them in order to receive our dopamine reward. It also generates motivation by helping to turn our emotional memory of something (for example, how pleasurable or painful it is) into movement and action.

It's worth noting that the kind of pleasure that the nucleus accumbens produces is primarily chemical. That means we don't always experience it at a conscious level *as* pleasure. Alcohol, nicotine, marijuana, cocaine, amphetamines – all these drugs cause an increase in dopamine activity in the nucleus accumbens, which is why they're usually so difficult to give up: no matter how much misery addiction may be causing, that dopamine rush can seem just too powerful to withstand. And, because the nucleus accumbens encourages us to repeat pleasurable activities, once that rush dies away we yearn to experience it again – even though our rational thought processes may be urging us to stay away from what produces it.

The idea of a 'pleasure centre' in the brain emerged from experiments on rats carried out in the 1950s by James Olds and Peter Milner. Olds and Milner introduced an electrode to a particular area of each rat's brain – the so-called medial forebrain bundle – and when the rat pressed a lever, an electrical charge was generated which stimulated the rat's pleasure centre. The rats were soon pressing the lever compulsively – generally between 3,000 and 7,500 times in a twelve-hour period (one poor rat pressed it 2,000 times an hour for *twenty-four hours*). So intense was the pleasure that the rats derived from pressing the lever that they preferred to do this rather than anything else, including eating, drinking and mating. In fact for some of the rats their frenzied activity came to an end only when they died from exhaustion.

*

What do you look for in a long-term partner? Well, the answer to that question may depend on whether you're a woman or a man.

Sex is clearly a major motivator for us all, at least at some point in our lives. But *how* exactly does it affect our behaviour? When it comes to the critical choice of long-term partner, research pioneered by the evolutionary psychologist David Buss (born in 1953 and currently based at the University of Texas at Austin) indicates that among the traits most likely to be sought after by both men and women are intelligence, kindness, empathy, dependability, healthiness, and mutual attraction or love. But after this happy consensus the sexes diverge. Men place far more importance than women on appearance and sexual attractiveness, and they also want their partner to be three or four years younger than themselves. Women, on the other hand, tend to favour men who are hard-working, ambitious and financially successful. Buss surveyed more than 10,000 people across the world, from Australia to Zambia, so these differences seem to be close to universal, rather than culturally specific.

Now, remember that men and women have more in common when it comes to mating (or, if you prefer a less clinical term, dating) preferences than they have differences. But differences there are nonetheless, so how do we explain them? The evolutionary perspective adopted by scientists like David Buss – and inspired of course by the work of Charles Darwin – locates the driving force for animal behaviour in the drive of species to reproduce and thrive. Key here is the *theory of parental investment*, developed in the early 1970s by the American evolutionary biologist Robert Trivers. Trivers argued that differences between the sexes (both animal and human) in mating behaviours make sense if we look at what's at stake for each of them.

The male, motivated primarily by the urge to perpetuate his genes, is free to walk away after sex, and indeed has an evolutionary incentive to find another mate as soon as possible (the more partners, the more chance of successful reproduction). The female, on the other hand, may have to contend with pregnancy and then a significant period devoted to caring for her offspring: ceaselessly switching partners is probably not a practical option. Because sex is likely to have far more of an impact on the life of a female than a male, it's natural that females should be much more choosy about whom they get involved with. Thus in the animal world males typically compete for the right to have sex with a female, who for her part carefully selects the best candidate – that's to say, the mate most likely to produce healthy, successful offspring. (This is not necessarily the male that would make the best long-term mate, as we'll see in a moment.) This doubtless explains why so many men would like a sports car. Certainly, male sexual desire seems, generally speaking, to be more powerful and constant than that of women – it is normally men who initiate sex – whereas female desire tends to peak at the time of ovulation (the time of maximum fertility).

Given that the consequences of sex may be so far-reaching for women, it's logical – according to the theory of parental investment – that they should prefer a long-term partner who's going to be able to provide lots of help with child-rearing, both emotional and material, instead of one who disappears after their brief night of bliss. (It's possible, incidentally, that the characteristics that make a man suitable as a short-term sexual partner are not necessarily those most valued in a long-term companion. Perhaps bearing this out, it's been estimated that around 14 per cent of the children of married couples have a biological father who is not their mother's husband.) And this explains why women say they want men who are conscientious, hard-working and successful. For men, the priority is successful reproduction, hence their preference for young and attractive mates (youth and attractiveness being a fairly reliable index of fertility).

Now, clearly human sexual life is often much more complex

than these rather broad generalizations suggest. Nevertheless, the research evidence seems to bear them out. How about the relationships in your own life?

Imagine that one afternoon you're walking down the street when a young, personable member of the opposite sex stops you. 'Excuse me,' they say with a winning smile, 'I've been noticing you around, and I find you very attractive. Would you go out on a date with me?' How do you think you'd respond (assuming you hadn't fainted with shock)? How about if they asked you to go back to their flat? And what would you reply if this stranger suggested you have sex with them?

This is an experiment that's been carried out several times over recent years. In one study on a US college campus, women approached by men accepted a date around 50 per cent of the time, but only 6 per cent agreed to go back to the guy's flat. How many women were willing to have sex? Precisely none. When the roles were reversed and it was women chatting up men, again around half of those approached agreed to a date. However, 69 per cent agreed to go back to the woman's flat, and 75 per cent were happy to have sex. Of the men who declined a roll in the hay, some explained sadly that they'd love to were it not for the fact that they had prior commitments. (Similar results were obtained on the other occasions this experiment was run.)

If the results of these studies are to be believed, not only are many men ready to have casual sex with a complete stranger, they'd rather do so than spend a little time on a date getting to know that same person. This kind of data provides support for the idea that men are much more motivated to engage in short-term sexual relationships than women, that they're much less choosy than women about sexual partners, and that they're far less inclined to monogamy than women (it's reasonable to assume that at least some of the men and women questioned in these experiments were in relationships).

If we accept the evolutionary explanation for differences between the sexes, the behaviour of the participants in the experiment makes perfect sense. Men are driven to have sex with as many women as possible in order to perpetuate their genes. Women, on the other hand, are far more selective, as is natural given that they can reproduce only approximately once a year. Compatible with this theory is the fact that men typically say they'd like around eighteen sexual partners in the course of their life, while women prefer four or five.

But it would be a mistake simply to characterize women as monogamous and men as promiscuous. The fact is that both sexes show great commitment to monogamous relationships – and both are promiscuous in certain circumstances.

For men the underlying motivation for promiscuity is the resultant increase in the likelihood of successful reproduction, but what evolutionary purpose does it serve for women? Three main factors have been identified. First – and, it seems to us at least, somewhat controversially – it's been suggested that women engage in short-term affairs for the material benefits they can bring (gifts, meals out, etc.). Second, it can help them to find a suitable partner, or perhaps to replace the one they already have with a better model. Finally, women often report that the sex in short-term affairs is much more exciting and pleasurable than the sex in their long-term relationship. But research is at an early stage here: women's short-term relationships weren't investigated until very recently, almost as if it was assumed that they weren't having any. This is plainly ludicrous: after all, if (heterosexual) men are having short-term sexual relationships, so too are the women they are dating. Indeed, mathematically speaking (and assuming that the population is evenly split between men and women) the average number of short-term partners must be the same for both men and women.

*

We began this chapter with a friendly dig at the plethora of books on 'motivation', pointing out (with perhaps a little academic pedantry) that their view of the subject was somewhat restricted – 'How can I get that promotion?', 'How can I make more money?', 'How can I be the best that I can be?' But achievement is crucially important. There's surely no one who has not, at some point in their lives, found it hard to get things done; hence the proliferation of books, CDs and DVDs on motivational skills.

So what is the secret? Well, one very important technique is *goal-setting* – that's to say, identifying the end point you want to achieve and any staging posts you'll need to visit on the way. (These staging posts are sometimes called 'sub-goals'.) But setting yourself a goal isn't necessarily sufficient: some goals are better than others. Ideally, your goal should be specific rather than vague or general: for example, rather than simply resolving to be fluent in Spanish by the end of the year, it would be more productive to aim to identify and attend a suitable evening class.

Your goal should be attainable relatively quickly: in fact the less time that elapses between you aiming for a particular goal and reaching it the better (within reason). This is because any goal that requires many weeks or months to achieve is likely to require superhuman levels of motivation. It's easy to feel discouraged if that end point still seems ages away after lots of effort. Clearly, however, many goals will require this level of sustained input, so you can overcome this difficulty by using lots of sub-goals and rewarding yourself each time you achieve one.

Next, your goal (and sub-goals) should be appropriately difficult. Make them too easy and you're unlikely to take them seriously. A goal to spend five minutes a day looking at a Spanish fashion or football magazine probably won't give you that feeling of achievement which is such a crucial part of motivation. On the other hand, selecting a goal that's too difficult is no better:

the chances are that you'll simply give up. Your goal should stretch you, but be realistic: if you don't believe you can achieve it, you're hardly likely to bother trying. Interestingly, studies have shown that the most highly motivated people set themselves relatively tricky (though still attainable) goals – they seem to thrive on the challenge of really raising their game.

Finally, no goal – no matter how well thought out – is likely to be achievable unless you really understand why it's important for you to succeed. Learning Spanish because Spain is a country you love visiting, and where you'd maybe like to live one day, is a goal with in-built motivation. Learning Spanish because there are no places left on the life-drawing course you'd really like to take is probably doomed to end in failure.

What gets you out of bed and on the way to work in the morning? Is it the comradeship of your workmates? The support of your boss? The sense that you're engaged in really worthwhile activity? What about money: how crucial a motivational factor is your salary-and-benefits package?

Your answer to the last question in particular might be very different if you were responding to a questionnaire issued by your employer. Research indicates that employees in such surveys consistently play down the importance to them of pay, even though these questionnaires are generally completed anonymously. Indeed, one study found that pay was ranked in these surveys, on average, as the fifth most important motivational factor at work, behind such factors as job security, opportunity for progression, interesting work, the nature of the company, and relationships with managers and colleagues. A scientific analysis of employee responses to various types of incentive, however, revealed that pay was the single most effective strategy for improving performance.

Thus we may claim that pay doesn't matter to us (much), but our actions belie our words. How to explain this discrepancy?

Perhaps we really do underestimate the power of financial rewards to motivate us. Or perhaps we're reluctant to admit publicly to the fact, money being generally regarded as a somewhat grubby motivation for almost any activity.

This appreciation of the significance of pay to employee motivation represents something of an ironic twist in the human-resources tale. Back in the early days of research into workplace motivation – the period from roughly 1900 to 1920 – money was seen as the motivator par excellence. If you paid your workers a healthy salary, so the thinking went, you could sit back and watch their performance rocket. Except, of course, that pay – though undeniably important – is rarely sufficient as a motivational force. People are unhappy or unproductive in even the best-paid jobs, and to get the very best out of everyone in the workforce a variety of incentives is needed.

What are the other incentives? Here's a list of eight of the most significant, a distillation of more than a century's worth of research into employee motivation. Which of them apply to you?

- A job that meets your emotional, practical, social, and intellectual needs.
- A job that suits your personality and that is compatible with your values (someone who is very shy is unlikely to enjoy working as a tour guide, say; equally, working for a meat producer may not be ideal for a vegetarian).
- A work environment that helps you to grow and develop your skills.
- Demanding but achievable goals.
- Rewards that you really want for meeting those goals (company merchandise, for instance, may be a pretty feeble motivational tool for many people).
- Feeling that you are being rewarded fairly in relation to your peers.

- A work environment that strengthens your belief in your own abilities.
- Believing that the management you work for are honourable, honest and trustworthy.

*

Techniques like goal-setting can help us all to boost our motivation and achieve the goals we're aiming for. But, as you've doubtless noticed, levels of motivation vary widely between people. Some of us just don't seem especially driven to achieve, while others are energetically ambitious in one, several or even every aspect of life.

The study of this aspect of human behaviour was pioneered by the psychologist David McClelland (1917–98), who spent much of his professional life at Harvard. McClelland termed it the 'need for achievement', or nAch for short.

Reasoning that people with strong nAch would reveal it in their responses to all manner of situations, his experiments included showing a number of individuals a picture of a man working at a desk on which was placed a photograph of a family. McClelland then asked the participants to describe what they thought was going on in the photo. (This kind of experiment is known as a 'projective' test, since it allows the participant to project their deep-rooted feelings and beliefs on to an ambiguous stimulus.) Some individuals chose to focus on the man's imagined family; others took a very different approach, commenting, for example, 'The man is an engineer at a drafting board. The picture is of his family. He has a problem and is concentrating on it … How can he get that bridge to take the stress of possible high winds? He wants to arrive at a good solution of the problem by himself.' The person who provided this response, according to McClelland, revealed a preoccupation with achievement – unlike those who concentrated on the mystery man's putative family life.

In another study, McClelland had participants try to throw a plastic ring over a post. How far away the participants stood was up to them. Those who'd scored modestly in tests of nAch tended to position themselves either close to the post (thus making the task comparatively simple) or far away (thereby virtually guaranteeing failure). However, the participants whose nAch score was relatively high typically elected to stand somewhere in the middle of these two extremes. Perhaps this was because people strong in nAch like to stretch themselves by setting challenging (though not impossible) goals.

Does our need for achievement influence our choice of career? McClelland thought so. He began by testing the nAch of a group of college students. Around a dozen years later he followed up the students and discovered that those whose nAch score had been high were more likely to be in 'entrepreneurial' roles, defined by McClelland as involving a significant degree of personal responsibility and risk.

Where does nAch come from? Is it innate, or the product of the experiences we accumulate throughout our life? Like all aspects of our personality, nAch is probably a consequence of both nature and nurture. Certainly the messages about achievement and ability we receive in childhood may have a powerful effect. Gail Heyman recently cast fascinating light on this issue in a number of experiments involving Californian schoolchildren aged eight to twelve.

Call a hypothetical child a 'maths whiz', Heyman found, and the other kids tended to assume that the child in question had always been good at maths and always would be. Ability was seen as something we're born with: you either have it or you don't. (The use of nouns such as 'maths whiz' implies that characteristics are constant.) When this kind of labelling was avoided, however, and it was simply stated that 'Joseph' did best at maths, the children were much more willing to attribute his success to other factors, such as effort. Similarly, when Heyman presented the children with accounts of academic performance that varied over time, they were much more receptive to the notion that their own performances could be improved than when they were told about (fictitious) children who had always been good (or bad) at a subject. If we believe that we can improve with effort, that's a pretty secure foundation for strong motivation and high nAch. If, however, we grow up convinced that ability is innate, and that nothing we do is going to change things much, our nAch is likely to be pretty weak. Motivation, after all, requires hope.

7. SLEEP

How long could you manage without sleep?

The current record-holder is Randy Gardner, who as a seventeen-year-old Californian high-school student back in 1964 went a staggering 265 hours – or eleven days – without so much as a nap. 'I was a science-fair geek in those days,' he recalled in 2006. 'My dad was in the Army and we travelled all over the place and I never failed to win first prize. When he got transferred to San Diego, I thought, "I'm going to have to come up with one hell of a winner to pull this off in a city this size."'

But pull it off he certainly did, exceeding the previous record – a David Blaine-esque stunt in 1959 by DJ Peter Tripp, who broadcast throughout his 'wakeathon' in New York City's Times Square – by almost three full days. Unlike Tripp, who consumed copious amounts of drugs in order to keep going, Gardner avoided stimulants entirely, resorting to not so much as a cup of coffee. How did he do it? 'It's mind over matter. Your body will shut down. If you don't override it with your mind, you're fucked. You're going to sleep. You're gone.' So Gardner kept busy with endless games of basketball, long walks, cold showers, and cognitive tests administered by the Stanford sleep scientist William Dement. He also relied heavily on round-the-clock encouragement and support from two friends.

'I wanted to prove that bad things didn't happen if you went without sleep,' he explained. Whether he was successful rather depends upon your definition of 'bad'. Certainly Gardner's extraordinary feat caused him no lasting physical or psychological damage. After sleeping for fifteen hours immediately after setting his record, his sleep swiftly returned to normal proportions, leaving him as right as rain.

Nevertheless, he'd endured many unpleasant experiences during the course of those eleven record-breaking days, including crippling exhaustion, forgetfulness, dizziness, slurred speech and blurred vision. He'd been moody and irritable, and unable to concentrate on the simplest tasks. He had even suffered hallucinations and delusions – on one occasion, for instance, imagining that he was the legendary San Diego Chargers running back Paul Lowe, and becoming irate when it was pointed out that he wasn't. 'We got halfway through the damn thing and I thought "This is tough. I don't want to do this anymore,"' Gardner admitted. 'But everybody was looking at me so I couldn't quit.'

Despite his remarkable achievement – with his record still unbroken almost fifty years later – Randy Gardner is something of a forgotten figure in his native US. 'The Japanese just love me. I'm a big hit with the kids' science shows. But in this country, nada. Nothing. Zippo. Basically, nobody seems to be interested. It's weird. Maybe because I didn't kill anybody while I was doing it. Or beat somebody up or drive a car through a building ... '

Birds do it, bees do it, even educated fleas do it – there's not an animal on the planet that doesn't need to sleep. Just how much sleep they require, however, and the techniques they deploy in order to get it, vary enormously. The aforementioned bees, for example, sleep for around six to eight hours a night. How can one tell if a bee is asleep? Checking whether their eyes are closed isn't an option: they don't have eyelids. But they do possess antennae, and these wilt listlessly during sleep.

Among the really big sleepers in the animal kingdom are bats, who slumber through twenty hours in each day, while pythons enjoy an impressive eighteen hours (much like newborn humans). At the other end of the spectrum, giraffes manage on the least deep sleep of any mammal: around two hours a night, in blocks no longer than an hour. Giraffes can snatch forty winks while standing up, but the laborious procedure involved in settling down on their haunches for a proper sleep leaves them so vulnerable to predators that they do it as rarely as possible. (Why evolution has not equipped giraffes with the ability to sleep while upright is a mystery, to us at least.)

Curiously, dolphins sleep with one half of their brain awake and with one eye open. They need to keep one side of their brain alert in order to process visual information from their open eye, and they must keep one eye open so that they can swim safely. But why do they need to swim? Unlike fish, which can simply find a congenial spot in which to sleep and stay there for as long as necessary, dolphins are mammals; as such, they must come to the surface from time to time in order to take in oxygen.

Other one-eyed sleepers are ducks – or at least ducks who have the misfortune to be stationed on the outside of the group in order to scan the environment for possible danger. As with dolphins, the side of the duck's brain responsible for handling data from the closed eye is free to shut down and sleep. After a while, the duck will change position so that the other eye – and other half of its brain – can take its turn sleeping. If a solitary duck sleeps alongside a mirror (admittedly not a common occurrence in the wild), the eye nearest to its illusory companion duly closes.

How much sleep do human beings require? The answer to that question depends principally on one's age. Here are the typical sleep times for the main age groups (though bear in mind that, since they are averages, many individuals may need more or less than these amounts):

Age	Average amount of sleep needed
Birth-2 months	10.5-18 hours
2-12 months	14-15 hours
12-18 months	13-15 hours
18 months-3 years	12-14 hours
3-5 years	11-13 hours
5-12 years	9-11 hours
Teenagers	8-10 hours
Adults (18-65)	7-9 hours
Older adults (65 and above)	6-7 hours

*

As very young children, we would make an annual visit to our great-aunt, a seemingly ancient woman, dressed from head to foot in black, who lived in a small house in which every available surface was piled high with mysterious trinkets and mementos. In a corner of the room that she called the 'parlour' sat a brass birdcage, and in the birdcage lived an aged dark-brown mynah bird. The bird did not care for visitors: as soon as we entered the room it would begin a frenzied chattering and whooping and shrieking that ceased only when our aunt draped a square of black fabric over its cage. Then it instantly fell silent. For a few moments we could hear it moving on its perch, and then nothing: it was as if the bird had vanished by means of some extraordinary conjuring trick. If the cover were removed, however, the bird would reappear, shuffling and twitching and muttering for a few seconds before resuming – louder than ever, because presumably crosser than ever – its cacophonous protest against our presence.

Our experience of sleep can seem rather like that of the mynah bird in its cage. We are awake, then oblivion descends upon us, and after that we know almost nothing at all – aside perhaps from a dream or two – until we eventually emerge blinking into the light. But of course our sleep is a much more complex and variegated affair than this – it's simply that we're not in a position to observe it. So let's look now at the five stages of sleep:

Stage 1. As we drop off to sleep, our brain activity begins to diminish, our heart rate drops, our muscles relax, our eyes roll, and our body temperature falls.

Stage 2. Now we're properly asleep, our brain waves become increasingly slow. Movement of our eyes and muscles continues to decline.

Stage 3. Deeper into sleep: brain activity lessens further.

Stage 4. The deepest type of sleep: our brain waves are at their longest, slowest and most regular. The eyes and muscles are virtually still. Stages 3 and 4 are regarded as the most essential portions of our sleep, and are crucial for the revitalization of the *prefrontal cortex* – the part of the brain that specializes in creative thinking, problem-solving, decision-making and verbal fluency.

Stage 5. Back in the 1950s, the Chicago researchers Eugene Aserinksy and Nathaniel Kleitman identified a distinct and previously undetected stage of sleep. They called it Rapid Eye Movement, or REM. It used to be thought that this was when we did our dreaming, but in early 1960s it was discovered that we also dream during non-REM sleep. Interestingly, the jerky eye movements that give this stage of sleep its name are neither connected with dreaming nor continuous throughout REM sleep (they occur only in short spells).

When we look at the brain's activity during Stage 5, it's pretty similar to what's going on when we're awake. Moreover, we tend to be much more sensitive to what's going on in the world around us then (a noise outside may wake us up, for example, or be incorporated into a dream). As such, REM is sometimes called 'paradoxical sleep': the sleep that resembles wakefulness.

In an average night's sleep, we might cycle through these stages five times, though the time spent in Stage 4 gradually decreases and that in REM steadily increases. It seems that our system is set up to ensure we get plenty of the really important deep sleep; after that, we're free to indulge in relatively inessential REM. All in all, Stage 1 comprises around 5 to 10 per cent of our night's sleep, Stage 2 about 50 per cent, Stages 3 and 4 about 10 to 20 per cent, and Stage 5 about 20 to 25 per cent.

Incidentally, you may be wondering about the purpose of REM sleep. It's been suggested that REM is designed to ensure that the frontal cortex – the rational, analytical part of our brain – does not lapse into complete inactivity during sleep (rather as though it's like a hugely sophisticated machine that is so complex to start up that one would rather keep it ticking over), or to help us gradually make the transition from sleep to wakefulness, or that it represents a relic from our time in the womb, when it provided stimulus for the development of a brain insulated from the outside world (unborn infants spend around eight to ten hours a day in REM sleep). But these are just theories: we still don't really know.

One day in February 1972 the French cave scientist Michel Siffre descended into the aptly named Midnight Cave in Del Rio, Texas. Two hundred and five days later he emerged.

Siffre's life underground was relatively comfortable – warm, with plenty of food and water, a bed, books, and regular phone contact with the team of scientists constantly monitoring his progress. But the cave was too remote from the outside world for natural light to penetrate, and Siffre had no means of knowing what time it was. Free to sleep when he liked and for as long as he liked, and deprived of the cues that signal the end of one day and the beginning of the next, Siffre nevertheless settled into a stable rhythm. His sleep–wake cycle, however, was not twenty-four hours long, as it is for the rest of us, but closer to twenty-five hours. As he explained in an interview in 2008, 'My sleep was perfect! My body chose by itself when to sleep and when to eat ... We showed that my sleep/wake cycle was not twenty-four hours, like people have on the surface on the earth, but slightly longer ... But the important thing is that we proved that there was an internal clock independent of the natural terrestrial day/night cycle.'

This 'internal clock' is one of the body's hundred *circadian rhythms* – 'circadian' being derived from the Latin for 'about a day'. (Other circadian rhythms include changes in body temperature, the cycle of hunger and feeding, and the schedule for release of particular hormones.) Under normal conditions – that's to say, when we have the rising and setting of the sun to help orient us, rather than being confined to a darkened cave hundreds of metres below the surface of the Earth – our body clock keeps to a fairly exact twenty-four-hour cycle.

The sleep-wake cycle is thought to be controlled by the brain's *suprachiasmatic nucleus* (SCN). Animals whose SCN is damaged do not maintain their normal patterns of sleeping and wakefulness. And when hamsters who normally operate on a twenty-five-hour sleep–wake cycle are implanted with the SCN of hamsters on a twenty-hour cycle, they change their habits accordingly. The SCN controls the release of the hormone *melatonin*: the darker it is, the more melatonin is produced, and the sleepier we feel.

As you'll have noticed, our need for sleep fluctuates over the course of a day. From around 6 a.m. we become gradually more lively, reaching a plateau at around 9.30 a.m. We dip in the early afternoon, before building to a daily peak of alertness between 6 and 8 p.m. We then gradually wind down, bottoming out between 2 and 6 a.m. This pattern doesn't hold for everyone, however. Some people (about 20 per cent of the population) are 'larks', at their best early in the day; another 20 per cent are 'night owls', who feel sharpest during the evening.

When we sleep, and for how long we sleep, is determined by our body clock, but also by how long it is since we last slept. If you've been dozing all afternoon, for example, you're going to find it pretty difficult to get to sleep at night, even if it is your normal bedtime.

Attempting to flout your body clock can have disastrous consequences. For example, lack of sleep is a major cause of road accidents. Indeed, 20 per cent of crashes on motorways in the UK are believed to result from drivers falling asleep at the wheel. These crashes generally occur in the early hours of the morning, when we're designed to be soundly asleep and not pushing at the speed limit down a dark and tedious carriageway. They also peak – though less sharply – in the middle of the afternoon. Again, this is a time when most of us are enduring a dip in energy levels. Anyone involved in a sleep-related accident is much more likely to be killed or seriously injured, because drivers aren't awake to brake or swerve.

Given this, it's safest to avoid driving in the early hours. If you do find yourself overcome by sleepiness while on the road, don't simply assume you can fight it off. The techniques most tired drivers use in a bid to stay conscious – turning the radio or CD player up loud, for example, or opening the window for a blast of fresh air – don't work for long. Instead, the best advice is to stop for a strong coffee and then take a fifteen-minute nap while the caffeine makes its way into your system. Don't sleep for longer, though, or you'll be too groggy to drive when you wake up.

Everyone needs sleep. Indeed, a person deprived of food will survive three times longer than someone denied sleep. But why? What's the purpose of sleep?

We still don't really know – which is a little surprising, given that the average person will spend around 200,000 hours asleep during their lifetime. That said, two theories now predominate.

(There's no need to choose between them, by the way, since they aren't mutually exclusive: both are useful.) The first focuses on the *adaptive* qualities of sleep, arguing that what determines animals' sleep patterns is the evolutionary advantage that these patterns confer. Or, to put it more plainly, how much you sleep depends on how beneficial it is for you to do so.

For many animals, sleep is an effective way of avoiding danger: the two-toed sloth sleeps twenty hours a day in the topmost branches of its chosen tree, for example. If you happen to be armour-plated like the armadillo, you can sleep as long as you like (armadillos normally enjoy at least eighteen hours a day). Predatory animals generally sleep for much longer periods than herbivores, which are obliged to remain constantly alert for trouble. Cats, for example, may sleep for fourteen hours a day, while cows and sheep in the fields normally manage fewer than four hours a night. For these latter animals sleep is a liability, though they'll indulge in much more of it when they're safe in a pen. Perhaps the amount of sleep typically required by humans, and the scheduling of that sleep, have their roots in the fact that our ancestors were most vulnerable to attack by predators in the dark and so spent these hours in the safety of the cave.

Similarly, many smaller animals rely on sleep as a means to conserve energy (body temperature drops during deep sleep, so fewer calories are consumed). For creatures like the mouse, if they're not busy finding food they're better off asleep: there's no advantage to be gained from sitting around watching the world go by, and, unlike larger animals, they lack the energy reserves to fund such unproductive activity. When the supply of food declines, smaller animals respond by lowering their body temperature or by sleeping more. Incidentally, while hibernation may seem to represent the ultimate example of such behaviour, it isn't really sleep at all but rather a much more intense form of 'cold storage' in which the animal's body temperature falls very dramatically. Hibernating animals actually 'wake up' in order to sleep.)

Energy conservation doesn't seem terribly relevant to human sleep, however, since we can achieve the same benefits simply by resting. Leading sleep scientist Jim Horne has put it nicely: 'The small further increase in energy saved by sleeping rather than resting ... is equivalent to only the calories provided by a slice of bread or a handful of peanuts.'

Sleep that knits up the ravelled sleeve of care,
The death of each day's life, sore labor's bath,
Balm of hurt minds, great nature's second course,
Chief nourisher in life's feast
 – **William Shakespeare**, Macbeth

The second major theory regarding the purpose of sleep highlights its *restorative* effects: sleep allows animals to recharge their batteries and repair the damage caused by the day's exertions.

But if sleep is restorative for humans, the nature of that restoration may surprise you. Exactly which areas of the human body are nourished by sleep rather than relaxation? Research has yet to find any – with a single exception, as we'll see in a moment. The so-called 'growth hormone' is secreted in large quantities during sleep, leading some scientists to posit a causal link between the two: that is, sleep aids growth. But if that's true, it's difficult to explain why this hormone should continue to be released in large quantities during the sleep of adults: after all, they've done all the growing they're going to do. Moreover, other hormones connected with growth don't seem any more plentiful during sleep than during wakefulness. (You're taller when you first awake, but that's only because the discs in your back have expanded during sleep. That extra height disappears the moment you step out of bed and place the full weight of your body through your spine once more.)

In fact for humans – and other large mammals – the one organ that really seems to need sleep rather than mere relaxation is the brain, and particularly the prefrontal cortex. When this is tired, concentration also suffers. People generally cope pretty well with sleeplessness. As long as it's not too prolonged, they're able to carry on functioning with surprisingly few problems, psychological or physical. But, as numerous experiments have shown, where they really take the hit is in the mental skills handled by the prefrontal cortex. Thinking flexibly, and making sound decisions in the light of changing circumstances, soon becomes incredibly tough. This can sometimes have devastating consequences.

At 11.38 a.m. on 28 January 1986, the space shuttle *Challenger* embarked on its tenth flight from Kennedy Space Center at Cape Canaveral in Florida. Among the astronauts on board was thirty-seven-year-old Christa McAuliffe, chosen from among 11,000 applicants to participate in NASA's Teachers in Space project. Seventy-three seconds after launch, however, *Challenger* suddenly broke up and plunged into the Atlantic, killing all seven members of the crew.

The technical reason for *Challenger*'s disintegration was a disastrous fuel leak caused by the failure of a seal in one of the shuttle's rocket boosters. That failure was triggered by the unusually cold temperatures in Florida in the days leading up to the launch. But investigators also concluded that lack of sleep had played a major role in the catastrophe. By the time *Challenger* launched, those making the key decisions in the control room had been on duty for over ten hours; moreover, they'd been able to snatch just a couple of hours' sleep the night before. Lack of sleep didn't prevent these managers from functioning at a certain level: had the launch been straightforward, their exhaustion would probably have been overlooked. But, as the warnings came in about the possible risk to the mission caused by the cold weather, the situation at Kennedy that morning called for creative, flexible thinking – precisely the kind of response that sleep deprivation makes so difficult.

We all dream, don't we? It seems highly likely, but in fact surprisingly little research into the prevalence of dreaming has been carried out. One honourable exception was a study of 1,000 Austrians, aged fourteen to sixty-nine. Here's what the researchers found:

- Sixty-eight per cent remembered dreaming at least once during the previous month.
- People under thirty recalled more dreams than those over fifty. Wealthy people remembered more dreams than poor people.
- Nightmares were reported by 4 per cent of the individuals surveyed. People on low incomes, and those living in communities numbering more than 5,000, were especially prone to these.
- Younger people were more likely to dream in colour; in all, 37 per cent of those surveyed reported doing so.
- Twenty-nine per cent of people had recurring dreams (i.e. the same dream occurring regularly), with women experiencing this more often than men.
- About a quarter of the people questioned said that they were sometimes aware that they were dreaming while dreaming (these are called 'lucid' dreams).

But if dreams are so prevalent, what causes them and what are they for? As with so many of the key questions about sleep, the answers remain elusive.

It's been estimated that we spend around a hundred minutes a night dreaming. We know now that dreaming is not confined to REM sleep, as was once believed, though non-REM dreams tend to be shorter and less wildly imaginative than those that occur during REM. We're also much more likely to remember our REM dreams, since this stage of sleep predominates towards morning. Even with REM dreams, however, we can often recall only their concluding moments.

It may be that speculating about the purpose of dreams is a mistake. Some experts believe dreams have no purpose: they're simply meaningless by-products of sleep. This may be why we remember so few of our dreams. But for Sigmund Freud dreams represented the 'royal road to the unconscious': with our conscious mind asleep, our basic (largely sexual) preoccupations can slip the leash and finally express themselves.

Freud's psychoanalytic theories have largely failed to withstand scientific scrutiny, but there may be some truth in the notion that dreams reveal thoughts and feelings of which we are generally unaware. Most dreams, however, are utterly mundane rehearsals of everyday life. And of course our efforts to understand our dreams take place when we're awake. Thus whatever we appear to 'discover' may tell us far more about how our waking mind works than it does about our dreams.

More recently, evolutionary scientists have suggested that dreaming may enable us to practise coping with danger. So prehistoric humans may have dreamed of sabre-toothed cats, thereby preparing them to deal with the threat should it occur for real. It's true that many dreams are frightening, but of course many others are not. And exactly how dreaming helps is far from clear.

Some experts have proposed that dreaming helps us lay down memories. Events of the previous day often crop up in our dreams, which may be the first stage of this process. And we also tend to favour events that occurred five to seven days ago, which may represent a further consolidation of our memories. Others argue that dreaming offers a safe and comfortable way to keep our brain ticking over during sleep, thereby ensuring that waking up is a relatively straightforward task. This may explain why blood pressure, heart rate and the rate of release of stress hormones like adrenaline and cortisol tend not to increase when we dream. Moreover, with the exception of our eyes (whose movements, remember, have nothing to do with dreaming), our body is paralysed during REM sleep. This is just as well, since we're thereby prevented from acting out our dreams. As we've mentioned, we do experience dreams during non-REM sleep but these tend to be much less dramatic, presumably making immobilization less essential.

'The worst thing in the world', wrote F. Scott Fitzgerald wisely, 'is to try to sleep and not be able to.'

Sleep plays such a crucial role in our lives that when it goes wrong for any extended period the consequences can be horrendous. But sleep problems are exceptionally common: on any given night, around one in three adults will be battling insomnia, and many others will be trying to cope with other sleep-related complaints. Here are the main ones:

Insomnia. The most common type of sleep problem, insomnia is a general term for a number of issues: finding it hard to fall asleep, struggling to stay asleep, not getting sufficient sleep, and not managing enough good-quality sleep.

Around one person in ten meets the criteria for 'clinical insomnia', the most severe and prolonged form of the problem. If you're taking longer than half an hour to fall asleep, have been experiencing this problem several nights a week and for more than a month, and find it very difficult to function properly during the day you may well have clinical insomnia. Women are twice as likely to be affected as men, which may be linked to their increased risk of depression and certain forms of anxiety.

Nightmares. Scientists still don't understand why nightmares occur. A theory that can probably be ruled out, however, is the one that gave them their name: that nightmares are caused by a demon crouching on us while we sleep ('mare' being the Old English word for demon). Nightmares are a product of REM sleep, so they tend to occur in the second half of the night.

If you're experiencing frequent nightmares, and they're causing you a lot of distress or are interfering with your day-to-day life, you may be suffering from *nightmare disorder.*

Sometimes people scream or struggle or yell, and wake up with their heart pounding, their body drenched in sweat, and gripped by a vague but extremely powerful sense of panic. This can seem like a nightmare, but may actually be a *sleep terror.* Sleep terrors usually happen during deep, non-REM sleep (hence they're unlikely to be caused by nightmares).

Sleepwalking also occurs during deep, non-REM sleep. This is why sleepwalkers are so difficult to wake, and why in the morning they usually have no memory of their nocturnal wanderings. It also means that when people sleepwalk they're probably not acting out a dream. (Because children get more deep sleep than adults, they're much more likely to sleepwalk and suffer sleep terrors.)

If someone is sleepwalking frequently, and it's causing them distress or interfering with their day-to-day life, a doctor might diagnose *sleepwalking disorder.* But sleepwalking can cause major problems whether or not such a diagnosis is applicable: moving around while asleep can lead to serious accidents.

Breathing-related sleeping disorders. Snoring is caused by a partial blockage of the airways, and it's a very common feature of sleep, especially as we get older or heavier or if we've been drinking or taking sleeping pills.

Heavy snoring can be a sign of *sleep apnoea*, in which breathing actually stops for several seconds. Untreated sleep apnoea can have dangerous consequences for the heart and the cardiovascular system. (Fortunately, extremely effective treatments are now available.) Other symptoms of sleep apnoea include snorts, gasps and choking sounds while asleep, morning headaches, and a very dry mouth. Older, overweight men tend to be most at risk.

Narcolepsy. The main feature of narcolepsy is daytime sleep attacks – the overwhelming and often irresistible urge to sleep, no matter where you are or what you're doing. Unsurprisingly, the consequences can range from the inconvenient and embarrassing to the downright dangerous.

But sleep attacks aren't the whole story. People with narcolepsy may also experience cataplexy (a sudden and total loss of muscle strength), sleep hallucinations and sleep paralysis – the terrifying sensation when waking up or falling asleep of not being able to move or speak.

Restless-legs syndrome. This involves an unbearable feeling of discomfort in the legs, which can be relieved only by moving them. Such sensations can strike at any time, but they tend to be worse when the person is inactive or at night. As a result, sleep can be severely disrupted.

Periodic limb-movement disorder can seem rather similar, but in this case the movement of the legs (and other limbs) is *involuntary*, a product of twitching muscles. Both problems are more common in older people.

*

Soap your head with the ordinary yellow soap; rub it into the roots of the hair until your head is just lather all over, tie it up in a napkin, go to bed, and wash it out in the morning. Do this for a fortnight. Take no tea after 6 p.m. I did this, and have never been troubled with sleeplessness since. I have lost sleep on an occasion since, but one or two nights of the soap cure put it right. I have conversed with medical men, but I have no explanation from any of them. All that I am careful about is that it cured me.

If you happen to be one of the 15 million adults in the UK who suffered from insomnia last night, you'll be relieved to hear that there is no need to follow the advice above, provided by a reader of the *Glasgow Herald* in the 1890s. As an editorial published in an 1894 edition of the *British Medical Journal* commented, 'We can not help thinking that some of our sleepless readers would prefer the disease to the cure.'

In the late nineteenth century it was widely believed that insomnia was a physical illness caused by problems with the circulation of blood around the body. (Sleeplessness was well known to doctors back then, but the term itself didn't exist until 1908.) Today we know that, although insomnia can sometimes be caused by physical ailments and certain types of medication, more often psychological factors lie at the heart of the problem. Happily, there are now several tried-and-tested ways to combat sleeplessness, no matter how severe it is – and they don't involve yellow soap:

- Exercise every day – it'll tire you out. (Don't exercise late in the evening, though: you'll just feel more awake.)
- Avoid caffeine, alcohol or nicotine in the evening.
- Develop a relaxing evening routine – maybe take a warm bath, or spend some time reading. Try listening to gentle music or doing a relaxation exercise.
- Don't let bedtime be worry time. Instead, try setting aside twenty minutes earlier in the evening to think through your problems. If you find yourself worrying while you're in bed, jot the thought down on a piece of paper ready for tomorrow's worry session and let it go for the night.
- Have a bedtime snack – but don't overdo it, or the effort of digestion is likely to interfere with your sleep. Instead, go for something healthy and relatively plain, like a glass of milk, a banana or maybe a piece of wholemeal toast.
- Get your bedroom right for sleep – that means a comfortable

bed and a room that's quiet, dark and your preferred temperature (around 18°C is usually best).

- Resist the temptation to lie in, and cut out daytime naps – you'll only find it harder to fall asleep at night.
- Learn to associate your bed only with sleep, so don't use it, say, for reading, eating, watching TV or writing a diary. (Sex is permissible, though, because it generally leaves us feeling sleepy.)
- Only go to bed when you're tired. Switch off the light as soon as you're comfortable.
- If you haven't fallen asleep within twenty minutes, get up and do something relaxing – listening to calming music or reading a book, for example. It's the same if you wake up in the night: if you haven't fallen back to sleep after twenty minutes, get up and only go back to bed when you're feeling tired.
- If your sleeplessness is made worse by nightmares, try the technique known as *imagery rehearsal*. Essentially, you need to retell the story of your nightmare, but this time you're in charge and you can change the story any way you like. Spend a few minutes every day running through this new version in your mind. Gradually you'll find that the events of your nightmare become much less disturbing.

8.FEAR AND ANXIETY

We are, perhaps, uniquely among the earth's creatures, the worrying animal. We worry away our lives.
 – **Lewis Thomas** (1913–93)

On New Year's Eve 2006, passengers on Ryanair's flight from Sardinia to Stansted were just settling down in readiness for take-off when a squad of armed police suddenly appeared. At gunpoint, five men were removed from their seats and escorted from the plane while bewildered passengers looked on. After a short delay, the Ryanair flight duly took its leave of the island and headed back to Essex.

The incident was the result of the extraordinary vigilance of just one man – as it happens, a British psychology lecturer. His suspicions had been first aroused in the departure lounge, when he had noticed the five men laughing together. Later, on board the plane, he was disturbed to see that the men were now sitting separately. Most troubling of all, one of them was reading a newspaper despite seeming to be blind. The lecturer took swift and decisive action, alerting the cabin crew and threatening to leave the plane unless the putative terrorists were removed.

But, as can occasionally happen, the psychologist was mistaken. The men forcibly ejected from the plane were not terrorists. They were musicians – members of the London-based calypso band the Caribbean Steel International Orchestra. They had been sitting separately on the plane because it is not possible to reserve seats on Ryanair flights. The blind 'terrorist' – tenor-pan player, and devoted Liverpool fan, Michael Toussaint – was not in fact reading a newspaper: he was listening to a fellow passenger read out the football scores. And the men had been laughing in the departure lounge while savouring their triumphant appearance the previous day at a Sardinian world-music festival.

It took the Italian police twenty minutes to establish that the five musicians were not a security threat. But the plane's captain refused to allow them back on board. Thus, rather than celebrating New Year's Eve with family and friends, they spent the night in a drab airport hotel before being put on a Ryanair flight the following afternoon. However, this flight was bound not for London but for Liverpool, where it arrived too late for the musicians to catch a coach home. Unable to find a hotel room in a rain-lashed – and fully booked – city centre, the five took refuge in a kebab shop before taking the first train to London the next morning.

By way of compensation for the musicians' 'inconvenience', Ryanair eventually offered them £100 each in traveller's cheques, together with vouchers for future flights with the airline. The courts took a rather sterner view, awarding each of the men £800 in damages, and another £190 in costs. A year later the Caribbean Steel International Orchestra played at the opening of Heathrow's Terminal 5. As for the psychology lecturer whose hair-trigger anxieties sparked the chaos in Sardinia, he appears to have vanished without trace, nameless and unmissed.

As the Caribbean Steel International Orchestra – now nicknamed the Talipan – would doubtless attest, fear and anxiety can quickly spiral out of control, skewing our perception of reality even in the face of clear evidence to the contrary. But it's not merely terrorism that spooks us. Anxiety in general is widespread – and it seems to be on the rise.

For example, an April 2009 report by the UK Mental Health Foundation found that 37 per cent of people (equivalent to 18 million UK adults) reported feeling frightened or anxious more often than in the past. Seventy-seven per cent believed that the world had become a more frightening place in the previous ten years. And 29 per cent admitted that fear and anxiety had prevented them from doing things they wished they had done.

Interestingly, women consistently report experiencing more fear and anxiety than men; in fact they are twice as likely to say they feel frightened or anxious a lot of the time. Younger people also seem to experience greater fear than older people, with 77 per cent of those aged eighteen to thirty-four admitting they feel frightened or anxious at least some of the time, compared to 65 per cent of those over fifty-five.

Fear and anxiety are, of course, anything but new. In fact they are part of our basic emotional equipment – indeed, arguably the oldest part – and function as an innate early warning system. They alert us to potential dangers, and prepare us to react: to fight or to flee, according to the classic formulation coined by Harvard physiology professor Walter Cannon in 1915. A series of physiological changes is set in motion, designed to help us focus entirely on dealing with the sudden threat to our existence. So, for example, our heart rate increases, allowing blood to reach our muscles faster. Our pupils dilate, relaxing the lens and allowing more light to reach the eye. Our digestive system is put on hold, resulting in reduced production of saliva – hence the dry mouth we often experience when we're afraid. Without fear and anxiety, humans would surely have disappeared long ago. After all, creatures that cannot recognize danger and respond accordingly are well suited only to being someone else's prey – just ask the dodo.

Even the word 'anxiety' is ages-old. Like its European cognates *angoisse* (French), *Angst* (German), *angoscia* (Italian) and *angustia* (Spanish), 'anxiety' has its origins in the ancient Greek *angh*. This appears in ancient Greek words meaning 'to press tight', 'to strangle', 'to be weighed down with grief', and 'load', 'burden' and 'trouble'. And its influence can be seen in Latin terms like *augustus*, *ango* and *anxietas*, all of which carry connotations of narrowness, constriction and discomfort – much like another Latin term that has become part of medical terminology: *angina*.

Incidentally, you may be wondering what the difference is between fear and anxiety. It's a good question – so good, in fact, that it has been the subject of debate among scientists for more than 200 years. The current consensus is that the two are pretty much interchangeable. If a distinction is to be made, it is that fear tends to have a clear and specific object (heights, for example, or spiders), whereas anxiety is a vaguer and more free-floating sense of unease. We generally know what is making us fearful. Anxiety, on the other hand, feels much more mysterious and complex.

What happens in our brains when we feel afraid? Until very recently – and specifically until the development of neuro-imaging technology, which allows biochemical activity in the brain to be recorded – the answer to that question could be only a matter of conjecture. Now, however, the picture is becoming clearer.

Deep within the brain, in the area known as the limbic system, lie two small pieces of tissue shaped, in the view of early scientists, like almond seeds. These tiny bits of grey matter, one on each side of the brain, are called the *amygdala* (the Latin term for 'almond seeds') – and they are largely responsible for our experience of fear and anxiety.

Scientists had long suspected that the brain's limbic system is crucially involved in the production of emotions. But the US neuroscientist Joseph LeDoux (b. 1949) was foremost in identifying the amygdala as the emotional computer of the brain, and as particularly important in relation to fear and anxiety. (LeDoux is a professor at the Center for Neural Science at New York University. He is also the guitarist in the neurologically literate rock band the Amygdaloids.)

The amygdala very rapidly processes the information the brain is receiving from the senses and decides whether we're in danger. If it believes that we are, it starts the physical, hormonal reaction that we know as anxiety or fear and that prepares us to deal with any threat. The amygdala is well placed to make this judgement because it is the storehouse of our unconscious, emotional memories, which allows it to assess a situation in the light of past experiences.

All this happens astonishingly quickly – well before the rational, analytical frontal cortex can kick into life. This speed can be a lifesaver, but it also increases the chance of errors. Our amygdala may be screaming 'danger' when the reality is much less worrying. All being well, the frontal cortex catches up and we are able to make a considered judgement of the situation. But the amygdala is amazingly powerful – which is why we're so often overwhelmed by our emotions.

If the amygdala is consistently overactive – as it seems to be in some people – it detects danger everywhere. Scientists believe this kind of amygdala malfunction plays a major role in a number of anxiety problems, including panic attacks and post-traumatic stress disorder, and also in night terrors. And if the amygdala is underactive? Well, the balance shifts in the other direction: instead of emotion, cold calculation. This most often shows itself in antisocial personality disorder – better known as psychopathy – in which individuals lack the capacity for empathy and remorse and instead show a fondness for bullying, lying and risk-taking.

One of the earliest – and most striking – demonstrations of the role of the amygdala was provided by the French doctor Edouard Claparède. In 1911 he treated a woman whose brain damage was so severe that she retained no long-term memory. When Claparède stepped out of the room for just a minute or two, the woman had no idea who he was when he returned.

This woman was the unwitting participant in a highly revealing experiment. On arriving for the consultation, Claparède as usual held out his hand in greeting. But when the woman shook it, she was pricked by a tack the doctor had hidden in his palm. Claparède later left the room, but when he returned the woman refused to shake his hand. She didn't recognize the doctor, and she was unable to explain why she was so determined not to shake his hand.

The woman's conscious memory of being pricked by the tack had vanished. But her unconscious, emotional memory, stored in her amygdala, remained intact, alerting her to a danger her conscious mind was powerless to detect. And this is how our undamaged brains work too. Our conscious memories may be fully functional, but our first – and frequently most powerful – assessment of threat comes from our amygdala, and its vital store of emotional memories.

Fear and anxiety have their origins in neurological events, which in turn bring about physical changes in the body. But, just as importantly, fear and anxiety are *psychological* phenomena, with distinctive effects upon how we think, feel and behave.

We know, for instance, that anxious people tend to assume the worst will always happen. For example, when researchers analysed the thinking of people with a spider phobia, they unearthed some very gloomy assumptions. Asked what they thought a spider might do if it was near them, the responses included 'bite me', 'crawl towards my private parts' and 'crawl into my clothes'. Tellingly, when questioned as to their own likely reaction when encountering a spider, the participants believed they would 'feel faint', 'lose control of myself', 'scream' or 'become hysterical'. These kinds of thoughts, of course, serve only to reinforce anxiety.

This tendency to imagine the worst outcome for any scenario is called *catastrophizing*. No matter how inconsequential the worry, the catastrophizer's thoughts spiral downward, step by step, into despair.

Imagine, for example, that you are having lunch with your boss. Into your head pops the thought 'I hope I don't spill this pasta sauce on to my shirt.' Naturally this would be inconvenient, since it might stain your shirt, and it might be a little embarrassing too. But the really practised worrier is unlikely to leave things there. Their train of thought might run like this: 'If I spill the sauce, it'll make a mark on my white shirt. I'll look messy and unprofessional. My boss is sure to notice – and she'll think I'm an idiot. My contract is up for renewal next month. She might decide not to renew it. I'll be out of work. This is a terrible time to find another job – what if I can't? I'll have to sell the car, cancel my holiday, maybe even put my flat on the market … '

To test your own powers of worrying, try this game of fretful consequences. Write down something you've worried about recently. Ask yourself what negative thing might follow if this event occurred. Then ask yourself what the negative outcome of that next event might be – and so on until you can't think of another disastrous consequence. The more anxious we are, the greater the number of consequences we're likely to come up with. Most people can think of between five and nine; anxious people can often manage ten or more.

Here are ten homophones – words that sound the same, but are spelled differently. Read out the first item of each pair to your friends, and ask them to write down the ten words.

- die/dye
- foul/fowl
- moan/mown
- groan/grown
- bore/boar
- pain/pane
- weak/week
- skull/scull
- bury/berry
- guilt/gilt

The more anxious someone is, the greater the likelihood that they'll opt for the more threatening spelling of the words (for instance, 'die' rather than 'dye'). This is because anxious people characteristically display what psychologists call an *attentional bias*. In essence, they focus on the negative (or the potentially negative) and overlook the positive. Thus someone who is anxious in social situations will seize upon a friend's remark that they are feeling tired and interpret this as a hint that the friend is tired of *them*, while remaining oblivious to the evident pleasure the friend takes in their company. A person worried about their health will be preternaturally alert for symptoms of possible illness, and yet utterly dismissive of all indications that they are in fact perfectly well. When we are anxious, we are hypersensitive to threat and hyposensitive to reassurance.

Interestingly, anxiety often manifests itself most forcibly not in worrying thoughts, but in alarming images. Thus, as the evening of a party draws near, the socially anxious person will find herself assailed by vivid mental pictures of her impending humiliation – standing alone in a corner for much of the night, or chatting inanely to a yawning acquaintance, her hair a mess and her clothes a horrible error. The hypochondriac sees himself in the doctor's office, perched in terror on the edge of his chair while the consultant shakes his head and gently explains that the prognosis, alas, is much worse than he had anticipated.

Many people attempt to cope with anxious thoughts and images by trying to suppress them. It doesn't work. This is because of the paradoxical way in which our mind functions: the more we attempt not to think about something, the more inevitable it is that we shall. You can test this out by having a go at the simple task that the young Dostoevsky reputedly set his brother: all you have to do is to try *not* to think about a white bear for sixty seconds. Now, how many seconds did you manage?

*

What causes anxiety, irrational fears, and phobias? Why are we scared of heights, or dogs or social situations?

For many years, the dominant explanation was that we learn our fears through a process known as *conditioning*, in which we come to fear an unthreatening object through its association with a threatening object. The theory had its origins in the work of the Russian scientist Ivan Pavlov (1849–1936). Pavlov famously demonstrated that, once a given stimulus (for example, a bell or a metronome) is associated with food, dogs will learn to respond to that stimulus in the same way as they react to food – by salivating – even when no food is present. The most influential proponent of conditioning, however, was the US psychologist John B. Watson. It was Watson who in 1920 conducted, with Rosalie Rayner, one of the most influential experiments in the history of psychology – though one that would surely fall at the first medical-ethics hurdle today.

Albert B. (or 'Little Albert') was nine months old, the son of a wet nurse at London's Harriet Lane Home for Invalid Children. Watson and Rayner began by testing Albert's reactions to a range of objects, including a white rat, a rabbit, a dog, cotton wool and burning newspapers. Albert – who, according to the psychologists, was a happy, healthy and stoical child – appeared perfectly content with them all. Some weeks later, Watson and Rayner showed Albert the white rat for a second time. On this occasion, as soon as Albert touched the rat, the psychologists slammed a hammer against a steel bar, producing a sudden and frighteningly loud noise. Over the next few weeks the psychologists discovered that Albert was now afraid of the white rat even when the steel bar wasn't struck. And not only that: the child was also scared of objects that in some way resembled the white rat, such as a rabbit or even Watson's hair. Watson and Rayner called this phenomenon 'conditioning', and argued for its fundamental importance in our experience of fear – and in particular how we come to develop phobias and other anxiety problems.

Conditioning is a powerful theory. The idea that we learn our fears through past experiences – albeit often not in the way that Watson envisaged – has remained central. But today this is seen as one of several factors involved (often in tandem) in the development of anxiety. We know, for instance, that our genetic make-up plays a role. Quite how significant that role is, no one can say for sure. The current view is that genes may amount to something like 30–45 per cent of the explanation for differences in levels of anxiety among the population.

While certain genes have been the focus of particular attention from scientists, the notion that there is a single 'anxiety gene' is highly improbable. Much more plausible is the theory that a complex combination of genes produces in some people a susceptibility to anxiety problems. But, in the absence of important environmental factors (an unhappy childhood, for example), this susceptibility will remain merely that.

Actually, our environment may well be the most decisive factor in determining whether or not we have problems with anxiety – regardless of our genetic inheritance. One of these environmental factors could be the lessons we learn from our parents. This was nicely suggested in an experiment carried out by the psychologists Friederike Gerull and Ronald Rapee. They showed thirty toddlers in Sydney, Australia, a green rubber snake and then a purple rubber spider, and studied their reactions. While the toys were on display, the children's mothers were asked to react in a happy and encouraging way or in a frightened or disgusted manner.

Later, the snake and the spider were shown to the toddlers a couple more times, though on these occasions their mothers' reactions were strictly neutral. Gerull and Rapee noticed that you could predict how a child would react to the toy when they saw it again, because the child mimicked the initial response of their mother. If the mother had feigned fear, the child was frightened. If the mother had appeared calm and happy, the toddler reacted likewise.

So it seems children may pick up their anxieties, their fears and phobias, from their most influential teachers: their parents. That may appear a very heavy weight of responsibility to carry. But remember: if our children are so ready to copy our negative behaviour, they will be just as receptive to our positive responses. We can help them to overcome their anxieties by maintaining a constructive, relaxed attitude towards life's difficulties in general and the situations they find frightening in particular.

Fear and anxiety are normal and natural: they are our early warning system, alerting us to possible danger. But that system can sometimes go badly awry. 'Anxiety', however, was a term scarcely used by doctors and psychiatrists until the late 1930s. Today it is one of the principal categories of psychological illness. What lay behind this sea change in the medical view?

Remarkably, it was largely due to the influence of one person: the founder of psychoanalysis, Sigmund Freud. He first set out his views on anxiety problems in 1895, arguing that 'anxiety neurosis' was the product of sexual frustration. Men or women who are unable to achieve sexual fulfilment, Freud suggested, suffer from an 'accumulation of excitation' that ultimately expresses itself in the symptoms of anxiety.

By the mid-1920s Freud's position on anxiety disorders had changed. He still saw them as linked to sexuality, but now the cause lay in psychical disturbances, not the build-up of physical sensations. When the wild and primitive sexual urges of the unconscious id can no longer be controlled by the ego (the part of the psyche responsible for tempering these urges), anxiety problems result. (The most famous – or infamous – of these urges is the supposed desire of sons to kill their fathers and sleep with their mothers: Freud's Oedipus complex.)

Recent years have seen psychoanalysis's influence wane, and Freud's views discredited. But their legacy can still be seen in the huge importance attached to anxiety disorders in current psychological and psychiatric thinking.

The *Diagnostic and Statistical Manual of Mental Disorders*, an official handbook for health professionals, lists six categories of anxiety disorder:

- phobias
- panic disorder, or PD
- obsessive–compulsive disorder, or OCD
- generalized anxiety disorder, or GAD
- social anxiety
- post-traumatic stress disorder, or PTSD

Nearly everyone is afraid of something, and for some people that fear can develop into a *phobia* – an intense feeling of fright and anxiety that is out of all proportion to the reality of the threat facing us. Phobias strike each time we're faced with the situation (or object) we dread – or even when we just *think* about facing them. We might worry about being harmed: for example, falling from a great height, or being bitten by a dog. Or we might be terrified of the way we believe we will react (perhaps by panicking or losing control): afraid, that is, of the fear itself. Naturally, individuals with phobias will go to great lengths to avoid the phobic situation.

Many people with a phobia feel as though they'll faint when confronted by the situation they dread – or even when they merely think about it. In fact fainting when we're frightened is a physiological impossibility, because our blood pressure goes up then. Fainting, on the other hand, occurs when blood pressure drops dramatically.

There is an exception, though. If you have a fear of blood,

your blood pressure may well drop at the sight of the stuff, and you may indeed faint. No one knows why this happens, but a good evolutionary reason may be involved. Besides fainting, one of the other consequences of lowered blood pressure is reduced blood flow – which, if you happened to be badly wounded, might just save your life.

More than one in ten of us suffer from a phobia at some point in our lives; in fact phobia is one of the most prevalent psychological problems. Animals come top of the list of subjects, with 5.7 per cent of us afraid of one type or another. Then come heights (5.3 per cent), blood and injections (4.5 per cent), enclosed spaces (4.2 per cent), water (3.5 per cent) and flying (also 3.5 per cent).

There are literally hundreds of phobias, many of them highly imaginative. Among our favourites are batrachophobia (fear of frogs), epistaxiophobia (nosebleeds), kenophobia (empty spaces), musophobia (mice), rhytiphobia (wrinkles), arachibutyrophobia (the fear of peanut butter sticking to the roof of one's mouth) and panophobia (fear of everything). Assuredly *not* one of our favourites is the dreadful phobia known in south-east Asia as *koro*. Those unfortunate enough to be afflicted with *koro* become terrified by the (fallacious) belief that their penis is retracting into their body. Disturbing though this event would be in itself, many sufferers believe that once the organ has completely disappeared they will die. They can therefore be moved to take drastic – and sometimes permanently disfiguring – steps to arrest the supposed retraction.

So much for phobias. What of the other five anxiety disorders?

If you're experiencing regular, unexpected panic attacks, you may be suffering from *panic disorder*. This kind of panic isn't the sudden sinking feeling you get when you arrive at the theatre to discover that you've forgotten your tickets. It's a white-knuckle ride of fear that can leave us breathless, dizzy and nauseous. A panic attack can feel like a coronary – and indeed our heart rate might rise by up to twenty beats a minute. We may believe we're going crazy, or about to collapse, or are on the point of death. These panics are so terrifying that sufferers are often reluctant to go anywhere they think might trigger an attack; thus they become agoraphobic.

People with *obsessive–compulsive disorder* (OCD) are plagued by distressing and constantly recurring thoughts (or obsessions) that they seek to cope with by means of elaborate rituals (compulsions). Thus a person obsessed with the idea of contamination may spend several hours every day cleaning their home. Someone who believes they are incapable of properly completing any task will be unable to leave the house until they've checked – over and over again – that the cooker is turned off and the doors and windows are securely locked. Most obsessions focus on issues of personal safety, either of the OCD sufferer or of other people. OCD thus resembles a ceaseless, exhausting and inevitably futile struggle against danger, real or imaginary.

Virtually everyone worries from time to time – in one study, 38 per cent of people reported worrying at least once a day, 19.4 per cent worried once every two to three days, and 15 per cent worried about once a month. But when things get truly out of hand – when we're so buffeted by vicious, unrelenting anxiety that it becomes nigh-on impossible to live our normal lives – we are in the grip of *generalized anxiety disorder* (GAD). This is a condition in which worry is off the leash and running amok. No incident is too insignificant to spark an anguished bout of worrying – an innocuous remark from a friend is taken as searing criticism; a tiny hole in a sweater is read as evidence of a moth infestation, necessitating an entire change of wardrobe; tiredness at the end of the day betokens imminent illness.

Social anxiety (also known as social phobia) is an extreme form of shyness. Both have at their root the fear that other people will think badly of us. Some people find all social situ-

ations frightening; others become anxious only in specific situations – for example, making a speech, eating in front of others,
or even using a public toilet (a condition known as paruresis
and experienced predominantly, though not exclusively, by men).
Understandably, people with social anxiety can be extremely
vigorous and resourceful in their efforts to avoid these dreaded
situations. If they are unable to escape, their anxiety may seem
overwhelming, encompassing physical symptoms such as nausea,
breathlessness, sweating, racing blood pressure, and anguished
worry and self-reproach.

Post-traumatic stress disorder (PTSD) was first recognized as
an illness as late as 1980, and then thanks only to the determined lobbying of American Vietnam War veterans, of whom
thousands were affected by what First World War doctors had
termed 'shell shock'. But PTSD is not confined to combat
veterans – indeed, 5 to 10 per cent of us will experience it at
some point in our lives. It can be triggered by any serious trauma,
from rape and violent assault to a serious illness, the death of
a loved one, or a natural disaster. People with PTSD are prone
to vivid, terrifying flashbacks; they endure a constant feeling of
being on edge; and they will go to great lengths to avoid any
reminder of the traumatic event, refusing to talk about their
experiences with loved ones, and frequently attempting to stifle
unwelcome thoughts and feelings through the use of drink or
drugs.

How can we overcome our fears and anxieties?

For many years, the preferred treatment for serious (and sometimes not so serious) anxiety was medication – and specifically
the so-called 'minor tranquillizers' or benzodiazepines, of which
the most well-known is diazepam (Valium). During the 1970s,
diazepam (dubbed 'mother's little helper') was the most widely
prescribed drug in the US, reaching its peak in 1978 when 2.3
billion tablets were sold. But benzodiazepines are rarely used to

treat anxiety today: they can cause some fairly unpleasant side effects, people taking them require ever higher doses to achieve the same benefits, and they can be frustratingly difficult to come off. Instead, a doctor is likely to prescribe one of the new class of antidepressants, the SSRIs (Prozac being the most well-known of these). SSRIs can be very effective in treating anxiety, though they too can have side effects. Moreover, many people find that their symptoms return once they stop taking the medication.

Increasingly, psychological therapy (particularly the variety called *cognitive behavioural therapy*) is being offered to people with anxiety problems, either in combination with medication or on its own. These techniques aren't a panacea: they don't work for everyone. But much well-validated research suggests that they are at least as successful as medication, and often more so. Indeed, the benefits of psychological therapy appear to be more durable than those of medication, with a significant reduction in the likelihood of symptoms recurring.

Moreover, psychological therapy isn't of value only to those with relatively severe anxiety disorders: there is substantial evidence to indicate that it can also help the much greater number of people struggling with relatively minor, everyday worries. And so here are five strategies, drawn from the techniques of psychological therapy, to beat anxiety:

1. **Face up to the situations you dread.** It's best to do this in a gradual way, beginning with relatively easy steps and building up. Psychologists call this technique exposure, and it shows people that they actually have nothing to fear.
2. **Drop your safety behaviours.** 'Safety behaviours' is the technical term for the props that people use to get through stressful situations – for example, sitting down when you think you're going to faint, or going to social events only with a friend. Safety behaviours fool us into thinking that we can't cope without them.

3. **Challenge your anxious thoughts.** Remember that thoughts aren't necessarily a reflection of reality. Write down all the evidence you can think of that supports or contradicts the thought. Try to imagine positive alternative explanations. Ask yourself what you'd advise someone in a similar position, or talk through your fears with a trusted friend.
4. **Use worry periods.** Reserve your worrying for a daily twenty-minute 'worry period'. If you catch yourself fretting outside your worry period, write down what's troubling you and then save it for later.
5. **Focus on problem-solving rather than worrying.** Define the problem as specifically as you can, and think of all the possible solutions. Weigh up the advantages and disadvantages of each, and try the one you think most promising.

9. HAPPINESS AND SADNESS

How happy do you consider yourself? Not sure? Then why not have a go at the following questionnaire. For each statement, the number below the response that you agree with is your score for that statement.

1. In most ways my life is close to my ideal.

Strongly disagree	Disagree	Slightly disagree	Neither agree nor disagree	Slightly agree	Agree	Strongly agree
1 ☐	2 ☐	3 ☐	4 ☐	5 ☐	6 ☐	7 ☐

2. The conditions of my life are excellent.

Strongly disagree	Disagree	Slightly disagree	Neither agree nor disagree	Slightly agree	Agree	Strongly agree
1 ☐	2 ☐	3 ☐	4 ☐	5 ☐	6 ☐	7 ☐

3. I am satisfied with my life.

Strongly disagree	Disagree	Slightly disagree	Neither agree nor disagree	Slightly agree	Agree	Strongly agree
1 ☐	2 ☐	3 ☐	4 ☐	5 ☐	6 ☐	7 ☐

4. So far I have got the important things I want in life.

Strongly disagree	Disagree	Slightly disagree	Neither agree nor disagree	Slightly agree	Agree	Strongly agree
1 ☐	2 ☐	3 ☐	4 ☐	5 ☐	6 ☐	7 ☐

5. If I could live my life over again, I would change almost nothing.

Strongly disagree	Disagree	Slightly disagree	Neither agree nor disagree	Slightly agree	Agree	Strongly agree
1 ☐	2 ☐	3 ☐	4 ☐	5 ☐	6 ☐	7 ☐

Diener, E., Emmons, R. A., Larsen, R. J., & Griffin, S. (1985). *The Satisfaction with Life Scale. Journal of Personality Assessment, 49, 71-75.*

Now add up your total score for the five statements. Here's what the figures may indicate about how content you are with your life:

35 - 30	Very high score; highly satisfied
29 - 25	High score
24 - 20	Average score
19 - 15	Slightly below average
14 - 10	Dissatisfied
9 - 5	Extremely dissatisfied

Depending on your answers to this questionnaire, you may or may not be pleased to learn that happiness doesn't simply feel better than unhappiness: it *is* better for us. Happy people are healthier, enjoy more success in their careers, and develop stronger social ties than unhappy folk.

In a fascinating study, LeeAnne Harker and Dacher Keltner traced the fortunes of more than a hundred Californian women over thirty years. They began by analysing the women's college yearbook photos, taken at age twenty-one. Virtually all the women were smiling, but only half were showing real happiness rather than a fake smile for the camera (one can assess this by looking at the contraction of the muscles around the eye: if you don't mean it, they don't move). When Harker and Keltner examined personality assessments completed by the women at the time the photo was taken, they discovered that the 'genuine' smilers were happier and more sociable than their classmates.

Now come the really intriguing findings. As well as the assessments from when the women were twenty-one, Harker and Keltner also had accounts provided at ages twenty-seven, forty-three and fifty-two. The women who'd been happiest in their yearbook photo were still the most content at every subsequent milestone; they were more organized, focused and motivated, and less prone to emotional problems. They were also more likely to be married at age twenty-seven, and to be still happily married thirty years later.

Happiness is strongly associated with optimism – and optimism, it seems, can help you live longer. The psychologists Christopher Peterson, George Vaillant and Martin Seligman followed the fortunes over thirty-five years of ninety-nine Harvard students whose pessimism had been assessed in 1946 (when they were in their twenties). The researchers found that the students who'd been most pessimistic as young adults were significantly more likely to experience ill health between the ages of forty-five and sixty.

Toshihiko Maruta and colleagues came to a similar conclusion when in 1994 they followed up several hundred patients who'd been admitted to hospital in the mid-1960s. As part of the admission process, each patient's level of optimism and pessimism had been measured. Thirty years later, it was the most pessimistic patients who were more likely to have died – and the optimistic ones who were most likely still to be alive.

So when it comes to happiness the stakes are high. But what

is happiness, and what causes it? Can we increase our levels of happiness? What does it mean to be sad, or depressed? And how can we overcome our low moods? Read on for the answers to all these questions, and more.

Sabera lives in the slums of Kolkata, one of a family of seven sharing a one-room slum apartment. Toilet facilities and running water are communal. Sabera's family owns a television and cooking equipment, but little else. Sabera has three children; two daughters died in infancy. All her time is spent caring for her family.

Rana cannot lay claim to even the meagre comforts available to Sabera. A fifty-five-year-old taxi driver, he is one of the 200,000 people in Kolkata who live on the city's streets. When the monsoon rains come, Rana sleeps beneath a tarpaulin.

With so much hardship in their lives, it would be natural to assume that Sabera and Rana are unhappy. After all, wouldn't you be? And yet research by Ed Diener, a key figure in the psychology of happiness – and, naturally, Joseph R. Smiley Distinguished Professor of Psychology at the University of Illinois – and his son Robert Biswas-Diener indicates that matters are not as clear-cut as one might imagine.

They interviewed eighty-three residents of Kolkata, all of them slum dwellers, prostitutes living in brothels, or homeless street people. For sure, these individuals were less happy than the middle-class students surveyed at the University of Calcutta – with the prostitutes more unhappy than the slum dwellers, and the homeless people most unhappy of all. Nevertheless, these desperately poor people – many of whom had recently endured ill health or bereavement – were broadly content with many aspects of their lives, and derived particular satisfaction from their social relationships, family ties, and religious convictions.

Now let's switch our focus to the very opposite end of the spectrum: the Western super-rich. This time Ed Diener (and his colleagues Jeff Horwitz and Robert Emmons) contacted 100 of those included in *Forbes* magazine's list of the 400 wealthiest Americans. They then compared the levels of happiness of these millionaires with those of 100 randomly selected adults from similar geographical areas. As you might expect, the millionaires were on average happier than the other guys – but not by much. Many of the millionaires scored lower than average for happiness, and the majority of those who weren't wealthy reported being very content with their lot. No one – regardless of their personal wealth – felt that money was important in achieving happiness. Friends, family, good health, accomplishing one's goals, and a devotion to God were all seen as much more significant.

So what do these two studies tell us about happiness? Well, it seems that money helps, but not nearly as much as we might imagine. And this is just one of the myths about happiness that research has exposed in recent years. Take youth, for example. Though our society appears to valorize being young to an extraordinary degree, it is actually older people who are most likely to be satisfied with their lives. Or health – as long as you're not chronically or critically ill, a spell of even moderately serious sickness is unlikely to make a great difference to your overall happiness. Spare a thought too for the massed ranks of teenage wannabes whose greatest desire is to be 'famous'. There is absolutely no evidence that fame routinely brings with it happiness (or, indeed, that it will allow you to live for ever). Which, given that the vast majority of the world's population has neither the opportunity nor the inclination to become a celebrity, is doubtless just as it should be.

How do levels of happiness vary around the world?

Professor Ruut Veenhoven and his team at Erasmus University in Rotterdam have analysed a mass of data gathered between 1945 and 2007 to produce the World Database of Happiness. Here's who came out top:

1. Denmark
2. Switzerland
3. Austria
4. Iceland
5. Finland

And here are the five unhappiest countries (with number 1 being the least happy):

1. Tanzania
2. Zimbabwe
3. Moldova
4. Ukraine
5. Armenia

Britain is ranked joint twenty-second – with Honduras. Australia is equal sixth; Ireland and Canada are among the nations tied in ninth; the US is seventeenth, France thirty-ninth and Japan equal forty-fifth.

To a certain extent, a nation's happiness is related to its wealth – rich nations tend to be happy, and very poor countries are generally very unhappy (though, as we've seen, even extremely poor individuals can enjoy a certain level of happiness despite the deprivations they endure). Once a country attains a certain level of wealth, however, that correlation breaks down. Japan, for example, is ranked forty-fifth in terms of happiness, but according to a 2006 study published by the World Institute for Development Economics Research its citizens are the richest on the planet (with average wealth of $180,837 per person). The super-happy Danish, on the other hand, average $70,751 per person. And Britain, where people have assets worth an average of $126,832, is tied in the happiness stakes with Honduras, whose citizens own $2,356. The net worth of the average Tanzanian is $681.

Why are the Danes so content with life? High-quality health-care, an excellent educational system, and high average prosperity are key factors in a nation's happiness. But Denmark isn't the only country with such advantages, so what makes it top in the contentment chart? One theory discounted by researchers was the notion that the Danes' happiness stems from their fondness for a drink or two, or, as another expert put it, 'One reason Danes seem smug may be that they were drunk when they participated in the Eurobarometer surveys.' Instead, two principal factors have been identified.

The first can be summed up in two names: John Jensen and Kim Vilfort. Or a date: 26 June 1992. For this was the day when Denmark – a nation of just 5.5 million people and a perennial minnow in world football – beat Germany, population 80 million and the then holders of the World Cup, to become European Champions. (Messrs Jensen and Vilfort scored the crucial goals.) This event has been called the greatest day in Danish history since 'the protracted history of Danish setbacks began with defeat in England in 1066, followed by the loss of Sweden, Norway, Northern Germany, the Danish West Indies and Iceland'. Although Danish levels of happiness have always been comparatively high in surveys, since 1992 they have reached new heights.

The second factor is encapsulated in the Danish term *Jante-lov*, meaning 'You're no better than anyone else.' A highly progressive tax system creates little incentive to choose a career simply on the basis of financial rewards or social status. Not only does this mean that Danes are more likely to end up working at a job they actually enjoy, it also results in minimal wealth inequality. This, combined with top-class health, education and welfare systems accessible to all, ensures that one of the major causes of unhappiness – comparison of your lot with that of others – is minimized in Denmark.

*

If the secret to happiness isn't youth, fame and fortune, then what is?

To answer that question, we turn now to one of the hottest new kids on the psychology block. Led by Martin Seligman, a professor at the University of Pennsylvania, *positive psychology* is dedicated to the investigation of 'what makes life worth living'. This represents a radical shift in focus for the discipline. As Seligman has written, 'For the last half century psychology has been consumed with a single topic only – mental illness.' Since the inception of positive psychology at the end of the 1990s, hundreds of scholarly articles, dozens of books, and several websites have appeared, all focused on understanding the nature of happiness and how we can go about increasing our personal stock of the stuff.

Positive psychology argues that there are three components to happiness – positive emotion, engagement and meaning – and the happiest people have them all.

Positive emotion. The term is dry and technical, but the feelings it denotes are anything but. These are the emotions we seem hard-wired to want more of – contentment, optimism, hope, joy, amusement and, arguably most of all, *pleasure*. Since the ancient Greeks, and specifically Epicurus (341–270 BC), the idea that the path to happiness lies in filling your life with as much pleasure as possible – a philosophy known as hedonism – has remained a potent force. (You can detect its influence, for example, in virtually all the advertising you see around you.)

Pleasure is important, of course – a life devoid of pleasure hardly seems worth living. However, if you want it to last it's best obtained not by short cuts (alcohol, for instance, or double chocolate-chip cookies), but by working out what you're good at – your 'signature strengths' – and using them as much as you can. So if you love learning new skills, for instance, take an evening class; if you enjoy helping people, maybe do some volunteering work; if you're creative, ensure your creativity has an outlet. Actually, this approach to happiness also has ancient roots, reaching right back to Aristotle (384–322 BC), who developed the idea of *eudaimonia* or being true to one's essential self.

Engagement. Perhaps you have been so deeply immersed in *Use Your Head* that when you eventually look at your watch you are astonished to discover that several hours have somehow slipped by unnoticed. (Then again, perhaps not.) This deep absorption in an activity is known as 'engagement' or 'flow', the latter a term developed by the psychologist Mihaly Csikzentmihalyi and the focus of much attention in recent years.

When we're experiencing flow, our mental resources are entirely focused on the task in hand. We're no longer aware of what's going on around us, and lose track of time. Self-consciousness fades away, and we become one with our activity. To produce this feeling of flow, a task must be well balanced: too easy and we become bored; too difficult and frustration results. Classic examples of flow-inducing activities are playing a musical instrument or sport; painting, writing or some other creative endeavour; or working on puzzles or other logical problems.

Meaning. Charles M. Schulz, creator of the 'Peanuts' comic strip, once wrote, 'My life has no purpose, no direction, no aim, no meaning, and yet I'm happy. I can't figure it out. What am I doing right?' This was probably somewhat disingenuous. Schulz, after all, reportedly took only a single holiday during the entire fifty-year run of 'Peanuts', a dedication to one's work that suggests not so much a life devoid of meaning or purpose but one absolutely full of it. And it doesn't matter where you find the meaning in your life – be it your career, your family, your religion, your political engagement – you cannot be truly happy without it.

*

Trying to be happier is as futile as trying to be taller.
– David Lykken and Auke Tellegen

Can this gloomy assertion be true? Is a long-lasting increase in one's level of happiness really impossible? It depends on which expert you consult. Many have argued that an individual's degree of happiness is largely pre-programmed, being a function of personality and genetic make-up. Thus happiness is essentially a matter of luck – and indeed the root of the word is the medieval English term 'hap' or chance (as in 'happenstance'). Proponents of this theory point to the fact that events that one might expect to make a very dramatic difference to one's happiness – winning the lottery, for example – often do nothing of the sort. The exotic holidays, fancy sports car and luxurious mansion certainly provide a short-term boost, but by the time a year has elapsed the individuals have usually returned to the level of happiness they enjoyed before their numbers came up. Studies of identical twins also seem to support the genetic argument for happiness. Twins who have been separated at birth, and who thus grew up in different environments, display levels of happiness that are more alike than could be expected by chance.

On the other hand, there are many experts – and especially those influenced by positive psychology – who believe that improving one's degree of happiness, substantially and permanently, is indeed possible. While our genes may well be a factor, they merely determine the lower and upper limits of our happiness – and those limits may encompass a very wide range of possibilities. But if this is true, how then do we set about increasing our happiness quotient? Here's what the UK government recommended in 2008, on the basis of advice from more than 400 specialists:

- **Connect.** Developing relationships with family, friends, colleagues and neighbours will enrich your life and bring you support.

- **Be active.** Sports, hobbies such as gardening or dancing, or just a daily stroll will make you feel good and maintain mobility and fitness.
- **Be curious.** Noting the beauty of everyday moments as well as the unusual and reflecting on them helps you to appreciate what matters to you.
- **Learn.** Fixing a bike, learning an instrument, cooking – the challenge and satisfaction bring fun and confidence.
- **Give.** Helping friends and strangers links your happiness to a wider community and is very rewarding.

The evidence suggests that you can also raise your levels of happiness by making sure you get sufficient sleep and by eating healthily. For example, one study followed more than 10,000 people in the UK between 2002 and 2004 and found that those who made major improvements in their diet (even without increasing the amount of exercise they took) reported feeling much happier, calmer and more peaceful.

Pessimists can learn to be optimists. When a pessimist experiences a negative event, they assume that

- Everything in my life is going to get worse
- Things won't improve
- It's my fault

An optimist, on the other hand, will conclude that

- It's not going to affect my life
- It's temporary
- It's not my fault

When you spot a pessimistic thought, challenge it. Ask yourself what evidence there is to support it – and to disprove it. What alternative ideas can you come up with? What would you advise a friend in a similar situation? And if there genuinely is a problem, ask yourself whether it is really as serious as it seems.

One approach currently generating a lot of excitement is *mindfulness*, a synthesis of modern Western psychological thinking and ancient Buddhist beliefs and practices, particularly meditation. Mindfulness, it seems, may help people both to increase their stock of happiness and to overcome problems such as depression and anxiety.

Mindfulness involves learning to live in the moment, developing your awareness of what it feels like to be alive in this present instant, and understanding that your thoughts and feelings are temporary, transient and not necessarily a reflection of reality. Mindfulness is best practised by means of regular meditation sessions, but you can get a taste right now: for the next few minutes, stop what you're doing and concentrate instead on the rise and fall of your breathing, the colour of the sky above you, the feel of your body as it rests.

Finally, here are some tips from the guru of positive psychology, Martin Seligman:

- Identify your top five strengths – perhaps your curiosity or enthusiasm for new experiences, your generosity or kindness – and think of ways to use them more often in your daily life.
- Each evening, write down three good things that happened to you that day.
- Every night for two weeks, write down five things in your life you are grateful for.
- Think of someone who has helped you in your life but whom you have never thanked. Write them a letter, call them up, or better yet pay them a visit – and express your gratitude.
- At least once every day, try to react in a positive and enthusiastic way to someone else.
- Set aside a day to do exactly what you want. Plan your day of luxury and pleasure in advance, so you maximize every moment.

- Savour and prolong moments of pleasure by focusing all your attention on the sensations you're experiencing. Share your pleasures with friends, and keep mementos.
- Identify the activities that provide you with flow, and do more of them.

*

In the *Simpsons* episode 'One fish, two fish, blowfish, blue fish', Homer's enthusiasm at Springfield's new sushi restaurant results in him inadvertently devouring the deadly *fugu* (together with everything else on the menu). Erroneously informed that he has just twenty-four hours to live, he resolves to break the habit of a lifetime and spend a little quality time with his kids. When he listens to Lisa playing her saxophone, he breaks down in tears – which, given the circumstances, is hardly surprising. But when Lisa hurriedly begins a more upbeat number, a miraculous transformation takes place. Homer is instantly consoled, joyfully dancing and singing his way around her bedroom and out the door: 'Oh I want to be in that rumba when the saints go over there!'

As Homer discovers (or not, as the case may be), music can have a powerful effect on mood. A great deal of research has been carried out on this topic, and the evidence is uncharacteristically unambiguous: sad music tends to lower our mood and happy music to cheer us up. (Which is not to say, of course, that sad music cannot be rewarding – indeed pleasurable – in its own way. As Shelley wrote in his ode 'To a Skylark', 'Our sweetest songs are those that tell of saddest thought.')

For this reason, you might consider putting together a compilation CD to play when you're feeling down or stressed. But what should you put on it? It may be wise to avoid Samuel Barber's *Adagio for Strings*, voted the saddest piece of music by listeners to BBC Radio 4's *Today* programme. When the mental-health charity Mind carried out a similar survey, these were the songs that sparked the biggest emotional reaction in respondents:

Happy	Sad	Chill out
"Let Me Entertain You" **Robbie Williams**	*"Everybody Hurts"* **REM**	*"Thank You"* **Dido**
"Walking on Sunshine" **Katrina & the Waves**	*"Creep"* **Radiohead**	*"Bridge over Troubled Waters"* **Simon & Garfunkel**
"Shiny Happy People" **REM**	*"Candle in the Wind"* **Elton John**	*"Porcelain"* **Moby**

*

Among the 600 islands that make up the Federated States of Micronesia is Ifaluk, just 1.5 square kilometres in size, and home to little more than 500 people. On Ifaluk, the emotion *ker*, which translates as 'happiness'/'excitement', is frowned upon, being regarded as likely to lead to smug and selfish behaviour. Far more preferable is it to experience *fago*, which is a kind of sadness experienced when loved ones are absent. The person capable of *fago*, the Ifaluk reason, is a person blessed with strong and loving relationships.

Like happiness, anger, disgust and fear, sadness has been identified as one of the five basic human emotions, present in us all at some time or other, and observable within the first weeks after birth. But what is sadness? Well, as the Ifaluk demonstrate, it is not necessarily a negative state, some sort of opposite emotion to happiness. Instead, its meaning may change according to culture and context. Some forms of sadness may even be pleasurable – leafing through an old photo album, or looking through childhood books, for example, can spark exquisitely bitter-sweet emotions. Sadness is a response to loss or failure; hence we're sad when we can't locate a treasured possession or are separated from our partner or children, or when we're unable to achieve the goals we set ourselves. If we're really sad, we may cry – a reaction of which no other creature is capable.

Sadness can get out of hand, of course, and veer into depression. More often, however, it's actually beneficial. It can, for example, result in us reassessing our behaviour. For instance, someone feeling down about losing contact with a friend might resolve to work harder at maintaining such relationships in the future. And sadness can help strengthen our social ties by prompting us to seek help from loved ones – finally making the phone call or visit we never got around to when things were going well.

*

The pain is unrelenting and what makes the condition intolerable is the foreknowledge that no remedy will come – not in a day, an hour, a month, or a minute. If there is mild relief, one knows that it is only temporary ... One does not abandon, even briefly, one's bed of nails, but is attached to it wherever one goes.
   – **William Styron**, *Darkness Visible* (1990)

Sadness, like many emotional and psychological states, exists as a spectrum, from mild and fleeting nostalgia to long-term misery. At the bleakest end of that spectrum lies depression, a condition now so prevalent that the World Health Organization has identified it as the principal cause of disability throughout the world. With depression estimated to affect up to 20 per cent of people at some point in their lives, there's a good chance that, if you haven't experienced it yourself, you know someone who has.

Depression can have a profound effect on body, mind and behaviour. People with depression feel down pretty much all the time. Life becomes an ordeal, devoid of interest or pleasure. Energy drains from the body. Even the simplest task appears impossible to complete. Sleep and appetite are disrupted. Negative thoughts fill the mind: we are worthless; the world is horrible; the future is unremittingly bleak. And behaviour changes accordingly: people with depression often withdraw into themselves, avoiding social contact and generally doing as little as possible. They might be irritable and agitated or, alternatively, noticeably sluggish in their thought, speech or movements. Tears, and long bouts of anguished brooding, are typical.

Given the widespread misery caused by depression, it has naturally been the focus of a great deal of research by psychologists over the last fifty years or so. We now know, for example, that depression is often triggered by extremely stressful life experiences, such as poverty, bereavement, unemployment or the end of a relationship. As with ordinary sadness, a sense of loss – of relationships, social status, or ideals, for example – often lies at the root of depression. Depression is especially likely if those stressful experiences involve humiliation or a sense of entrapment: perhaps being fired from your job, or feeling mired in a relationship you're unable to abandon. As you might expect, those who've suffered neglect or abuse in childhood are vulnerable to depression. And people who can't rely on a decent support network when times are tough are at greater risk of slipping into depression than those who can.

Arguably the greatest contribution to our understanding of depression has been made by the American psychiatrist Aaron T. Beck (born 1921), now a professor emeritus at the University of Pennsylvania. Beck is a lapsed psychoanalyst, his belief in Freud's theories gradually disintegrating when he began subjecting them to scientific scrutiny in the early 1960s (an endeavour that, even before he'd drawn any firm conclusions, saw him refused membership of the American Psychoanalytic Institute).

For Beck, depression involves three key processes. And, crucially, these processes aren't buried deep in the psyche: with the appropriate training, they are in fact eminently observable. In fact, once you're aware of their existence, you can identify them in yourself. As Beck puts it, 'There is more on the surface than meets the eye.'

Negative automatic thoughts. Beck argues that depression is triggered less by the events that happen to us than by our interpretation of those events. Stifle a yawn in front of a depressed person, for example, and they will probably assume you're bored with their company, rather than simply trying to cope with a late night. Why? Because the thoughts that spring automatically to their mind are pessimistic ones about themselves, the world and the future.

Logical errors. When we're depressed, we don't think straight. Instead, we are prone to all kinds of logical errors, such as *overgeneralization* ('X didn't like that film I suggested; she and I never agree on anything'), *catastrophization* ('I forgot my appointment at the dentist yesterday; I'm losing my mind') and *dichotomous, all-or-nothing thinking* ('If I don't do this perfectly, I've failed').

Negative schematic beliefs. Underlying a depressed person's negative automatic thoughts and logical errors are deep-seated and profoundly unhelpful beliefs ('schemas') about themselves and the world around them – for example, 'I am worthless'; 'I am a failure'; 'I am unlovable.' These kinds of belief are often triggered by childhood experiences, such as losing a parent, being bullied, or being let down by people one has trusted.

Alison had suffered from depression periodically since her university days. Usually she was able to ride it out and keep functioning pretty well. But sometimes she felt so low that work and family commitments became impossible. Instead, she closed the curtains and took to her bed, occasionally for two or three weeks at a stretch. It was during one of these dark periods (literally and metaphorically) that we met her a few months ago. Alison was an old family friend: our fathers had worked together back in the 1970s, and we had seen a lot of her and her siblings while growing up.

We sat in her shadowy living room and drank the tea we had made for ourselves in her kitchen. She confessed that she had not set foot outside the house for a month (her partner did all the shopping and domestic chores), but thought she could now feel the depression beginning its very gradual retreat. We reminisced about the past, and particularly the holidays the two families had taken together. But Alison – normally so acute in her memories – seemed unable to recall many of the incidents we mentioned. 'Do you remember the time Chris [her older brother] threw you into the swimming pool at that camp site?' we asked. Alison was non-committal. 'Chris was always a nightmare,' she replied, somewhat vaguely. 'And he still is.' 'What about that disco when that German boy you fancied finally asked you to dance?' 'I don't remember. All those guys were creeps.'

In fact Alison's shaky memory is typical of people with depression. First, they're much more likely to recall negative rather than positive experiences. And, second, they find it difficult to remember specific incidents in their past; instead, they over-generalize. The British clinical psychologist Mark Williams, who discovered this 'autobiographical memory bias', has speculated that it may be a protective strategy, shielding the individual from potentially distressing recollections: if you don't recall events in detail, they are much less likely to upset you.

This memory bias is often combined in depressed people with a tendency towards *rumination* – that's to say, endlessly dwelling on the same negative thoughts. In fact the more people ruminate, the greater the risk that they'll develop serious depression (and/or anxiety problems). When people who are feeling low ruminate, they tend to focus on unpleasant experiences, to see their present problems more pessimistically, and to worry more about the future – all of which, it's easy to imagine, can help tip someone over the edge and into fully fledged depression. And if they ruminate *while* depressed, their illness is likely to be more severe and longer lasting.

Intriguingly, there appears to be both 'good' and 'bad' rumination. The former consists of simply recalling your feelings; the latter of analysing those feelings. So trying to pinpoint exactly the way you felt last night is fine and perhaps even beneficial; repeatedly attempting to discover why you reacted in that way and what it signifies is unhelpful, because if you're already miserable you'll probably take a pessimistic, self-blaming viewpoint.

These insights into memory bias and rumination, and Beck's discoveries, make it clear that depression operates on two psychological levels. The first is our depressed thoughts ('I am unlovable'; 'Everything I do ends in failure'). The second is the very skewed ways in which we think about our experiences. To tackle depression, you have to address both levels. And this is just what therapies such as cognitive behavioural therapy (CBT), which Beck invented, and its spin-off mindfulness do, often with great success. (You can read more about CBT on pp. 258–9.)

Some psychological statistics are contentious. One that is undisputed is the fact that women are twice as likely to suffer from depression as men. In this instance, the debate focuses not on whether but *why* this should be the case.

There's no conclusive evidence to suggest that the difference is biological (no wombs wandering around the body to cause hysteria, for example, as was once believed) or genetic. Instead, the focus has fallen on environmental factors: that's to say, the life events that women experience and the ways in which they respond to them.

Before we look at the main candidates, a word of caution and qualification: this difference between the sexes is age-related. Pre-adolescent boys are more likely to be depressed than girls, and after the age of fifty-five the rate of depression in women declines so much that men actually overtake them. The fall in women's rates of depression in later life has been attributed to the menopause, but because the evidence points away from physiological factors it seems as if social and psychological changes must be responsible (though what those might be isn't yet clear).

Marriage. In many Western societies, married women are at greater risk of depression than single women, possibly from the stress of having to manage a household alongside other commitments such as work. The opposite is true for married men, who have lower rates of depression than single men, and also for women in Mediterranean countries where, it's suggested, the traditional home-making role is held in higher esteem.

Children. As any parent can testify, looking after small children can be an inordinately stressful as well as rewarding experience. Hence it's little surprise that women (and particularly young women) caring for pre-schoolers are especially vulnerable to depression. But there may be more to this than simply the demands of parenthood – which still, of course, tend largely to be shouldered by mothers rather than fathers. We know that paid employment can be an important source of self-esteem, fulfilment and pleasure. But many mothers are either unable to work or must fit their jobs around their childcare responsibilities (thus generating additional stress).

The kinds of pressure faced by mothers are much more likely to result in depression if the women in question are poor and/or bringing up their children alone. (This news may not come as a shock to you.) For example, the risk of working-class mothers developing depression is three times greater than that for middle-class mothers or women without children.

Low self-esteem and difficult close relationships. For a year, the psychologist Antonia Bifulco and her team tracked the fortunes of more than a hundred working-class mothers in London. All these women were struggling with low self-esteem and/or conflict-ridden relationships with partners, children or other close family members. None, however, was depressed when the study began. Bifulco found that more than a third of the women developed depression during the year, and especially if they'd experienced a serious problem or setback in that time.

Women who had suffered from depression in the past were particularly vulnerable, with those at greatest risk being the individuals who had first developed the illness in their teens. Data on the role that childhood abuse (of which girls are at greater risk than boys) and neglect play in the onset of later depression is thin on the ground. But in almost every case the women in Bifulco's study who had become depressed as adolescents had experienced these kinds of difficulty in their childhood.

Rumination. As we've seen, people who dwell on their worries are more likely to suffer from depression. And women are more prone to rumination than men.

Investment in relationships. According to the 'cost of caring' theory, women develop stronger ties to family and friends than do men. Clearly this tendency can be a great strength: the relationships so assiduously nurtured by many women can provide a source of support that men often lack. But it also constitutes a point of vulnerability: it's not simply one's own problems that are likely to get one down, but also those experienced by those that one cares for.

10. MEN, WOMEN AND COMMUNICATION

Who is the best-selling relationship author of all time? According to his website (and we've no reason to quibble), it's John Gray, whose sixteen books have reputedly sold more than 40 million copies and been translated into over forty-five languages. This enviable success has been built on the back of his 1992 blockbuster *Men Are from Mars, Women Are from Venus*.

As its title makes abundantly clear, *Men Are from Mars ...* presents a picture of two sexes baffled by each other's strangeness. As different as the proverbial chalk and cheese, women and men speak wildly divergent emotional and psychological languages. We may spend much of our adult lives in romantic relationships with members of the opposite sex, but these relationships are often founded on mutual mystification and incomprehension.

Forty million copies sold suggests that John Gray's theories strike a chord with very many people. Indeed, they seem to fit perfectly so many of our beliefs about the opposite sex. But are men and women *really* so dissimilar?

Before we explore the scientific evidence, let's take a look at the biological characteristics of sexual identity. At the most basic level, what does it mean to be male or female?

Our biological sex is determined by five interrelated factors. The first and most fundamental is *genetic*: humans inherit two sex chromosomes from their parents (chromosomes are structures of DNA; these particular chromosomes contain the genetic blueprint for our sexual development). One of these chromosomes originates from our mother, and the other comes from our father. Girls normally inherit one so-called X chromosome from each of their parents, giving them a chromosomal sexual identity of XX. Boys, on the other hand, acquire one X chromosome from their mother and a Y chromosome from the father (XY) – it's the Y chromosome that encapsulates a boy's 'maleness'.

Our genetic make-up determines the pre-natal growth of our reproductive organs: the *gonads*. For females this means the ovaries, and for males the testes. Once these are in place, sexual development is largely influenced by our *hormones* (essentially forms of chemical released by cells in our body). Male sexual hormones are called *androgens*; the one everybody has heard of – and the most significant – is testosterone, which is mainly produced by the testes. Among the hormones generated by the ovaries are oestrogen and progesterone. It's worth remembering that these 'male' and 'female' hormones aren't the exclusive property of one sex or the other. Males and females create both androgens *and* oestrogen and progesterone. What sets them apart is the quantity produced: males typically secrete a greater number of androgens than do females, who in turn normally create more oestrogen and progesterone.

Fourth in the list of biological factors are the *internal features* of the body that facilitate reproduction. For females these include the Fallopian tubes, the womb and ovaries, while for males it's the prostate gland, sperm ducts, the seminal vesicles (the glands that produce much of the liquid that becomes semen) and the testes.

Finally, each sex is distinguished by its *external genital organs*:

the penis and scrotum in the case of males, and the exterior lips of the vagina (the labia majora) in females.

Incidentally, you may be wondering what the difference is between our sex and our gender. The two terms are often used interchangeably (and for simplicity's sake we're going to use them like that here). But, where they aren't, 'sex' refers to our biological designation as either male or female, and 'gender' to the set of culturally determined behaviours associated with a particular sex. So carrying a baby in one's womb is a sexually determined role; feeling a responsibility to perform most of the childcare is (at least partly) a reflection of gender expectations.

'The general discussions of the psychology of sex, whether by psychologists or by sociologists show such a wide diversity of points of view that one feels that the truest thing to be said at present is that scientific evidence plays very little part in producing convictions.' The previous sentence was written almost a hundred years ago by the American psychologist and feminist Helen Thompson Woolley. Today the debates – at least in the academic world – may be more scientifically grounded, but that certainly doesn't mean the experts are all in agreement. Are the psychological (as opposed to biological or anatomical) differences between the sexes few or many? Are those that do exist the result of nature or of nurture? The answers to these questions are still disputed.

That said, if there is a consensus it's that the psychological differences between men and women are far fewer than traditionally believed. There's relatively little scientific evidence to support the idea that men and women are fundamentally dissimilar, and much more to suggest that they are alike in most respects. Indeed, when the psychologist Janet Shibley Hyde analysed current scientific research on male and female psychology, in 2005, she found that 30 per cent of the reported differences were close to zero and another 48 per cent were only small. The psychological differences between the sexes, for so long assumed by scientists and non-scientists alike to be vast, actually turn out to be relatively modest. (Some experts have argued that academic studies highlighting apparent differences are far more likely to be published than studies that find no such variation between males and females, so the research Hyde assessed may already have been skewed in its emphasis on dissimilarity.) The 'gender similarities hypothesis' has been summarized by Hyde thus: 'Males and females are similar on most, but not all, psychological variables. That is, men and women, as well as boys and girls, are more alike than they are different.' Whichever planet men are from, therefore, it's almost certainly the same as the one inhabited by women.

The superiority of men, opined the French psychologist Gustave Le Bon at the beginning of the twentieth century, is 'so obvious that no one can contest it for a minute'. Le Bon was repeating a widely held scientific view that, because men's brains are larger than women's (as is indeed generally the case), this ensured that they were more intelligent too. Unsurprisingly, there's no evidence to support this position – nor, for that matter, to suggest that women are more intelligent than men. For example, women and men are fundamentally alike in the size of their vocabulary and their ability to read and understand written texts, as well as in their competitiveness, their enjoyment of sex, their effectiveness as leaders, their degree of impulsiveness, their gregariousness, and the factors that motivate them at work.

(We should bear in mind, however, that some of these areas have been studied in much more depth than others, and that no one really knows how a small statistical difference in a labora-tory experiment will translate into men and women's relative performance in real-life situations. Moreover, any difference between the sexes is much less significant than the variation *between* members of the same sex: even in tasks where one sex tends to perform better than the other, a member of the less proficient sex may well score higher than a member of the more proficient sex. These kinds of data describe general trends, not specific individuals.)

Arguably the major difference between men and women concerns their respective sexual orientations. The overwhelming majority of men (perhaps 94–98 per cent) are sexually attracted to women, and a similar proportion of women are attracted to men. There's also a good deal of data to back up the idea that men are more physically aggressive than women (at the extreme end of this spectrum, a murderer is ten times more likely to be male than female), and more dominant and assertive in their behaviour. The average woman, on the other hand, is likely to be relatively caring, empathetic and conciliatory. After this, however, the evidence becomes much less clear-cut, and such differences as do show up are generally extremely subtle.

It's generally assumed, for example, that males are stronger at maths than females. Actually, although on most tests the difference is negligible, it favours women not men. That said, older boys and young men (college students, for instance) tend to do better than their female counterparts on some problem-solving assessments. Similarly, most people tend to think of women as being better at verbal skills than men, yet the research indicates that any advantage is minimal and, as with almost all these tests, varies depending on which particular aspect of the ability is being assessed. For example, women tend to score more highly than men in tests of verbal fluency, but there are no differences between the sexes when it comes to vocabulary or comprehension skills.

The clearest difference in cognitive ability between the sexes relates to what are known as 'visuospatial' skills (that's to say, how we perceive the spatial relationship between objects), though even here both sexes perform similarly on certain tests. Men generally do significantly better than women at mental rotation

– imagining how an object will look when it's rotated – and at other spatial perception tests, which may explain why men are generally regarded as better map-readers than women. But for visuospatial skills, as for virtually all psychological and cognitive abilities, any differences between the sexes are much smaller than the variations within a particular sex. Thus *on average* men are better at mental rotation than women, but this certainly doesn't guarantee that a particular man will score more highly than a given woman at this.

Here's a little anthropological fieldwork for all the parents of young children reading this book. Next time you drop your child at school, spend a few minutes carefully observing the way the kids act in the playground or classroom. How similar is the behaviour of the girls and the boys? What differences do you see?

Identifying physical characteristics is a relatively simple task: males tend to be taller, heavier and stronger than females. And, as we've seen, there are some pretty unarguable biological variations between the two sexes. But to what extent do these distinctive physical and biological characteristics translate into differences in the ways males and females think, feel and behave? Scientists who've studied the social interactions of children have identified just three areas in which boys and girls are significantly dissimilar – which perhaps isn't many given the prevalence of the notion that males and females come from different planets.

The first difference – and the one that is noticeable earliest in a child's life – is the fact that boys and girls have distinct preferences when it comes to the toys they like to play with. Even at the extremely tender age of one, boys tend to opt for vehicles and guns, whereas girls would rather play with dolls, prams, tea sets and other domestic-themed toys. (If you're surprised by the precociousness of this development, you're not alone. But the evidence is substantial.) The respective differences are maintained throughout childhood. One study that looked at letters to Father Christmas composed by eight-to-eleven-year-olds, for example, found that more than 50 per cent of the boys asked for a vehicle of some type, while fewer than 10 per cent of the girls did. On the other hand, over 25 per cent of the girls wanted a doll, compared to less than 1 per cent of the boys.

The second major difference between boys and girls lies in their choice of playmates. Children typically develop a rough-and-ready awareness of gender by the time they reach the age of three. At this point they can usually identify both their own gender and that of people they see around them. (They may still be foxed by appearances, however: ask a three-year-old about a man with long hair and they may well tell you that he's a girl.) With gender awareness comes a distinct preference for playmates of their own sex: boys like to hang out with boys; girls would rather play with other girls. Again, this is a tendency that persists throughout childhood. Psychologists who observed the behaviour of a group of eight-to-eleven-year-olds at school, for instance, discovered that more than 50 per cent spent absolutely no time socializing with children of the opposite sex.

The third and final difference in the way that boys and girls interact socially concerns their style of play. Boys generally prefer physical activity (sometimes pretty rough and even aggressive), and they often hang out in large groups. So you'll probably see primary-school boys playing football in their break times, for example, or charging around the playground chasing one another. Boys don't tend to talk to each other a great deal, except insofar as it relates to what they happen to be doing. Girls' play, on the other hand, is typically a far more sedate and intimate business – perhaps involving role play or just chatting with one another about mutual interests – and generally the social units are much smaller, often comprising just two or three close friends. Girls can certainly be aggressive, but rarely physically. Rather than hitting someone, girls are much more likely to make an unkind remark or try to exclude that person from the social group.

How do we explain these differences between girls and boys? Are they the result of innate, biological factors ('nature') or socially learned behaviour ('nurture')? Let's look at these alternative accounts.

Meet Baby X. Just six months old, with gorgeous big brown eyes, auburn curls, and an irresistibly cute smile, Baby X is dressed in a fetching pink romper suit, decorated with bunnies and kittens and complemented by matching booties and bonnet: the very picture of chic and contented infancy. Now, based simply on the scant information we've given here, write down five adjectives you'd use to describe Baby X.

What if Baby X were dressed all in blue? Would it affect the words you choose? Psychological research suggests that it probably would. In the most famous experiment of this type, carried out in the mid-1970s, John and Sandra Condry showed adults a video of a baby staring and then bursting into tears as a jack-in-the-box sprang open. Half the participants were informed that the baby was a boy, while the other half were led to believe it was a girl. Those who thought the child was male described its reaction to the jack-in-the-box as 'anger'; the others labelled the emotion 'fear'.

The fact that we modify our behaviour towards children depending on whether we presume they are male or female is often cited in support of the idea that gender is (at least partly) learned rather than innate. If the sexes differ in various ways, the explanation may lie not simply in our genetic and biological make-up, but in the particular roles that society has developed for females and males.

For example, many researchers have drawn attention to the differing ways in which parents tend to treat their sons and daughters. A newborn baby girl is likely to be seen as 'soft'; a boy, on the other hand, is 'strong'. Parents talk more to their baby daughters, and favour physical play for sons. And they may well decorate their child's room in gender-specific ways (blue paint and pictures of vehicles for boys, perhaps; pink, pastels, fairies and cuddly animals for girls). In some cases, parents may be responding to their child's preferences (we've already seen that children as young as one make distinctly gendered choices when it comes to toys). But it's safe to say that whatever preconceptions a parent has about what defines a boy or girl will be communicated, subtly or with the clarity of a megaphone, to their offspring.

But we don't learn only from our parents. In fact the idea that children acquire their understanding of gender principally by imitating their same-sex parent has been superseded by the perception that children learn by observing the behaviour of males and females in general. That education seems to begin remarkably early in a child's life: by the age of two or three a child will tell you what boys and girls like (they might say, for instance, that girls love to play with dolls, or that boys enjoy building with Lego). As they get older, their knowledge of gender characteristics becomes increasingly nuanced: they realize, for example, that some girls have short hair and wear trousers, and that not every boy likes playing with trains.

Of course, a society's idea of what's 'normal' for males and females can easily take the form of simple stereotypes, with un- appealing consequences for individuals who run up against them. For instance, women who are seen as assertive or forceful (tradi- tional male qualities) can pay a heavy price in the workplace. One study found that women showing these characteristics were much less likely to get hired for a managerial position than men who behaved in a similar way – even though the job description specifically called for the ability to be sensitive and empathetic (qualities generally associated with women). Men, on the other hand, still frequently believe that it's inappropriate for them to show 'weakness', with the result that they often endure a protracted struggle with their problems rather than asking for help.

Bruce Reimer was born in 1965 in Winnipeg, Canada. Following a disastrous circumcision that irreparably damaged his penis, his parents agreed to have the twenty-two-month-old baby surgically castrated. Female hormones were administered, a rudimentary vagina was created, and Bruce was renamed Brenda.

As she grew up, Brenda adopted the characteristic behaviour of many girls – for example, taking a keen interest in her appearance. But all was not well: teased by her classmates, Brenda had few friends and believed that it was boys, and not girls, who 'had a better life'. Distressed and confused by her gender identity, she rejected further vaginal surgery at the age of fourteen (by which time she had developed breasts), changed her name to David, and began to live as a boy. Sex-change surgery a couple of years later was a disaster – the 'penis' David was given was a very poor likeness of the real thing, and he twice sought to commit suicide. However, life improved significantly following a second, much more successful, operation when David was twenty-one, and he met and married a single mother with three children. Yet the torment of his adolescence seemed to have left permanent psychological scars: after many years of depression, and following the breakdown of his relationship, he killed himself in 2004 at the age of thirty-eight.

No case could be a more powerful reminder of the crucial influence on sexual identity of our basic biological make-up. David Reimer was genetically male – at birth and throughout his life. Changing his sexual organs and raising him as a girl was not sufficient to make him *feel* as if he were female.

Reimer's desperately sad story forced a rethink among those scientists who had insisted on the malleability – or 'plasticity' – of gender. (Many experts in the second half of the twentieth century had argued that children were essentially blank slates upon which parents and the wider society 'inscribed' a gender.) Clearly our sexual identity isn't only the product of our upbringing: it has extremely deep roots in our biology. For example, when girls are exposed to unusually high levels of male hormones in the womb – as occurs in the case of children with the genetic disorder congenital adrenal hyperplasia – they subsequently prefer to play with 'boys'' toys such as trains, cars and trucks. They're less likely to favour the company of other girls (as we saw earlier, girls and boys generally prefer to play with children of their own sex). And they're also prone to dissatisfaction in general with their identity as a girl.

Or take the extraordinary case of the Batista boys. Natives of a small village in the Dominican Republic, these four brothers were actually born as girls (they possessed female genitalia) and were raised as such. But at the age of twelve an enormous and very belated surge of testosterone caused their vaginas to disappear and be replaced by testicles and normal-sized penises. The Batista children went on to lead normal lives as men – marrying, and comfortably adjusting to their new sexual status. The transition from female to male was made easier for them by the fact that more than thirty other children in the village had experienced exactly the same metamorphosis, the result of a mutant gene active only when passed on by both parents (all the affected families are descended from a common ancestor).

All this does not mean, however, that our gender is entirely determined by our biology. Instead, how we act as men or women is – in most situations – most likely to be the result of a combination of innate, biologically determined, predisposition and learned behaviour.

The babies were just a day old, temporary residents of the Rosie Maternity Hospital in Cambridge. They were pretty young to participate in a psychological experiment, but participate they certainly did. The hundred babies were shown the smiling, friendly face of a young female psychologist, Jennifer Connellan; they were also introduced to a rather bizarre-looking mobile – roughly spherical and about the size of a human head, but clearly mechanical. (The researchers nicknamed it the Alien.) When hours of video footage of the babies were analysed, a remarkable finding emerged. Girl babies spent most of their time gazing at Connellan's face, whereas male babies preferred looking at the Alien.

This experiment was led by the distinguished Cambridge University psychologist Simon Baron-Cohen, a pioneer of research into the causes and treatment of autism (and, incidentally, the cousin of the comedian Sacha Baron Cohen). The babies' reactions seem to fit with Baron-Cohen's influential recent theory regarding the differences between men and women. Males, Baron-Cohen argues, are predominantly 'systemizers' – exhibiting what he describes as 'the drive to understand a system and to build one'. Now, these systems aren't simply restricted to machines, but encompass everything from mathematics and music to sports, business and politics. What the average male isn't so good at, however, is empathy: 'effortlessly putting yourself into another's shoes, sensitively negotiating an interaction with another person so as not to hurt or offend them in any way, caring about another's feelings'. Empathy is a female strength, though women tend to fall behind men when it comes to systems. Thus the female babies in Baron-Cohen's experiment responded to the person, while the males were primarily interested in the inanimate mechanical object. (Baron-Cohen sees autism – a disorder that overwhelmingly affects boys – as an extreme example of an systemizing/empathizing imbalance.)

What lies behind this essential difference between the sexes? Baron-Cohen believes it is caused principally by innate biological factors, and specifically by the male hormone testosterone. The more testosterone a child is exposed to in the womb, the more likely they are to favour systemizing rather than empathizing. Boys, of course, typically generate much higher levels of testosterone than girls. These male hormones, Baron-Cohen argues, affect the relative growth of the left- and right-hand hemispheres of the brain. Androgens cause the right hemisphere (associated with spatial ability, upon which systemizing draws so heavily) to develop more than the left (which is thought to specialize in language and communication: that's to say skills essential for empathy). Moreover, this male right-hand bias isn't confined to the size of the brain's hemispheres: Baron-Cohen cites intriguing research suggesting (albeit tentatively) that a man's right foot and right testis tend to be larger than their left-side counterparts, and conversely that a woman's left foot, ovary and breast are generally bigger than those on the right side of the body.

Baron-Cohen is at pains to point out that these are general observations: many women are excellent systemizers, just as many men are gifted empathizers. And his arguments seem to tally both with much scientific research and with many people's everyday experiences. But his theory has been controversial nonetheless. Some experts have disputed the extent of the demarcation between the sexes, pointing out, for example, that there's very little difference in male and female mathematical or verbal ability. Other critics have read Baron-Cohen's ideas as a rationalization of existing gender imbalances (the relatively small number of women working in science, for example, or the fact that so few men opt to stay at home and look after their children). This is a charge that Baron-Cohen passionately denies:

> Don't assume that the better parent in a child custody case is the mother, since it could be that the father is a wonderful empathizer who can tune into his child's needs, while the mother cannot ... And don't assume that a young woman won't survive the university maths course she has applied for. She may be a talented systemizer ... Individuals are just that: individuals.

*

Having looked at the similarities and differences between men and women, let's now turn the spotlight on what happens when the two sexes try to communicate with one another. Did you know, for example, that it's possible to predict the longevity of a relationship simply by observing the first few minutes of a discussion between the partners?

The psychologists Sybil Carrère and John Gottman recruited 124 newly married couples and observed each of them having a fifteen-minute talk about an issue causing tension in the marriage. They then followed the fortunes of the couples over a six-year period. At the end of those six years, 17 of the 124 couples had divorced. But what was so striking was the fact that the researchers could tell whether a marriage was going to succeed or fail simply by analysing the first *three* minutes of the discussion. The more positive the interaction – for example, in the tone of voice the couples used towards each other, the things they said, and the expression on their faces – the more likely it was that the couple would still be together six years later. It was the couples who communicated most negatively who subsequently ended up in the divorce courts.

If anyone needed a reminder of the importance of good-quality communication to a relationship, Carrère and Gottman's research surely provides it. If communication should break down, it's almost inevitable that the couple will eventually split up. When a relationship founders, the responsibility normally lies with both partners. But men do seem to be worse at communication than women. (This is a generalization, of course: we're referring to broad trends here, not individuals. Moreover, research into communication is notoriously tricky.)

Most of us think of 'communication' as the things that people say to one another. Verbal communication is critically important (as we'll see in a moment), but just as crucial is the *non-verbal* sort. Without speaking a word, we're constantly sending out messages about how we feel – for example, by our facial expression, the clothes we choose to wear, or the movements we make. And we're remarkably sensitive to many of these signals: one study found that it took participants just three-quarters of a second to accurately identify facial expressions of happiness, sadness, anger, disgust and surprise.

You can tell a lot about a relationship by observing the partners' non-verbal communication. When things are going well, for instance, the partners are likely to stand a lot closer to each other than when they're unhappy (if we're not intimate with someone, we normally feel uncomfortable if they come closer than about half a metre away). Lovers look at each other more often, make more eye contact, and touch one another far more (as do women and men when they're flirting). The tone, volume and rhythm of the voice (so-called 'paralanguage') are also revealing: for example, lovers often use 'baby talk' to communicate with one another, they spend more time being silent, and the female partner frequently adopts a much more submissive manner than she does with other people.

Do men and women differ in their use of non-verbal communication? It appears that they do. For example, women smile more than men, regardless of how they're actually feeling. In conversations, men tend to behave in a relatively dominant fashion, looking at the other person more when they themselves are speaking than when they're listening (when people talk as equals it's the other way around). This kind of behaviour sends out an unmistakable message about which of the interlocutors merits attention. Men also use the bodily poses associated with power more routinely than do women: they sprawl and stretch out, commanding the space around them. And men are much more likely to touch women than vice versa – again, a gesture often asserting dominance.

Here's a poser for you: name the subject that couples like to talk about least. Money? Sex? Housework? The in-laws? In fact, and with a pleasing irony, the number-one taboo topic for couples is the state of their own relationship. Researchers found that more than two-thirds of the men and women they questioned confessed to steering clear of the subject with their partner (which doesn't necessarily mean they aren't interested, just that it's often unproductive to raise the issue). Other topics it might be wise to avoid mentioning include past relationships – and (surprise, surprise) any others that you might be having at the moment …

Taboo topics aside, the kind of subjects that people discuss with one another can be a telling index of the nature of their relationship. Generally, the more intimate our connection with another person, the greater the range of conversational topics and the more we reveal our own opinions and experiences. In fact it's almost impossible to build any kind of close relationship without being open. It's a reciprocal process: you divulge personal information, and the other person responds in the same fashion; gradually, intimacy is built. And research suggests that the more partners share their thoughts and feelings with one another, the more content they are.

Other types of verbal communication also mark out the successful relationship. For example, lovers often adopt a private language, full of in-jokes, idioms and personalized slang, that may be utterly intelligible (and somewhat nauseating) to anyone else who happens to hear it.

Men and women are pretty similar when it comes to verbal communication (though, as we've seen, they often deploy the non-verbal variety quite differently). However, men tend to be more assertive and dogmatic when they talk: women sprinkle their conversation with questions and qualifications. Women, on the other hand, are typically much more comfortable discussing their feelings than are men. To use the jargon, women 'self-disclose' more readily than their male partners. As a result, their friendships can be a lot stronger than those that exist between men, who generally stick to impersonal topics. (Would we be the first people to wonder whether men would sit together in stony silence were it not for the existence of sports and cars?) Picking up on these tendencies, some experts have argued that women are much more likely to view language as a means to express themselves, whereas men regard speech primarily as a tool to get things done.

Men's reluctance to discuss personal issues doesn't merely characterize their friendships: it's quite often carried on into their romantic relationships. That said, men are much more comfortable discussing personal issues with their female partner than with their male friends, with whom they're more likely to *do* things (go to the pub, watch football, and so on). In fact, because they're so unwilling to open up to anyone other than their partner, men may have no one else to turn to when times get tough – unlike women, who typically have a very well-developed network of female friends to rely on.

Given the importance of communication to a successful relationship, what can we do to improve it? Actually, there are some pretty simple steps you can take to ensure your communication is as good as it can possibly be:

Don't mind-read. It's difficult to communicate properly if you assume you know what your partner's thinking. So don't jump to conclusions, and don't take things personally: the way your partner's behaving probably has nothing at all to do with you.

Remember that communication is not simply about the things you say. It's also the hugs and kisses, the smiles and caresses, and the willingness to make eye contact – in other words, the full range of non-verbal signals that we're constantly sending out to our partner.

Show your partner that you understand and empathize. We all know the middle-aged man's chat-up line, 'My wife doesn't understand me.' This phrase has become a bit of a joke, but it does contain an important truth, because it's critical that you make every effort to understand your partner's views and feelings. Even more important, you need to *show* your partner you understand, by your facial expression, the nod of your head, the words you use, and the actions you take. Simply recapping what your partner has told you will help enormously ('I understand that you're exhausted after your day at work and that you don't want to cook every night').

Set aside a regular time to talk together. Let your partner know how you're feeling, discuss how you think the relationship is going, whether your needs and expectations have changed, and work together to solve problems.

Be clear and specific if something is troubling you. Resist the temptation to make sweeping, general complaints ('You never lift a finger around the house'). Instead, focus on the particular ('We need to work out a rota for the washing-up and the hoovering').

Let your partner talk. No matter how badly you need to get things off your chest, don't simply rant on. Be as calm and measured as you can, and keep things short and sweet and to the point. Leave gaps for your partner to speak.

Be positive. No one likes being criticized, so don't focus on the negative aspects of your partner's behaviour. Instead, present any requests in terms of positive actions you'd like them to take. For example, instead of 'You're always undermining me,' try 'I'd like you to back me up even if you don't always agree.' Remember that the best way of changing someone's behaviour isn't to criticize what you don't like: it's to praise and encourage what you do like.

Use 'I' and 'we', not 'you'. Don't point the finger at your partner ('You're always ... ', 'You never ... '); be up front about your own wishes ('I'd like ... ', 'I think we need to ... '). It's a way of signalling that you're willing to take your share of the responsibility for solving the problem, rather than simply allocating blame. Using 'we' will work wonders too: a subtle but eloquent sign that you want to work together to sort things out.

Negotiate. Winning an argument with your partner may feel like a victory, but in reality it's anything but. All you're doing is breeding frustration, anger and resentment – and thereby priming the pumps for further conflict. So make agreement and compromise the end point of any arguments.

Listen. This might be the most important communication skill of all. Give your partner the space and time to tell you what's on their mind. Don't interrupt, don't mind-read, and don't let your attention wander. Try not to dismiss what they say; be open-minded and flexible. Make listening your priority.

11. FRIENDSHIP, ATTRACTION AND LOVE

For all my education, accomplishments, and so-called wisdom ...
I can't fathom my own heart.
  – **Woody Allen**, *Hannah and Her Sisters* (1986)

What's the secret to happiness? As we saw in Chapter 9, this is one of the hottest topics in psychology today. There's at least one key factor on which all the experts agree: the stronger our relationships, the happier we are likely to be. Human beings are social creatures: to feel truly content with life, we typically need at least a few close friends, a supportive family, or a loving romantic partner. Anyone fortunate enough to enjoy all three has really got it made.

But, though our friendships and romantic relationships are crucial to our well-being – influencing our physical health as well as our happiness – they often seem bafflingly mysterious experiences. How do we make friends? Why are we attracted to certain people and not others? What is love? How do we know whether someone is right for us? What can we do to make our relationships as successful as possible? These are questions often enveloped in a quasi-mystical haze, but the answers are actually rather more straightforward than you might expect. So let's begin our exploration of the supposedly unfathomable depths of the human heart with a look at the rules of attraction.

Everyone, it's probably safe to say, remembers their first day at secondary school. For one of the authors of this book, at least, the memory is remarkably vivid, even though many more years than he would wish to count have elapsed since then. Trooping nervously into an eerily silent and unfamiliar class-room containing three columns of antiquated, graffiti-covered wooden desks, each of them built to accommodate two students, we learned that the seating arrangements for the year followed a simple formula. At the very front of the nearest column would sit the students whose surnames were closest to the beginning of the alphabet; the sequence would continue until it reached its conclusion at the end of the furthest column, to which outer darkness were consigned those whose names started with the letters W and Y (there were no Xs or Zs in our class).

Two years later, and though by then we were free to sit with whoever we chose, the author's best friend remained the boy with whom he had found himself sharing a desk on that first momentous day. He got on well with the students who had occu-pied the desks immediately in front and behind his own during their first year at school, but even after all those months he scarcely knew some of those who had sat on the other side of the classroom – almost as if the few metres separating the desks had concealed an invisible wall.

Trivial though this anecdote is in itself, it does exemplify one of the most fundamental – albeit prosaic – truths about attrac-tion, whether romantic or otherwise: that the single most important factor determining whom we get to know, like and even love is simply *proximity*. This was demonstrated in a famous study conducted in the 1950s, which found that students living in graduate accommodation at the Massachusetts Institute of Technology were much more likely to name as close friends people living on the same floor as themselves – even though the students had had no say in which accommodation they were allocated in the seventeen buildings. The correlation between proximity and friendship was so pronounced that students were almost twice as likely to be very friendly with their next-door neighbour than with the person living just one room further down the corridor.

Spending a lot of time with someone isn't necessarily going to make you like them – in fact, if they're really not your type, the frequent contact might drive you crazy. But, if there's a chance that you might get on, proximity provides the most fertile soil for a relationship. (Think of your own experiences: the chances are that your best friends, and your partner if you have one, are people you've spent a lot of time with – at school, university or work, for example.)

Why does proximity exert such a potent influence on our feelings? Well, if you see someone regularly, they soon become pretty familiar. Most of us prefer the familiar to the unfamiliar, perhaps because it helps us feel that we have the measure of our environment. Several experiments have demonstrated that familiarity alone – for example, recognizing someone's face even when we know nothing else about them – predisposes us in people's favour. Seeing a lot of someone, of course, also affords us ample opportunity to get beyond superficialities, to discover what we like about them, and to build a relationship. And if we know we're likely to be in regular contact, we're more likely to make an effort to get along.

'Love looks not with the eyes, but with the mind,' wrote Shakespeare in *A Midsummer Night's Dream*, 'And therefore is wing'd Cupid painted blind.' Unfortunately for those of us who happen to possess neither the face nor the physique of a supermodel, Shakespeare's assertion is over-optimistic. When it comes to attraction, physical appearance matters very much indeed, for women and men alike.

Although notions of beauty vary somewhat from culture to culture and over time, there's still a remarkable degree of agreement across the world as to what makes a person physically appealing. Men, for example, tend to prefer women who are younger than themselves, who wear their hair long, and who are neither very overweight nor (contrary to the impression one might derive from many women's magazines) especially thin. When it comes to a woman's figure, men go for curves, and specifically a waist-to-hips ratio of 0.7 – that's to say, where the circumference of the waist is 70 per cent of that of the hips. Women, on the other hand, generally like their men to have a waist-to-hips ratio of around 0.9. Women and men both agree that the male partner should be taller than the female. And, despite the billions of pounds that women spend each year on perfumes, scent is less important to a man than it is to his (prospective) partner.

When it comes to faces, men and women both seek out symmetry, proportionality and 'normal' features (we prefer the average face to the unusual one). One extraordinary study asked eighty-two women to smell eighty T-shirts, each of which had been worn in bed by a different man for two nights. The shirts rated by the women as smelling the most pleasant and sexually alluring turned out to be those that had been worn by the men with the most symmetrical faces. However, not every woman responded in this fashion: only those who were at the most fertile stage of their menstrual cycle were able to pick up the scent of symmetry. Similarly, women about to ovulate tend to prefer more rugged and stereotypically masculine faces than they do at other times of the month. Men, on the other hand, react most enthusiastically to women's faces that are relatively delicate and child-like.

Physical appearance is generally a more powerful factor in sexual attraction for men than for women, but there are a couple of very important caveats to this observation. First, for short-term relationships women are just as likely to be seduced by good looks as are men. Second, men and women agree that what they value above all in a long-term partner is someone who is intelligent, kind, empathetic, dependable, healthy and loving. Thus women are less impervious to physical beauty, and men more capable of seeing past it, than common wisdom might indicate.

Nevertheless, as we saw in Chapter 6, differences between the sexes do exist. After surveying more than 10,000 people around the world, the evolutionary psychologist David Buss discovered that, while men placed a very high premium on appearance, women wanted long-term partners who were materially successful, hard-working and ambitious. (Hence when the Beatles sang that money can't buy you love they were mistaken – as in fact Paul McCartney, who wrote the song, apparently later acknowledged.)

Male and female attitudes towards physical appearance have been explained by evolutionary scientists in terms of the sexes' respective approaches to reproduction. Facial symmetry, for example, is a pretty reliable guide to genetic health and, as such, an indicator that the person in question would make a prudent choice of mate. Women's liking for rugged, masculine faces during times of maximum fertility, and for a male waist-to-hips ratio of a slender 0.9, can be understood in the same way. Men's preference for younger women of average weight, for long hair, and for the 'hourglass' waist-to-hips ratio of 0.7 has a similar rationale, since these too are indicators of good health and fertility. But the perpetuation of one's genes requires more than a physically suitable mate: for offspring to enjoy the best chance of survival, the parents must be able to provide a safe and supportive environment. Historically, this requirement has been especially acute for women, for whom the consequences of a sexual encounter can be very much more dramatic and far-reaching than for a man – hence the priority women place on partners who can provide reliable, long-term emotional and material support. (For more on this topic, see pages 101–4.)

But good looks aren't simply an advantage when it comes to

romance. Attractive people also tend to be more popular in general, with more friends (as well as more sexual partners) than plainer folk. No doubt part of the explanation for this is simply that the rest of us enjoy being around pretty people because they're nice to look at. But we also tend to assume that if someone is attractive they're likely to be intelligent, funny, socially adept, successful and kind. Indeed, study after study has shown that, whether we're male or female, our perception of a person's capabilities and personality is heavily influenced by how physically appealing they seem to us (regardless of how long we've known them). And thus, as well as getting more dates and winning more friends than the rest of the population, attractive people also do better at work. One study even put a figure on the value of being easy on the eye, finding that handsome MBA graduates earned $2,200 more than their unattractive peers in first jobs. For some reason, pretty women didn't benefit during the hiring process, but their reward followed in due course: compared to physically unprepossessing women, attractive female graduates eventually enjoyed a $4,200 salary advantage.

How much do you have in common with your friends? And how similar would you say you are to your partner?

There are exceptions, of course, but most people gravitate towards those who are like them – in intelligence, social class, personality, beliefs, racial background, looks and even weight. (We also tend to like people who are of similar age, though when it comes to long-term partners both sexes prefer the man to be a little older than the woman.) Indeed, after proximity and physical appearance, *similarity* is one of the most powerful drivers of attraction, for friends and lovers alike. There's a degree of realism at work here: most of us would love to date a stunningly attractive person, for example, but we know that it just isn't going to happen. So, instead of risking rejection, we set our sights on someone we're confident might actually welcome our advances. As any glance at the gossip magazines will tell you, very average-looking people – usually older men – do sometimes win the hearts of young and exceptionally beautiful individuals, but generally only when they have something of similar value to offer in return for that beauty, namely money and status. (Interestingly, this matching of levels of physical attractiveness extends not only to our lovers, but to our friends as well.)

However, our preference for people who seem similar to us isn't simply pragmatic: it's also a profoundly positive instinct. How exhilarating does it feel when you first realize how much you have in common with someone? And how much easier – and enjoyable – does the time you spend with them become? The stock of shared experiences that similarity entails hands us ready-made building blocks to construct a relationship. This isn't essential, but it definitely helps. Moreover, as we saw when we looked at the power of proximity to generate close relationships, we're drawn to the familiar. Difference can be exciting, for sure, but most of us, most of the time, prefer the security of what we know. And what could be more familiar than someone who shares our upbringing, or political attitudes, or even our level of attractiveness?

But similarity doesn't simply boost our estimation of the other person: it's also a self-affirmation. It shows us that we aren't alone; we aren't odd. There are people out there just like us – people who are fun to hang out with and, even better, who seem to enjoy our company.

Happy relationships are usually built on what two people have in common, rather than what divides them, though they may also benefit from different but complementary characteristics (for example, one member of a couple might be happy to take on responsibility for practical issues around the house, while the other prefers to organize their social commitments). That said, even if the members of a couple are quite different when they first meet, by the time they've been together for a number of years they become increasingly alike. Moreover, the longer your relationship (whether romantic or as friends), the larger the pool of shared experiences you build up.

Some experts have argued, however, that couples are often rather more dissimilar than they might imagine. But this doesn't matter, because it's not the reality of the situation that counts: it's what each member of the relationship *believes* to be true. A little compromise and sensitivity never hurts: deep down you may not share your partner's passion for foreign travel, burn with the same fierce political idealism, or care quite so much about the state of the house, but if you're happy to accommodate their enthusiasms then your relationship is likely to be all the better for it.

A close friend invites you to a dinner party. 'You must come,' they insist: 'X is going to be there and has told me how much they like you.' This doesn't involve romantic interest, and you hardly know X, but how do you think you'd get on with them when you meet?

Now consider your reaction should your friend accompany their invitation with the words 'Don't let it put you off, but X is going to be there. I know they're not all that keen on you, but I'm sure they'll be on their best behaviour. You'll have a great time!' This is the first you've heard of X's antipathy towards you. Would it affect the way you behave towards them at the party?

A very similar scenario was presented to participants in a classic psychological experiment carried out in the mid-1980s. When individuals were led to believe (falsely) that the people they were chatting to liked them a lot, they responded accordingly, displaying much more warmth, openness and all-round friendliness than if they were told (equally falsely) that their companions didn't care for them. What's at work here is the fourth law of attraction, after proximity, physical attractiveness and similarity: *reciprocity*. Simply put, we like those who like us. And, because we tend to get back what we give, acting positively towards someone encourages more of the same in return. Behave as though someone likes you and the chances are they soon will. Enter a conversation expecting hostility and you may well encounter it.

Reciprocity is so powerful because it goes right to the heart of our sense of self. When we spend time with someone who likes or loves us, their emotions can feel like a validation of our personality and abilities, providing a delightful shot in the arm for our self-esteem. (Perhaps because people who already enjoy high self-esteem aren't so much in need of this kind of boost, reciprocity is often a less significant factor in their friendships.) Equally, if we find it difficult to form close relationships, only the most self-confident person will be able to withstand the thought that they are somehow lacking.

It's lovely to be liked, but even sweeter if your friend is someone who used to dislike you. We tend to like these people more than those who were always warm towards us. At the other end of the spectrum, we reserve our fiercest animosity not for those who we've never got along with, but for the former friends who have rejected us.

'Professions pass for nothing, and actions may be counterfeited; but a man cannot help his looks ... First impressions are often the truest, as we find (not infrequently) to our cost ... A man's look is the work of years, it is stamped on his countenance by the events of his whole life, nay, more, by the hand of nature ... ' Thus wrote the English philosopher and literary critic William Hazlitt in his essay 'On the Knowledge of Character', published in 1822. Whether or not Hazlitt was correct in his estimation of the accuracy of first impressions – and there's no evidence to suggest that his faith in the revelations of physiognomy was justified – it's clear that our initial judgement of someone often plays a major role in determining what sort of relationship, if any, we subsequently have with them.

To see the power of first impressions in action, we can turn to a revealing experiment carried out by the American psychologists Michael Sunnafrank and Artemio Ramirez, Jr. They separated a class of 248 university students into same-sex pairs, none of whom had ever spoken to each other before. Each pair spent a few minutes (either three, six or ten) chatting, and then the students were asked to assess how much they liked their partner, how much they had in common, how well they thought they'd get on in the future, and how beneficial they anticipated the relationship would be for them. Nine weeks later, Sunnafrank and Ramirez interviewed the students again. They discovered that the nature of a pair's relationship could be accurately predicted simply by looking back to their initial impressions of one another – whether the students had spent ten minutes chatting or only three – and specifically to their rating of the advantages the friendship was likely to provide.

Why do first impressions exert such a powerful influence upon us? On some occasions, an initial encounter may genuinely provide us with the information we need to make a realistic judgement of a person's character and the costs and benefits of engaging with them. But, as we saw in Chapter 4, human beings are often poor decision-makers. Rather than taking the time to think things through logically, we rely on rapid short cuts, guesses and generalizations. Imagine, for example, that you are considering candidates for a job in your team. How would you feel about someone described by a referee as 'envious, stubborn, critical, impulsive, industrious and intelligent'? Tempted to hire them? How about candidate number two: according to their referee, if you go for this person you'll be getting someone who's 'intelligent, industrious, impulsive, critical, stubborn and envious'? Most people opt for the latter person, even though the characteristics mentioned by the referee are identical, albeit presented in reverse order. We seize upon the first information we're given, and base our judgement on that alone. (This is what's known as a *primacy effect*.)

It's especially difficult to reason logically when love – or at least sex – is involved. Sometimes the people least adept at understanding a relationship are the very individuals who should be in the best position to do so: the couple themselves. Emotion blurs reality; we just don't see things as clearly as we probably should. How often have you wondered what on earth a couple can see in each other, or anticipated their break-up months before it actually happens? When researchers asked three different groups to predict the longevity of undergraduate relationships, they found that the most accurate judges were the students' room-mates. The parents of the young people involved – sometimes living hundreds of kilometres away – proved the second most successful analysts. Trailing in last of all were the students themselves: they were prone to poignantly optimistic forecasts of romantic bliss. Knowing that even their parents had seen the split coming can't have made it easier to bear.

We all know friendship when we see it, but defining its essence can be tricky. In an attempt to do so, the British psychologists Michael Argyle and Monika Henderson surveyed people in the UK, Italy, Hong Kong and Japan. The result was the following 'rules of friendship':

- Volunteer help in time of need.
- Respect the other's privacy.
- Trust and confide in each other.
- Keep confidences.
- Stand up for the other person in their absence.
- Don't criticize each other in public.
- Show emotional support.

- Look the friend in the eye during conversation.
- Strive to make the friend happy while in each other's company.
- Don't be jealous or critical of each other's relationships.
- Be tolerant of each other's friends.
- Share news of success with the other.
- Ask for personal advice.
- Don't nag.
- Engage in joking or teasing with the friend.
- Seek to repay debts and favours and compliments.
- Disclose personal feelings or problems to the friend.

A strong friendship and a successful romantic relationship share many characteristics – for example, trust, respect, honesty, empathy, supportiveness, intimacy and enjoyment of one another's company – but our feelings towards a friend are generally less intense than towards a lover. (If they aren't, trouble may well be brewing.) We'll probably spend a lot less time with our friends than with our partners, and won't feel anxious or jealous about their life without us. And friendship doesn't normally involve sexual attraction – again, if it does, things are likely to get pretty complicated. (Most friendships are same-sex, and most people are heterosexual, so these kinds of difficulties don't often arise.)

You can't build a close friendship (or indeed a romantic relationship) unless you're prepared to open up and share your innermost thoughts and feelings. But there's a protocol that must be followed. Pouring out your life history the first time you meet someone is unlikely to elicit the response you want. Rather than reveal their own deep secrets, the other person will probably back off instead.

What's required is a measured, reciprocal process, with each person matching the level of intimacy and candour exhibited by the other. According to *social penetration theory*, as the relationship progresses, the participants become increasingly open with one another. Once two people have become really close, and the bedrock for the relationship has been laid down, the emphasis shifts away from personal disclosure and towards mutual support. Which isn't to say that the individuals stop confiding in one another – unless, of course, the relationship is under stress, when the exchange of confidences is likely to dry up. On the other hand, a failing friendship can sometimes bring with it even more openness, but this time of a peculiarly toxic type, as the individuals reveal what they *really* think of each other. Whether the level of disclosure increases or tails off, a struggling relationship is one undergoing what's known as *depenetration*, as the two individuals gradually extricate their lives from one another.

As we saw in Chapter 10, women tend to be more comfortable with disclosure than men; as a result, their friendships are often more intimate and therefore stronger. Men talk to one another, of course, but the subject of their conversation is much more likely to be events and activities rather than thoughts and feelings. It's a rather sweeping generalization, but there is some truth in the idea that men's friendships are primarily conducted 'side by side', whereas women's are largely 'face to face'. Part of the reason for this reluctance to open up is doubtless the belief that 'real men' don't show their feelings. Similarly, men in the UK and the US are much less likely to make any physical contact with their same-sex friends than are women, though – as with male attitudes to self-disclosure – things are different elsewhere in the world.

To illustrate this difference between the sexes, researchers presented a group of men and women with an account of a visibly distressed aircraft passenger. When the person in the adjacent seat asks sympathetically whether the problem is a fear of flying, the passenger either pretends that it is or, in a second version of the story, reveals that the trouble is concern about the health of their absent mother. Asked for their reactions to this scenario, women and men agreed: if the passenger were a woman, the right thing to do would be to open up and share their anxieties with their neighbour; a man, on the other hand, ought to keep his problems to himself.

Making a perhaps unexpected recent return to British television schedules has been the quintessential 1970s game show, *Mr and Mrs*. Originally presented by Derek Batey, the show tests couples' knowledge of one another. In keeping with contemporary preferences, the modern version – *All Star Mr and Mrs* – features celebrities and their partners rather than 'ordinary' people. But the questions haven't changed a great deal: 'Who is the most jealous: you or your partner?', 'Who is the most stylish?', 'What is your partner most scared of?', 'What's your partner's favourite flavour of crisp?', 'What's your partner's favourite car?' (Actually, the questions may have been updated a little. Here's one from the heyday of the show: 'When you're having a meal at home and there's no one else around, just you and your wife, do you always have serviettes, sometimes have serviettes, or never have serviettes?')

The appeal of *Mr and Mrs* lies in its jocularly affectionate exploration of that most mundane of subjects: the long-term romantic relationship. And what it celebrates is a particular type of attachment, known to psychologists as *companionate love*. Despite countless centuries of philosophical, literary and artistic speculation, very little scientific research has been undertaken into the nature of love. But the consensus among experts today is that there are probably two main forms of romantic love. *Passionate* love denotes the euphoria of a relationship's early stages, when our desire – physical as well as emotional – for the loved one is so fervent that it resembles intoxication. Interestingly, passionate love seems to be associated with changes in the brain, notably an upsurge in secretion of the neurochemical dopamine. This is no surprise: dopamine plays a critical role in our experience of pleasure.

Passionate love, however, does not last. Without wanting to sound too unromantic, this is probably just as well: sustaining a relationship at such fever pitch would be exhausting and impractical (it's hard to get much else done in your life when you're first in love). Instead, what develops is companionate love: a relationship that is deeply rooted and – if all is going well – deeply sustaining. The highs are fewer, but this is a love on which we can truly build our lives.

Perhaps you've wondered what it is about someone that made you fall in love with them. As we've seen, attraction is usually the result of four intertwining factors: proximity, physical appearance, similarity and reciprocity. But love may also have its roots in a simple misunderstanding. When we feel intense attraction to someone, a series of chemical changes is triggered in our nervous system. These changes generate a state of arousal – which is a psychological term for heightened awareness, rather than sexual excitement. Arousal can be caused by all manner of experiences and emotions: fear, elation, sleeplessness, drug or alcohol use, as well as attraction. Our heart may beat faster, our mind race, and our stomach fill with butterflies. But is it possible for us to misinterpret the cause of our arousal? Might we assume our feelings have been sparked by the presence of an attractive person when really their origin lies elsewhere?

According to some experts, this kind of error is entirely possible. Among the evidence is a terrific experiment devised by Donald Dutton and Arthur Aron in Vancouver in 1974. Eighty-five unaccompanied men aged eighteen to thirty-five were approached as they began to cross one of two different bridges: a small, low one spanning a stream or the frankly terrifying Capilano Canyon Suspension Bridge, which swayed each time there was a gust of wind, offered only a low wire handrail by way of protection, and was seventy metres high and just a metre and a half wide. The men were handed a picture of a young woman and asked to write a short story about it while standing in the middle of their respective bridge. A male and female research assistant were on hand to help, and the participants could also telephone the assistants after the experiment should they be interested in learning more about the study.

Dutton and Aron discovered that men who crossed the suspension bridge and were approached by the female research assistant were much more likely to include sexual imagery in their stories and subsequently to phone the assistant. Men on the small bridge didn't respond in this fashion, even when the same female researcher came to talk to them, and nor did those who were joined by a male research assistant while on the Capilano Canyon bridge. The men on the suspension bridge were misreading their fear-induced arousal as sexual attraction. Which suggests that anyone having trouble getting dates might want to start hanging out in scary places ...

What are the ingredients of a successful romantic relationship? Well, it turns out to be a fairly complex mix, including some or all of the following:

- shared decision-making
- trust
- intimacy – physical, emotional and psychological
- sexual attraction
- time and energy working at the relationship
- agreement about who does which household chores
- emotional support for each other
- positive actions, whether it be giving your partner a hug, bringing them a cup of tea in bed, or being ready to listen when they need to talk
- clear communication (for more on this, see pp. 183–5)
- tolerance, flexibility and patience
- negotiation skills

To get a sense of your satisfaction with your own relationship, try the following questionnaire. Again, for each statement, the number below the response that you agree with is your score for that statement.

1. Please indicate the degree of happiness, all things considered, of your relationship.

Extremely unhappy	Fairly unhappy	A little unhappy	Happy	Very happy	Extremely happy	Perfect
0 ☐	1 ☐	2 ☐	3 ☐	4 ☐	5 ☐	6 ☐

2. In general, how often do you think that things between you and your partner are going well?

All of the time	Most of the time	More often than not	Occasionally	Rarely	Never
5 ☐	4 ☐	3 ☐	2 ☐	1 ☐	0 ☐

3. Our relationship is strong.

Not at all true	A little true	Somewhat true	Mostly true	Almost completely true	Completely true
0 ☐	1 ☐	2 ☐	3 ☐	4 ☐	5 ☐

4. My relationship with my partner makes me happy.

Not at all true	A little true	Somewhat true	Mostly true	Almost completely true	Completely true
0 ☐	1 ☐	2 ☐	3 ☐	4 ☐	5 ☐

5.   I have a warm and comfortable relationship with my partner.

Not at all true	A little true	Somewhat true	Mostly true	Almost completely true	Completely true
0 ☐	1 ☐	2 ☐	3 ☐	4 ☐	5 ☐

6.   I really feel like *part of a team* with my partner.

Not at all true	A little true	Somewhat true	Mostly true	Almost completely true	Completely true
0 ☐	1 ☐	2 ☐	3 ☐	4 ☐	5 ☐

7.   How rewarding is your relationship with your partner?

Not at all	A little	Somewhat	Mostly	Almost completely	Completely
0 ☐	1 ☐	2 ☐	3 ☐	4 ☐	5 ☐

8.   How well does your partner meet your needs?

Not at all	A little	Somewhat	Mostly	Almost completely	Completely
0 ☐	1 ☐	2 ☐	3 ☐	4 ☐	5 ☐

9.   To what extent has your relationship met your original expectations?

Not at all	A little	Somewhat	Mostly	Almost completely	Completely
0 ☐	1 ☐	2 ☐	3 ☐	4 ☐	5 ☐

10. In general, how satisfied are you with your relationship?

Not at all	A little	Somewhat	Mostly	Almost completely	Completely
0 ☐	1 ☐	2 ☐	3 ☐	4 ☐	5 ☐

For each of the following items, select the answer that best describes *how you feel about your relationship*. Base your responses on your first impressions and immediate feelings about the item.

11.	Interesting	5	4	3	2	1	0	Boring
12.	Bad	0	1	2	3	4	5	Good
13.	Full	5	4	3	2	1	0	Empty
14.	Sturdy	5	4	3	2	1	0	Fragile
15.	Discouraging	0	1	2	3	4	5	Hopeful
16.	Enjoyable	5	4	3	2	1	0	Miserable

Now add up your total score for the sixteen questions. If it's more than 51, your relationship looks to be in good shape. A score of between 47 and 51 indicates mild dissatisfaction, and a total of 46 or less suggests that your relationship is causing you distress. If you fall into the last category, you may want to investigate possible strategies to get things back on track.

12. BABIES, CHILDREN AND PARENTING

'I still remember Harry's first smile,' our friend remarked wistfully, his eyes moistening as if he were gazing into the cot right now rather than listening to the continuous dull thump of a CD player from above as Harry – now a broad-shouldered youth of thirteen – busied himself with his homework (or at least that's what he seemed to have muttered over his shoulder he was going to do as he disappeared upstairs).

'He was three weeks old. A gorgeous boy. No trouble at all.' At this point there came an enormous crash from Harry's bedroom, something like the noise a huge and very full wardrobe would make if you were to push it down a very steep flight of stone steps. Our friend winced, sighed, and retreated back into the past.

'I can see it as clearly as if it were this morning. We'd just woken him up so the health visitor could check him over. I was standing over him, watching his eyes gradually open and scan the room. After a few seconds, he noticed me. I gazed at him and smiled. His eyes darted from my face to the health visitor and then back to me again. And then, just as I was about to lift him out of the cot, he smiled. It was the most beautiful thing I'd ever seen.

'"He's a bit young for a smile," the health visitor said. "Probably wind." She was a *sour* woman.'

Young babies do suffer from wind, of course, but they aren't simply the sum of their bodily functions (really, they aren't). In fact they begin their emotional and psychological development pretty much from the moment they enter the world. And they start communicating their feelings through their facial expressions just as soon. Babies convey emotions such as interest, distress, disgust and happiness right from birth. Between the ages of two and seven months they add to their repertoire fear, surprise, delight, sadness and anger. And by the time they reach the grand old age of two they can show much more sophisticated emotions such as shame, guilt, envy, pride and embarrassment, which seem to rely on the ability to appreciate both their own identity ('I did it!') and the fact that there are accepted standards for behaviour – no mean feat for a toddler.

It may seem that babies have limited means at their disposal to communicate their desires. They can't talk, after all. Nevertheless, they have at their disposal a variety of techniques to let you know how they're feeling and what they want. For example, babies often instinctively engage in a sucking motion when they're unhappy, and it seems to ease their distress. If you spot this behaviour, you know that your help is required. The same goes, of course, for crying – a sound so terrible that parents will do whatever's needed (often just a cuddle) to make it stop.

One enormously successful technique used by babies to communicate with their carers is smiling. Nothing is more likely to secure adoring attention from an adult: who can resist a smiling baby? Babies smile instinctively from birth, but they don't begin to smile *at* things – usually people – until they're about six weeks old (so perhaps that health visitor was right). From their earliest days babies also love looking at their carers – and they want their carers to look back. If for some reason the carer doesn't return their gaze, the baby is likely to get quite upset. And babies instinctively adapt their bodies to that of their carer when they're cuddled – thus encouraging the adult to do more of it.

However, infants aren't simply discovering how to express their own desires: they're also learning to read the emotions of the people around them. By about seven to ten months they begin to use adults' reactions as a guide to how they should respond to a given situation (this is called *social referencing*). A one-year-old, for example, will play with a new toy if the person standing nearby is smiling, but avoid it if that same person looks frightened. So parents have a lot of power to shape their child's emotional make-up: run screaming from the room when you see a spider, for instance, and your little one may well learn to do the same.

Over the next few pages, we'll explore children's emotional and psychological development. We'll look at the role of parents and the influence of siblings, and we'll reveal exactly how much harm a working mother may be doing to her little ones.

Increasing numbers of British urbanites are now discovering the pleasures of keeping chickens and other fowl. (As far as we know, no one has produced a reliable figure for the number of people raising these birds, though in 2006 a report for the Department for Environment, Food and Rural Affairs speculated that it might run to hundreds of thousands.) Deliciously fresh eggs, the pleasing chatter of the birds as you potter around the garden, and the satisfaction of knowing that in some small way you are evading the clutches of the food industry – the attractions are clear. But a word of caution for those tempted by this image of quasi-rural bliss: chickens imprint.

And what, you may ask, is *imprinting*? Well, imagine that you are a chick who has just emerged from the egg and is taking its first steps in the world. What on earth, you wonder, are you supposed to do now? How will you survive in the vast and bewildering space in which you find yourself? Suddenly you become aware of a large figure towering over you and clucking contentedly. You are smitten: this mysterious being will henceforth be the focus of your every waking moment. You will see many other such creatures in your life, and most of them will closely resemble this one, but you saw her first and so it is she who has won your heart. You will look to her for safety, food and comfort; she will be your role model; you will never let her out of your sight – you will, in short, imprint upon her.

Chickens (and some other birds) imprint on the first creature they see moving once they themselves are mobile, whatever or whoever it is. Normally, of course, that creature is another chicken – generally the chick's mother. And thus, from an evolutionary viewpoint, imprinting makes sense: it forges an unbreakable bond between the chick and the animal that will care for it until it is old enough to fend for itself. But, as the Nobel Prize-winning scientist Konrad Lorenz (1903–89) famously demonstrated (in his case with geese), if the chick happens to catch sight of, say, a middle-aged scientist rather than its mother, it is the scientist who will be the unlikely recipient of the chick's unwavering devotion.

Human beings do not imprint – which is probably just as well. But the bonds we form with those who care for us are just as critical. Indeed, according to many experts, nothing is as important for our well-being as the relationships we experience with those who care for us during the first years of life. The child psychiatrist John Bowlby, who had been much influenced by Lorenz's research into imprinting, called this bond *attachment*:

> No variables have more far-reaching effects on personality development than a child's experiences within the family. Starting during his first months in his relation to both parents, he builds up internal working models of how attachment figures are likely to behave towards him ... and on all those models are based all his expectations ... for the rest of his life.

Bowlby prioritized the relationship between mother and child, arguing that 'Mother-love in infancy is as important for mental health as are vitamins and proteins for physical health.' Perhaps he was merely giving voice to the precepts of the Edwardian age in which he grew up, one of six children of an eminent surgeon and his wife. And not just its precepts: Bowlby's mother was a remote figure by contemporary standards, though her lack of involvement in the day-to-day care of her children was normal for women of her class at that time. From the age of seven, Bowlby saw even less of her, since he was sent away to boarding school.

Bowlby trained for a career in the navy, but soon abandoned the sea in favour of psychiatry and psychoanalysis, eventually becoming head of the Department for Children and Parents at London's Tavistock Clinic soon after the Second World War. Although his theory of attachment has drawn much criticism, and has been revised and refined by many other child-development specialists, it remains a hugely influential account. So let's look in a little more detail at what attachment entails.

Young babies tend not to be very concerned about which person is providing the care and attention they require; hence they're very happy to be passed from one adoring relative to another, even if they've never laid eyes on them before.

That all changes, however, between the ages of seven and nine months. Gradually, the baby develops an attachment – defined by the psychologist Jerome Kagan as 'an intense emotional relationship that is specific to two people, that endures over time, and in which prolonged separation from the partner is accompanied by stress and sorrow' – to one person in particular. Generally this is the mother, since she's usually the prime carer, though it could be anyone who happens to be occupying that role. The baby cries when the mother leaves (this is known as *separation anxiety*), and clings to her when unfamiliar people are nearby (so-called *stranger anxiety*). Bowlby argued that this desire for attachment is innate: like imprinting chickens, we're genetically hard-wired to form such bonds, because they represent our best chance of survival. Over the following months, the infant may develop attachments to many other figures in its life, though the bond with a primary caregiver – be it the mother, the father or someone else entirely – tends to remain the most important.

It's clear now that our first attachments are far from the only influence on our emotional and psychological development: our personality, the experiences we accrue during our lives, and our later relationships with friends, siblings and lovers all play an important role. Nevertheless, there does seem to be a clear association – though no one has managed to prove a clearly causal relationship – between the nature of the attachments we form as very young children and our later well-being.

Bowlby's very first research study, carried out in the late 1930s, highlighted the links between the psychological problems of forty-four patients at the London Child Guidance Clinic and the absence (temporary or permanent, for example through bereavement) of their mothers, an experience he termed *maternal deprivation*. It was a seam he was to continue to mine throughout his career, including a landmark study for the World Health Organization in 1951 in which he analysed the effects on children of growing up away from their parents – a common consequence of the Second World War.

Today, Bowlby's emphasis on the child's relationship to its mother seems too exclusive. Infants can form deep attachments to fathers, grandparents, childminders and nursery workers. Indeed, children develop attachments to anyone who provides them with attentive, loving care. And the trauma that Bowlby attributed to maternal deprivation might well have been the product of other stressful aspects of the children's lives (being separated from siblings, for example, living in an unfamiliar city, or being subjected to neglect or abuse). Be that as it may, the consequences when children aren't able to form healthy attachments – and studies indicate that as many as a third of children may be in this boat – can be profound. These children often find it harder to make friends, and are withdrawn, cautious and shy. They're reluctant to try their hand at new tasks, presumably fearing failure, and are at greater risk of experiencing anxiety and depression. As they get older, they're also more likely to develop behavioural problems and to skip school. As adults, they are are less self-confident, possess lower self-esteem, and suffer more relationship problems.

If, on the other hand, our attachments are healthy – or 'secure' – we have both a dependable source of love and support as we make our way in the world (a 'safe base') and a positive model for all future close relationships. So children who are securely attached at the age of one tend a few years later to be more outgoing, more popular, better at problem-solving, and more socially skilled than children who've not been so lucky in their relationships. Generally speaking, they're also happier, have more close friends, and go on to enjoy more successful adult romantic relationships.

This seems logical. Unless later events dictate otherwise, securely attached children are likely to grow up with a deeply rooted optimism about themselves, the people around them, and the relationships they forge. Our earliest caregivers seem to send us a message that is difficult to forget. For the securely attached child this message is something like this: *You are loved. You will always be able to rely on this love as you make your way in the world. And other people will come to love you too.*

What can we do to ensure that the attachment our children form to us is a secure one? There's no mystery: give them as much love and support as you can; be sensitive to their needs; and try to make their home stable and harmonious.

*

Attachment may well be a crucial concept for understanding children's emotional and psychological development, but how on earth do we go about measuring such an elusive quality?

In fact it's possible to get a pretty reliable sense of a child's attachment style merely by observing them for around thirty minutes (and remember that we very often take our childhood attachment pattern with us into adulthood). This is done by using the 'Strange Situation' technique devised in the 1960s by Mary Ainsworth (1913–99). Ainsworth was born in Ohio, but moved to Canada as a small child, training as a psychologist at the University of Toronto. Soon after the Second World War she accompanied her husband to London and landed a job at Bowlby's Tavistock Institute. Although Ainsworth worked closely with Bowlby for a number of years, she developed the Strange Situation test some years after having left the Tavistock. Some experts have disputed the validity of the test, and others have criticized it for causing children distress, but it remains widely used today.

So what is this Strange Situation, and what can it tell us about a child's attachment style? The first thing to mention is that this is a test optimally given to a child at about the age of one: much earlier and the baby may not yet have developed a particular attachment to a parent or caregiver; much later and the child is likely to have acquired a range of relatively sophisticated techniques to deploy when meeting strangers – which, as we'll see in a moment, is a key feature of the test.

The Strange Situation begins with the researcher welcoming the baby – let's call her Olivia, since that seems to be a current favourite in the English-speaking world – and her mother to the room where the experiment is going to take place. The researcher leaves, and baby Olivia is free to explore the exciting toys distributed throughout the room. A few minutes later a stranger enters. The stranger is silent initially, but after a minute or so begins chatting to the mother; then the stranger greets Olivia. The mother departs; three minutes later she returns, and the stranger exits. The mother leaves Olivia on her own for a couple of minutes before the stranger reappears. Then the mother returns, the stranger departs, and the experiment is over.

What's crucial here is the reaction of the baby to the mother's absence and return. *Securely attached* children are happy to explore the room while their mother is present, but are moderately distressed when she leaves and delighted when she returns. Insecurely attached children fall into three categories.

Those who are *anxious/resistant* stick closely to their mother, no matter how alluring the toys scattered around the room, and are distraught when she leaves. Although the anxious/resistant child will run to her mother when she returns, she'll then push her away, or even hit her. This kind of behaviour often reflects a child's attempts to deal with inconsistent and unpredictable parenting, in which the kind of reception they can expect depends entirely on the parent's mood at that moment.

The *anxious/avoidant* child tends to ignore their mother when she's around and not be too concerned when she leaves. When the mother reappears, she'll get the same aloof treatment as before. This kind of attachment is typically produced either by parents who frequently ignore their children or by those who fuss over them excessively.

Finally, the *disorganized* child – often the victim of severe neglect or abuse – seems utterly bewildered by the whole experience, and swings between wanting the mother and shunning her. This may be because, for all the desire for contact and love, they have learned that these can be dangerous.

How common are these various types of attachment? Around 65 per cent of one-year-olds are securely attached, 20 per cent anxious/avoidant, 10 per cent anxious/resistant, and 5 per cent disorganized. Insecure attachment is more likely in children whose parents are struggling with their relationship, their finances, or drug or alcohol problems.

*

On Christmas Day 1989, in the small Romanian city of Târgoviçte, Nicolae Ceauşescu and his wife, Elena, were sentenced to death after a cursory trial and immediately executed by firing squad. Over the weeks and months that followed, the grim consequences of Ceauşescu's twenty-four-year rule of Romania became clear to Western observers.

Arguably none of these consequences was grimmer than the fate of Romania's 150,000 orphans, consigned to dilapidated orphanages and supervised by staff who had been instructed to avoid prolonged interaction with the children. The eminent British child psychologist Michael Rutter has provided a disturbing picture of these children's lives: 'The children were confined to cots without toys or playthings, carers scarcely talked to them and feeding time was usually a bottle full of gruel … Washing often consisted of being hosed down with cold water, and sometimes drugs were used to keep the children calm. There was physical or sexual abuse … '

None of these children – most of whom had arrived at the orphanages as tiny babies – had had the opportunity to form close attachments with any adult, let alone a parent. How did this deprivation affect them? Were the consequences as devastating, and permanent, as Bowlby predicted?

Some of the Romanian orphans were adopted by families in the UK, allowing Michael Rutter and his team to compare their progress to age six with that of a number of British adoptees (none of whom had suffered deprivation or abuse). When the Romanian children arrived in the UK, they were often ill and frequently very malnourished, and more than half were far behind where they should have been in their cognitive and psychological development.

Just a few years later, however, the advances they had made were truly remarkable. They were a little shorter than their British counterparts, but their weight was normal, and their average IQ had shot up by around forty points. The children who'd come to the UK before the age of six months registered IQ scores on a par with the British adoptees; those who arrived after the age of two, however, were on average two dozen points below their British peers. Clearly, the longer the children had spent in the orphanages, the greater the impact on their IQ.

Again, in the case of the orphans' social development, most problems were seen in those who'd come to the UK relatively late. For example, they were less keen on imaginative play, and the older ones were more likely both to touch strangers and to be inappropriately friendly. Interestingly, around 6 per cent of the Romanian adoptees (and none of the British children) showed autistic-like characteristics – for example, finding it difficult to interact with people, to read social situations, or to carry on a conversation. Unlike children with autism, however, these problems improved dramatically over time, suggesting that they were a consequence of life in the orphanage.

The experience of the Romanian orphans indicates that depriving young children of love and attention can have profoundly negative effects, which is surely no surprise. But it also shows that Bowlby was too pessimistic: given the right kind of support later in childhood, there is a way back from the precipice. However, although some of the Romanian adoptees who'd spent longest in the orphanage were free of any behavioural, emotional or psychological problems by the age of six, children generally fare better the sooner proper support can be given. Children are remarkably resilient, but the longer the abuse and neglect continue, the more difficult it becomes to undo the psychological damage.

Here's a story about a little boy named Maxi.

Using his pocket money, and after very careful deliberation at the sweet shop, Maxi has bought himself a delicious bar of chocolate. However, Maxi is anxious that his little sister may discover the chocolate and devour it before he can taste so much as a mouthful (she has form in these matters). So he hides it in the blue cupboard in the kitchen and heads off to his room to fetch his favourite toy, a large green tractor, which he intends to play with while keeping guard over his chocolate. While Maxi is upstairs, however, his mother finds the chocolate and moves it from the blue cupboard (which is where the pasta, rice and noodles live) into the green cupboard (home of biscuits, cake and other delights). Now, when Maxi returns from his bedroom, which cupboard will he look in for his chocolate?

This shouldn't be too much of a challenge for you. Maxi will look in the blue cupboard, because that's where he left his chocolate. But this is a scenario that will totally fox the average three- or four-year-old. They know that the chocolate has been moved to the green cupboard, and they conclude therefore that Maxi must know it too. Until they reach the age of four or five, most children lack the ability to think themselves into a situation like Maxi's, to imagine the world as he might see it. They lack, in short, a *theory of mind*.

The term 'theory of mind' was coined in a famous article published in 1978 by the psychologists David Premack and Guy Woodruff: 'Does the chimpanzee have a theory of mind?' (In case you're wondering, Premack and Woodruff concluded that it does.) What it encapsulates is the capacity to understand not simply that we ourselves have thoughts and desires and feelings, but that other people have them too. Without this ability it's incredibly difficult to form relationships: empathy is tricky, and the people we encounter can seem mystifyingly obscure and capricious. Indeed, it's been suggested that what lies behind the difficulties in communication and social interaction experienced by many people with autism is precisely a deficiency in theory of mind – what Simon Baron-Cohen, director of the Autism Research Centre at the University of Cambridge, has described as 'mind-blindness'.

The formation of a theory of a mind is clearly a huge

milestone in a child's psychological development, but of course that's not to say that younger children have no insight into other people's thoughts and feelings. After all, even a young baby can read basic emotions on a person's face and understands what to do in order to elicit a particular response (I laugh and you pull a funny face, for example, or I cry and you stop trying to feed me that revolting puree of mixed vegetables).

It's still not clear exactly which gears must click into place in our young brains in order to facilitate a theory of mind. Perhaps it's dependent on reaching a certain level of linguistic proficiency. Several studies have shown that children who excel at language tasks tend to be equally successful in tests of theory of mind; other researchers have argued that the more a child talks about their feelings and thoughts with their siblings and peers the better their performance at theory-of-mind tasks. Whatever the explanation, the breakthrough children make at about age four is only one of the steps: we continue to refine our understanding of how other people think, feel and behave throughout our lives.

How do people parent, and what works best for their children?

There seem to be four main styles of parenting:

Authoritarian parents lay down the law and expect their children to stick to it. Any query is likely to be met with a firm 'Because I said so!' To keep their kids in line, this kind of parent tends to use punishment rather than, say, negotiation.

Authoritative parents set rules, and expect them to be followed. But they will explain their thinking and may involve the children in deciding how best to achieve an objective – so, for example, an authoritative parent concerned about the amount of television their kids are watching may ask them to help draw up an acceptable timetable for viewing. This kind of parenting is more pragmatic and collaborative, and a great deal warmer and more sensitive than the authoritarian style.

Permissive parents take a pretty laissez-faire attitude towards their offspring. Generally they're content to allow their children to express themselves as they wish, and don't attempt to direct how they spend their time. This isn't neglect – permissive parents do care about their children – but rules and discipline do not feature prominently on the agenda.

Uninvolved parents are so distant that it can seem as if they're trying to pretend their children don't exist. It's what permissive parenting looks like without the love – remote, uncaring and even hostile.

Which style of parenting is most likely to help children do well – and which will, to use Philip Larkin's famous phrase, 'fuck you up'? In a classic study carried out by the developmental psychologist Diana Baumrind in the 1960s (and whose conclusion have been supported by much subsequent research), it was the children of authoritative parents who had the best chance of thriving – emotionally, academically and in their relationships with adults and peers.

Children whose parents used an authoritarian style, on the other hand, often appeared difficult, sulky and unhappy. Their academic record, and social skills, were OK, but generally average rather than outstanding.

Permissive parenting tended to be associated with children who were self-centred, impulsive, bossy and (particularly in the case of boys) aggressive. These children displayed poor social skills – which, given the characteristics we've just itemized, is hardly surprising. Their academic achievement was below average too.

But it's the children of uninvolved parents who really struggled. Even at a relatively early age, they were often wild and unruly, prone to temper tantrums and other hostile behaviour. Predictably, these children tended to fare very poorly at school, and as they reached adolescence they were much more likely than other kids to drift into alcohol and drug abuse, truancy, crime and sexual misadventures.

But it's worth remembering that parents are not solely responsible for the person their little one turns out to be. (If you have children, this is probably a sentence that you would do well to memorize.) Indeed, some experts have argued that children's relationships with their peers have much more of an impact than do their parents. And children themselves can exert a significant influence on the kind of approach their parents adopt.

Because of their personality – which is substantially determined by genetic factors – some children are simply much easier to raise than others. Many parents will swear that their child's personality was evident even when they were a newborn baby, and certainly not only are some infants much more active in the womb than others, but this characteristic persists throughout later life. So a naturally impulsive, lively and moody child, for example, may push her exasperated parents into implementing a more authoritarian style than they'd ideally choose. And it may be that, for this particular child, this is what it takes to improve the child's behaviour. Probably more likely, however, is that this reaction will only generate more of the behaviour that it's intended to prevent.

In the UK, 55 per cent of mothers with children under five now work outside the home. In the US the story is very similar, with almost two-thirds of mothers with children under the age of six engaged in some form of paid employment. As we all know, we're a very long way indeed from the days when fathers worked (that is, worked for money) and mothers 'kept house'.

By now this demographic shift, though admittedly dramatic, is hardly novel. But the relevant statistics can still trigger an impassioned debate in the media. This debate usually boils down to one central question: are working mothers somehow damaging their children by their absence from the family home? Many of us seem to believe that they are. For example, in one recent survey, conducted by experts at the University of Cambridge, more than half of those questioned believed that family life suffers when a mother goes out to work – and women were almost as likely to take this view as men. This opinion is even more widespread in the United States. Society is broken; children are running wild; and the mothers who should be tending hearth and home are out at work. (Bowlby himself argued that working mothers were inflicting 'maternal deprivation' upon their children.)

But are working mothers really such a pernicious influence on their children's well-being? The evidence suggests not. To take just one representative example, one study of more than a thousand children in the US found that neither the amount of time spent each week in non-parental childcare nor the age at which childcare began had any impact on the bond between mother and child, nor on the child's overall level of happiness. Provided the childcare is of high quality, children will thrive just as much as they would if they spent the day with a parent. In any case, it's not the care children receive while their parents are out at work that has the biggest influence on their well-being – it's the care they receive when back home.

What about the effect on children of divorce? This continues to be a very live issue indeed, given that in 2007 there were approximately 140,000 divorces in the UK. In the US, around half of marriages fail, resulting in about a million divorces each year.

Divorce is, of course, traumatic for children and parents alike, and especially during the first year after the break-up. Children of divorced parents are more likely to suffer from anxiety and depression. Moreover, because their mum and dad are probably equally distressed, they may well not be able to call on the kind of parenting that would help them deal with their problems. (Boys seem to find it especially difficult to cope, though it's not clear why this should be the case.) And the effects can persist well into adulthood – children whose parents have divorced, for instance, are more likely to have their own marriages break down, perhaps because they lack a ready model of how a successful long-term relationship should function.

However, children are often much more resilient than their parents imagine. Most do manage sooner or later to come to terms with the end of their parents' marriage. And many – perhaps as high as 75 per cent – don't experience any major emotional or psychological problems. Finally, although divorce is potentially profoundly disruptive for children, research indicates that the consequences of warring parents staying together can often be worse.

Many children seem to have a somewhat fractious relationship with their siblings – though of course we do not write from personal experience: we have always got along just fine. Sibling rivalry is normal, fuelled by a perception on the part of the older child that they now have competition for their parents' love and attention. (Clearly, this isn't simply a matter of perception, at least when it comes to the amount of time a parent can devote to each sibling: the day does not elongate in line with the number of children one has, though it may sometimes feel like it.) If you're currently struggling with sibling rivalry – as a parent, that is – the best advice is to ensure that your older kids receive as much affection and one-on-one time as you can manage. And try to involve them in caring for their younger sibling: this will give them a pleasurable sense of their own importance, and give you the opportunity to spend time together rather than having to choose between children.

Nevertheless, for all the squabbles, bickering and point-scoring that siblingdom can involve – and, chillingly, one expert has noted that young children can have as many as fifty-six minor spats in a single hour – on the whole it seems to exert a positive influence on a child's development, providing them with a playmate, confidant and ally against the world. Siblings tend to fight less as they get older. And younger children benefit from having an older sibling to teach and look out for them, and to provide a role model; older siblings learn how to care for another person, simultaneously boosting both their maturity and their self-esteem. (When researchers analysed how people in more than 150 societies raised their children, they discovered that in more than half those societies an older sibling was the main carer for pre-school kids.)

Siblings are more likely to get on well if their parents also have a strong relationship, if the parents intervene to sort out arguments rather than succumbing to the admittedly powerful temptation to leave their children to it, and if they show no favouritism – which doesn't mean, alas, that your child will never complain that you're always taking their brother or sister's side ...

Siblings, then, frequently play a hugely positive role in a child's life. But this doesn't mean that only children are at any great disadvantage. In fact all the evidence suggests that on average only children fare at least as well as children with siblings in measures of self-esteem, self-discipline, and social skills and peer relationships, and even marginally better in tests of intelligence. Lacking a sibling, only children are perhaps able to draw from friendships the kind of companionship and support that other children derive from their brothers and sisters.

13. GROUPS

Imagine that you are woken in the small hours by a woman's scream. It seems to be coming from the street outside, and as you haul yourself out of bed and over to the window you see that a man is dragging a woman into an alleyway. What would you do?

The answer seems obvious: you'd try to help the woman. If you were feeling especially courageous you might go outside and confront the man; at the very least you'd telephone the police. But no one intervened when Kitty Genovese, returning home from work at 3 a.m. in New York City in 1964, was attacked and murdered. How could this happen? Why was it that not a single soul from the dozens of nearby apartments took it upon themselves even to call 911 – despite the fact that no fewer than thirty-eight of them came to their windows, and even though the assault lasted more than half an hour? This was the question that the psychologists Bibb Latané and John Darley set out to answer.

They quickly discovered that many of the explanations then doing the rounds didn't hold water. It wasn't that the neighbours were jaded, cynical city-dwellers, indifferent to the needs of the anonymous hordes around them. On the contrary, they'd been aghast when they'd seen what was happening to Kitty Genovese. And of course people living in cities do help each other sometimes. In fact the reason no one helped Kitty Genovese was simply that so many other people could have done, thus allowing individuals to feel that they themselves didn't need to. This has become known as the *bystander effect*.

We tend to assume that other people's behaviour is a consequence of their personality: X didn't put the milk back in the fridge because she's lazy; Y remembered my birthday because she's so thoughtful; Z is so rude – he completely ignored me in the street yesterday. Interestingly, when it comes to our own behaviour we're much more likely to acknowledge the role that external circumstances play: I didn't put the milk away because I was late for work; thank goodness my friend reminded me it was Y's birthday or I'd have forgotten it completely; I didn't spot Z because I was too busy worrying about my appraisal.

Besides explaining why the unfortunate Kitty Genovese was left to die, the bystander effect is a perfect illustration of the way in which *everyone's* behaviour is often determined less by personality than by the situation in which we find ourselves. What happened to Kitty Genovese wasn't down to the kind of people she happened to have for neighbours. If any one of them had believed they were the sole witness to the crime it's likely that they would have tried to help (research carried out by Latané and Darley, and others, suggests as much). What sealed her fate was the *social context* in which those neighbours made their judgement calls, that's to say the impact of other people on their own behaviour. Seeing themselves as part of a group, they were able to renounce personal responsibility.

In this chapter we'll look in detail at the influence upon us of other people, and specifically of groups. On the way, we'll find out how many of us would administer a deadly electric shock to someone we've never met before, debate whether two heads are really better than one, and discover whether prejudice is inherent in us all.

*

Take a look at these four lines:

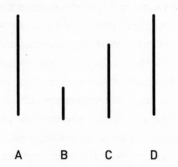

A   B   C   D

Which one is the same length as line A? Is it B, C or D?

No, this isn't a trick question: you're right – the answer is D. Solomon Asch used this task in a classic experiment he carried out in 1951. When participants were shown the lines with no one else in the room, more than 99 per cent gave the correct answer. And this is hardly surprising: as you've seen for yourself, it's a pretty easy exercise. (What's really surprising is that anyone should have offered a wrong answer.)

Asch also tested participants when they were gathered together in groups of seven. However, in each group six of the seven were researchers pretending to be participants. The procedure went like this: each group member was asked to call out which line most resembled line A. The first four people questioned were 'fake' participants; they all gave the same wrong answer. These responses bamboozled many of the real participants, who plainly couldn't believe what they were hearing. And yet, when they were then asked for their own view, *more than a third* offered the same response as the previous speakers. Over a number of trials, 75 per cent of participants gave at least one wrong answer – even though, as they explained afterwards, they knew full well that it was erroneous.

Why would so many people knowingly offer an incorrect response in an utterly trivial task such as this? The answer seems to lie in our powerful desire to *conform* to the views of the majority – even when, as in Asch's experiment, we neither know who they are nor are likely ever to meet them again. (Asch also investigated whether the size of the majority influenced the likelihood of conformity. Up to a point, it did. But once the number of fake participants reached three, there was little difference in the responses of the sole real subjects in the groups.)

Critics have argued that the pressure to conform today is much less pronounced than it was when Asch carried out his experiments in the early-1950s US. Well, perhaps, but it's hardly vanished entirely. But why? What lies behind this drive to conform?

Two main theories have been suggested. The first argues that we sometimes adopt the views of the majority because we recognize this as an effective means of gaining knowledge (so-called 'information influence'). Thus, for example, although we have never visited Estonia, we are happy to take on trust the commonly accepted facts that its capital is Tallinn and its population around 1.3 million, and that it includes fourteen hundred lakes.

But the informational theory can't account for what Solomon Asch discovered – after all, the data supplied by the majority in his experiments was worthless and the participants knew it, though this didn't stop three-quarters of them conforming nonetheless. What seems to have been going on was something called *normative influence*: we conform because we have an innate drive to fit in with the group, almost regardless of what it may be (and even though we may privately disagree with many of its precepts). No one – or perhaps almost no one – wants to be an outsider; instead, we long to be part of a community. And if that means wearing particular clothes or having our hair cut in a certain style, choosing an 'acceptable' career or area of town in which to live, or even proclaiming that a very short line actually looks identical to a much longer one, then we'll do it.

*

In 1963 the psychologist Stanley Milgram recruited forty men aged twenty to fifty from the city of New Haven, Connecticut, to take part in a psychological experiment. No details about the nature of the experiment were revealed to the volunteers, who were simply told that it was an opportunity to 'learn about themselves'. This proved to be something of an understatement.

When each of the participants arrived at Milgram's lab, it was explained that their role as a 'teacher' in the experiment was to punish any mistakes made in a memory test by a 'learner'. (This learner was actually an actor, but the participants believed them to be another volunteer.) The punishment was to take the form of an electric shock. The teacher was introduced to the learner, who explained that they were suffering from a heart condition, but during the session they sat in separate rooms.

With each mistake made by the learner, the teacher was instructed to intensify the strength of the electric shock. Gradually the learner could be heard shrieking with pain and begging for the session to end. Even when the learner was eerily silent – perhaps unconscious or even dead – the teacher was instructed to keep administering the shocks. And *two-thirds* of the participants did just that, right up to a level of 450 volts, even though they believed – erroneously – the shocks to be real and the actor to be just like them: a volunteer from the streets of New Haven. Milgram wrote:

> I observed a mature and initially poised businessman enter the laboratory smiling and confident. Within 20 minutes he was reduced to a twitching, stuttering wreck ... At one point he pushed his fist into his forehead and muttered 'Oh God, let's stop it.' And yet he continued to respond to every word of the experimenter, and obeyed to the very end.

These results shocked Milgram. Not only had he failed to anticipate such wholesale obedience, nor had any of the groups –

ranging from members of the general public to psychiatrists – he'd questioned before the experiment. The psychiatrists, indeed, had predicted that 99.9 per cent of the participants would eventually refuse to continue administering the shocks. We are, it seems, easy prey for groups in authority.

When that authority is questioned, however, we are much more likely to rebel. Milgram found this, for example, when he moved the site of the experiment from the leafy campus of Yale University to a dingy office offsite, when the role of the experimenter was played by a distinctly unprofessorial-looking individual, and when Milgram arranged for other apparent 'participants' to question the experimenter's instructions. In such situations, compliance fell from around 66 per cent to sometimes closer to 20 per cent.

Over the years these experiments have been replicated by scientists in many different countries, and – unlike Milgram's initial research – involving women as well as men. But nothing has changed: the results of these studies have been remarkably similar to those produced by Milgram.

It's worth remembering, incidentally, that Milgram began his research less than twenty years after the Second World War, and in part it represented an attempt to understand how so many individuals could subjugate their morality to participate in the Holocaust. (Milgram had in fact in his early career been a research student of Solomon Asch, pioneer of the study of conformity.) The first languages into which his work was translated were German and Hebrew.

The Hollywood screenwriter Joe Eszterhas, author of such classics as *Basic Instinct*, *Jagged Edge* and *Showgirls*, once wrote that 'the inner dynamics of Hollywood are like politics. Say you give a script to a group of executives – they sit around, afraid to voice an opinion, saying nothing, waiting to know what the consensus is.'

What Eszterhas is describing here is something known in the psychological literature as *groupthink*. You might think that bringing a group of people together is the perfect way to access a wide range of diverse opinions on an issue. Well, of course it *can* work like that. But sometimes the very opposite happens: the group becomes entirely focused on achieving consensus, and will not tolerate any dissent. This is groupthink, and it is generally agreed to have played a part in such notorious disasters as the loss of the space shuttle *Challenger* in 1986 – when NASA managers were so intent on a prompt launch that information that might have prevented the catastrophe was received with intense scepticism – and the Kennedy administration's calamitous 1961 invasion of Cuba at the Bay of Pigs, when enormous pressure to conform was brought to bear on those who had the temerity to question the wisdom of the enterprise. (One of Kennedy's advisers confessed that he hadn't spoken up because 'Others would regard it as presumptuous of him, a college professor, to take issue with august heads of major government institutions.') Groups that are dominated by a particularly forceful leader, that are dealing with very stressful situations, and that are isolated from external influences seem especially vulnerable to groupthink. Those, on the other hand, that actively encourage freethinking are much less likely to fall victim.

It is often taken as axiomatic that decisions made by a group are more reliable than those made by an individual (two heads, as we all know, are better than one). But in fact the reverse seems to be true. And the cause doesn't lie simply in the temptations of groupthink. Numerous laboratory studies involving tests of relatively simple factual knowledge have shown that group judgements are around *20 per cent* more inaccurate than the average score of the group members when questioned individually. Why exactly this should be so isn't clear.

Groups are also prone to another powerful influence. Imagine, for instance, that you are engaged in jury service and have retired to reach a verdict on the case of a man accused of assaulting a stranger in the street. The evidence against the man seems fairly convincing, though you and several other jurors have some minor concerns. However, as the discussion progresses, you find yourselves not only agreeing that the accused is guilty, but far more convinced of the fact than at any time during the trial. Your jury team has just experienced the phenomenon called *group polarization*: the tendency for a team of people to adopt a view that is much more extreme than that held previously by any of the individuals.

Why does this happen? Partly it can be explained by our innate drive to conform to the opinion of the majority. Then there's the fact that the information we use to support our decision is skewed. Instead of a balanced debate between opposing viewpoints, the group spends its time rehearsing the arguments in favour of its initial position, and thereby reinforcing it. The greater the opposition a group senses from outside, the more entrenched and extreme its views are likely to become.

'OK, everyone: let's take ten minutes out and brainstorm this problem a little.'

Just how deeply you are gripped by despair at these words probably depends on the number of brainstorming sessions you have attended to date. But, although brainstorming may not always be fun, at least it gets results. After all, it's got to be much more productive to have a group of people thinking about an issue rather than one person alone. It's a question not merely of numbers (the 'two heads are better than one' theory), but of individuals sparking off each other to generate ideas they'd never produce by themselves. Alex Osborn, the US advertising executive who devised the brainstorming technique in the late 1940s, estimated it would double a group's output of ideas.

But is this true? Is brainstorming really such an effective technique? Unfortunately, much of the research carried out in recent years suggests not. Individuals working alone generally produce more and better-quality ideas than those in a group. And the bigger the brainstorming group, the more likely it is that problems will occur.

One of the reasons for this somewhat counterintuitive finding is probably that it's easy for people to hide in group sessions, letting others do the work (this is a tendency known as *social loafing*, of which more below). When we do have an idea, we may not have the self-confidence to share it, particularly in front of our bosses or people we don't know well. Keeping quiet can seem like the safest strategy.

Perhaps most importantly, however, brainstormers are often victims of something called *production blocking*. Because it's generally seen as inappropriate to speak when someone else is already talking, participants in a brainstorming session aren't as free to share their ideas (or to comment on other people's suggestions) as it might seem. And the delay between the arrival of an idea and the chance to communicate it can be ruinous. By the time the opportunity to speak presents itself, the individual may have forgotten what it was they wanted to contribute, or decided against mentioning it. That's if they have been able to come up with an idea at all: many people need silence and solitude to really think creatively, not a crowded room in which someone is always speaking, often at great volume. The power of production blocking was demonstrated in an experiment carried out by Wolfgang Stroebe and Michael Diehl, who found that individuals who were able to contribute whenever a thought came to them produced twice as many ideas as those who could speak only when everyone else was silent.

No matter how miserable the prospect of another Monday may be, for some of us there is always a glimmer of comfort: the weekend is over, work looms, but at least we no longer have to report for *choir practice*.

When we were at school, the very worst thing about Mondays was the two-hour-long session in the music room, endlessly repeating tiny phrases from Brahms's Requiem, or whichever choral masterpiece we were shortly to bludgeon into bloody submission in front of our aghast relatives and friends. But, however painful it was for us, it must have been many times worse for our music teacher, Mr Chisholm, a man for whom the term 'long-suffering' might well have been coined. Again and again he was driven to the very brink of madness by our inability to sing even the shortest passage of music without someone in our ranks sounding like a rodent being strangled or an asthmatic pipe organ. Eventually Chisholm would point in exasperation to the section of the choir from which this cacophony seemed to be emanating and ask each of us to sing the line in question solo. Usually this was accomplished with remarkable success. But as soon as we sang together the result was always the same: half-hearted, slapdash and teeth-clenchingly unmusical. This was surely the moment at which yet another small fragment of Chisholm's beleaguered being shrivelled into nothingness.

Abject though we were as a choir, we did at least perfectly exemplify the phenomenon known as *social loafing*. As we've seen, and contrary to what one might expect, groups do not always outperform individuals. Social loafing is another illustration of this tendency. Rather than group members working together to achieve an outcome far superior to that which any of them could accomplish individually, what often happens is that they *reduce* their effort, taking advantage of the relative anonymity offered by the group to idle along in neutral.

Of course social loafing isn't inevitable. If the task in hand is accepted as important by the group members, it's much less likely to occur. The same is true if the group itself, rather than the task, is valued by its members. (Most of those in our school choir, however, regarded membership as a punishment rather than a source of pride.) Knowing that you can be held personally to account is also a strong motivating factor – which doubtless explains why our solo performances in rehearsal were so much better than our collective efforts.

It's been suggested, incidentally, that the Beatles were guilty of social loafing. The songs written together by John Lennon and Paul McCartney up until 1967 – so the theory goes – were much better, and much more successful, than those they produced as a duo in the last years of the group. Why? Well, it's suggested that from late 1966 onward the group members became increasingly distanced from one another. Thus, when Lennon and McCartney worked together, perhaps neither was willing to supply the level of commitment and creative energy of previous years. Instead, they saved their best work for their solo compositions.

'An individual in a crowd', wrote the French social psychologist Gustave Le Bon in 1895, 'is a grain of sand amid other grains of sand.' Identity is lost, and the individual 'descends several rungs in the ladder of civilization, he is ... a creature acting by instinct ... [He can be] induced to commit acts contrary to his most obvious interest and best known habits.'

Le Bon's view of crowds as inherently wild, irrational and violent remained the standard theory for many years. And when one thinks for example of rioting football supporters (thankfully now a rare occurrence in British soccer, though far from extinct), or the mobs that often gather outside the courts whenever a high-profile murderer is taken off to prison, it certainly appears plausible. Perfectly sane and stable individuals can seem to lose their very identity in a crowd – a phenomenon termed *deindividuation*. Normal standards of behaviour are waived, and the crowd is at liberty to become a sprawling, brawling monster.

However, Le Bon's ideas seem much more plausible in regard

to crowds we've witnessed rampaging on the TV news than they do when we think back to those of which we've formed part. This very morning, perhaps, you were among a large group of people travelling to work, making your way through the train station or along the high street. Or you might think back to your experiences as one of several thousand people at a music festival. Or to the hundreds of football matches you've attended without incident. Crowds, after all, are generally pretty unthreatening entities, and the people who compose them no more given to mindless acts of aggression than anyone else.

This isn't to say, though, that our sense of who we are never changes when we're in a crowd. Often it does, but that change takes the form of a strong identification with the values and norms of that specific group. If it's a violent gathering, we may find ourselves acting violently too. But if it's good-natured and peaceful we'll behave accordingly. *The* crowd doesn't exist: only particular crowds, each with its own distinct character. As several experiments have demonstrated, ask someone to dress up as a member of the Ku Klux Klan and you'll get the behaviour to match; on the other hand, give them a nurse's uniform and you'll find that they are suddenly polite, friendly and solicitous.

In an analogous fashion, it seems that our sense of identity can change in line with the roles we play in day-to-day life. Probably the most famous illustration of this was a notorious experiment carried out in 1971 by an old South Bronx schoolfriend of Stanley Milgram (he of the electric-shock study), the psychologist Philip Zimbardo.

Zimbardo recruited twenty-four male students for a two-week study of prison life; half were randomly assigned to the role of 'prisoner', while the remainder became 'guards'. Zimbardo accepted only the most psychologically stable of the volunteers – 'an average group of healthy, intelligent, middle-class males'.

To their surprise, the prisoners were arrested at home on a Sunday morning and taken to the prison – really the basement of the Stanford University Psychology Department building – in handcuffs. They were searched, stripped naked and deloused, and given an ID number, which was always used instead of their name. The guards wore khaki uniforms, and mirror sunglasses to hide their eyes, and carried a billy club.

So cruel and abusive were many of the guards that by just the second day of the experiment the prisoners rioted. In the wake of the rebellion, and amid rumours that a mass breakout was being planned by the prisoners, the punishments inflicted by the guards became increasingly demeaning. Prisoners were forced to do multiple push-ups (sometimes with a guard or another prisoner on their back); their bedding was removed; they were denied the right to use the toilet when they chose; and they were ordered to strip naked for the amusement of the guards.

Unsurprisingly, many of the prisoners developed emotional and psychological problems. Visited by a priest, more than half of them gave their prison ID number and not their name. The idea of simply quitting the experiment did not seem to occur to them. Within less than a week, the experiment had spiralled out of control. Zimbardo called a halt after just six days of the planned two weeks:

> We had created an overwhelmingly powerful situation – a situation in which prisoners were withdrawing and behaving in pathological ways, and in which some of the guards were behaving sadistically. Even the 'good' guards felt helpless to intervene, and none of the guards quit while the study was in progress. Indeed, it should be noted that no guard ever came late for his shift, called in sick, left early, or demanded extra pay for overtime work.

*

What makes a good leader? Write down the first five qualities that you'd look for in such a person.

Now, read through this list of names:

- John F. Kennedy
- Mahatma Gandhi
- Queen Elizabeth I
- Bobby Moore
- Emmeline Pankhurst
- Martin Luther King
- Winston Churchill
- Eleanor Roosevelt
- Vladimir Lenin
- Nelson Mandela

How many of these people – all of whom are generally regarded as great leaders – meet the criteria you've just jotted down? And how much would you say they have in common with one another?

According to conventional wisdom, leaders are born and not made. This is known as the 'great man' – nowadays often amended to 'great person' – theory of leadership. But, as you may have discovered when tackling the little exercise above, it's far from easy to identify personality traits that are common to all successful leaders. Hence it's not surprising that most psychologists today consider the 'great man' theory to be largely a red herring. (Its traditional identification of leadership and masculinity is also well past its sell-by date: studies show that women are just as likely as men to make fine leaders.) But, though the differences between effective leaders may vastly outnumber any similarities, there do seem to be a few consistent characteristics. Successful leaders, on the whole, tend to be more self-confident, extrovert, hard-working and intelligent than other people. They're also generally taller and better-looking.

But if personality isn't all there is to effective leadership, what other factors are involved? It's been suggested that what really matters is the degree to which the leader embodies the aims and characteristics of the group. Certainly, most if not all the leaders we've picked out above meet this criteria, being utterly committed to their respective cause – whether it be women's suffrage, national independence or the quest for the World Cup.

Other experts have argued that how successful a leader is depends largely on the kind of circumstances in which they're attempting to lead. In the 1960s Fred Fiedler, one of the most influential industrial psychologists, developed what he termed *contingency theory*. He argued that, broadly speaking, there are two main types of leadership style. The first is *task-oriented*. As the name suggests, leaders taking this approach put the highest priority on identifying and accomplishing the goals of the group, and generally don't spend too much time worrying about the feelings of their subordinates. On the other hand, leaders adopting the second approach – which Fiedler called *relationship-oriented* – focus on the morale of the group. These leaders work to ensure that their team members are happy and fulfilled, and that their own relationship with each individual is as strong as possible.

Incidentally, though Fiedler believed that leaders normally fall into one or other of these categories, recent research has suggested that individuals may move between them according to which approach they think best fits their current situation.

Fiedler stressed that both approaches could be successful, but only in the appropriate context. He argued that the task-oriented style is especially well suited to situations in which the leader has either a lot of control (when, for example, the objective of the group is very clear, relations between the team and the leader are good, and the leader enjoys considerable power) or very little (the relationship between the leader and the team is broken, the task is ill-defined, and the power of the leader is limited). In the first situation the leader has no need to build relationships: everything is already in place for the group to function effectively. In the second situation relationship-building is a luxury, and perhaps even impossible: the leader must focus on figuring out what needs to be done and then directing the team to do it. A relationship-oriented approach, however, is generally best when the leader has a middling level of control: in these situations, getting the team on board can make all the difference.

How well do these categories fit your experience of working with a team?

In the early 1950s twenty twelve-year-old boys turned up for a two-week camp in Robber's Cave State Park, Oklahoma. In itself this was hardly unusual, summer camp constituting a staple part of middle-class American childhood. But there was more to this particular camp than met the eye. The boys were, in fact, unwitting participants in an experiment devised by the pioneering social psychologist Muzafer Sherif (1906–88), who was born in Turkey and went on to teach at Princeton, Yale and the University of Oklahoma.

On their arrival at Robber's Cave, the boys were randomly assigned to one of two groups. The groups were then separated in order to allow the members of each one to bond. This didn't take long; pretty soon each group had given itself a name (the Eagles and the Rattlers), and placed an appropriate symbol and flag above the entrance to its respective dormitory. Strikingly, the boys also asserted that their own group was better than the other, and proposed a competition to prove it. Sherif duly obliged, and the Eagles and Rattlers did battle at events such as baseball and tug of war. These events only intensified the rivalry between the two groups. Each was convinced not merely that the other group was less skilled at particular sporting activities, but that its members were actually less pleasant people.

Sherif was interested in how groups form, and how they relate to each other. What he discovered was just how quick prejudice is to develop between groups – and how it's often based on the flimsiest of foundations. Sherif argued that this prejudice resulted from the fact that the groups were competing for scarce resources – that is, success in the various tournaments and challenges. And this theory may offer part of the explanation for prejudice – think of the rise of fascism across Europe in the years of the Great Depression, for example, or the fact that lynchings of black people in the southern USA between 1882 and 1930 corre-lated inversely with the price of cotton (the higher the price, the fewer the number of murders). But competition seems unlikely to be the sole explanation. After all, prejudice may become less overt during times of relative plenty, but there's no evidence to suggest it disappears completely. And in Sherif's summer-camp experiment it was notable that hostility between the groups began almost as soon as they were formed. Could prejudice result simply from the fact that we belong to different groups?

It would appear so. Henri Tajfel (1919–82) divided up a group of strangers into groups on the basis of nothing more signifi-cant than their preference for the paintings of Klee or Kandinsky. When the group members were then asked to allocate notional 'rewards' to the other participants, all of whom were listed anonymously, they automatically favoured those who were in the same group – even though they hadn't met them and didn't know their names, or even what they looked like. Group member-ship – albeit clearly trivial, indeed virtually meaningless – was enough for the participants to discriminate between individuals.

(Tajfel, incidentally, had more than an academic interest in how people are categorized into groups. A Polish Jew, he was captured by the Nazis while serving in the French army. The military uniform saved his life: wearing it made him a prisoner of war; without it he would have been just another Jew destined for the death camps.)

On the basis of these experiments, one could be forgiven for concluding that prejudice is innate and therefore inevitable. At a fundamental psychological level, we do seem naturally to favour the 'in group' (that is, the group of which we're part) and to disparage the 'out group' (the group against which we define our own identity).

But prejudice can be overcome. Contact between groups is a good start, but what really helps is *collaboration* on a joint project, as Sherif found by having his two groups work together to cope with a broken-down supplies truck, and many subsequent studies have produced similar results. In tackling a task that neither group can accomplish alone, the boundaries between two opposing groups are transcended. Instead of in groups and out groups, one new, inclusive, group comes into being. And the benefits endure even after the goal has been achieved.

14. PSYCHOLOGICAL DISORDERS AND THEIR TREATMENT

It must be admitted that no definition adequately specifies precise boundaries for the concept of 'mental disorder' ... different situations call for different definitions.
– The Diagnostic and Statistical Manual
of Mental Disorders, 4th edition

As you'll have gathered by now, *Use Your Head* is an attempt to explain how the human mind works. In this chapter, however, we turn to what happens when things go wrong.

And go wrong they certainly do, with huge implications both for individuals and for society as a whole. For example, the cost to the UK taxpayer of mental illness was put at £77 billion for England alone in 2009. The US government estimates the annual cost of mental ill health at $193.2 billion, with untreated and mistreated mental illness responsible for $105 billion in lost productivity each year.

So just how common are psychological problems? In a survey of almost 9,000 randomly selected adults conducted for the UK's Office for National Statistics, around one in six people had suffered from anxiety or depression in the previous week. The most common symptoms (in order of frequency) were difficulties sleeping, fatigue, irritability, worry, poor concentration and forgetfulness. Women were more likely than men to experience these problems, and the rates among people over sixty-five were the lowest of any age group (the rates were highest among people aged forty to fifty-four). Around 0.5 per cent of those surveyed had suffered from psychosis – that is, very severe mental illness – during the past year.

Approximately 7.5 per cent met the official criteria for alcohol addiction, while a quarter of those questioned were described as having a hazardous pattern of drinking, defined as 'an established pattern of drinking which brings the risk of physical and psychological harm'. Thirteen per cent of people had used illicit drugs – usually cannabis – in the previous twelve months, with the highest rates among those aged twenty to twenty-four. Around 3.7 per cent were addicted to one or more drugs.

Meanwhile, figures from the US indicate that a majority of Americans (57 per cent) will experience a psychological disorder at some point in their lives. Take a twelve-month snapshot and 32 per cent of the population will be suffering from at least one such problem. Almost a third of people in the US will experience an anxiety disorder during the course of their life, with phobias being the most common type, and 21 per cent will suffer from depression. Over the course of a single year, 19 per cent will suffer from anxiety and almost 10 per cent from depression. Thirty-five per cent of Americans will battle a so-called substance disorder during their lives: around 30 per cent will be addicted to nicotine, 13 per cent will abuse alcohol or become dependent on it, and 8 per cent will abuse or become addicted to other drugs.

In 1486 two German monks, Heinrich Krämer and Jakob Sprenger, published *Malleus Malificarum*, a highly imaginative handbook for the identification and punishment of witches that was to remain in print right through to the eighteenth century. Sadly, most of those unfortunate enough to fall victim to the suggestions contained in *Malleus Malificarum* (Latin for 'Hammer of the Witches') were women who today would probably be diagnosed as suffering from some type of psychological disorder.

Krämer and Sprenger's treatise formed part of an age-old tendency to regard mental illness as the product of supernatural forces. Exorcism, for example, was widely practised in Europe during the Middle Ages in order to rid the individual of the evil spirits supposedly causing their illness. Other similarly motivated 'treatments' including shaving a cross into the hair of the possessed, chaining them near a church to ensure they were within earshot of the word of God, and dangling them over a seething mass of venomous snakes. The Swiss physician Paracelsus (1493-1541), on the other hand, argued that psychological well-being was determined by the configuration of the moon and stars – a theory that led to the coining of the term 'lunatic' and that still survives today in the form of astrology.

The idea that psychological problems were a supernatural phenomenon competed with the belief (which finally succumbed to the weight of scientific consensus only in the nineteenth century) that their cause, like that of all illnesses, actually lay in physical factors, and specifically the imbalance of the body's four essential 'humours' – black bile, yellow bile, phlegm and blood – which we met in Chapter 1.

The study of mental disorders really gathered pace during the eighteenth century, a process that also resulted in the emergence of professional psychiatry and, in the second half of the nineteenth century, of psychology. Hugely influential figures such as Philippe Pinel (1745–1826), a psychiatrist working at Paris's La Bicêtre hospital and then at the world-famous Salpêtrière; William Tuke (1732–1822), an English Quaker tea merchant who established the York Retreat in 1796; and Benjamin Rush (1745–1813), a physician and one of the founding fathers of the United States, argued that psychological disorders were in part the product of stressful life situations (a theory, incidentally, first proposed by Plato). As such, they could be cured by providing patients with an environment that was restful, hygienic, and socially and intellectually stimulating. This so-called 'moral therapy' transformed asylums and mental hospitals. Formerly places simply of confinement – and therefore run very much like prisons, with patients often shackled and brutally punished for transgressions – the aim was now to turn them into truly therapeutic institutions.

These advances did not last. By the latter part of the nineteenth century the wards were once again overflowing, and the care and attention that could be offered to individuals were often minimal at best. Psychiatry's growing conviction that psychological disorders were biological in origin – a belief strengthened by the discovery that the delusions and hallucinations experienced by some patients were actually the result of the organic disease syphilis – did not help. After all, if mental illness was caused by the physical degeneration of the brain, what possible benefit could psychological therapies offer?

Although the disciplines of psychology and psychiatry were well established by the middle of the twentieth century, there was little consensus about the nature of mental illness. How should one define a psychological disorder? What symptoms should one look for? What was normal and what was abnormal? How many psychological disorders existed? What caused them? All these questions remained the subject of vigorous debate.

Emil Kraepelin (1856–1926) – regarded by many as the father of psychiatry – had drawn up the first modern classification of mental illnesses in 1913. Influential though Kraepelin's work undoubtedly was, classificatory systems proliferated. No single system was universally accepted, meaning that clinicians might easily disagree not only on the nature and causes of an individual's illness, but also on whether she or he was ill at all. Under such circumstances, standardization of diagnosis and research was virtually impossible.

The first tentative steps towards such standardization were taken in 1948 when the World Health Organization included information on mental illness in its *International Classification of Diseases and Health Related Problems* (ICD). This was followed in 1952 by the American Psychological Association's *Diagnostic and Statistical Manual of Mental Disorders* (DSM). But neither made much impact. As David Barlow and V. Mark Durand have noted, 'As late as 1959 there were at least nine different systems of varying usefulness for classifying psychological disorders worldwide.'

A second edition of the *DSM* appeared in 1968, but the real leap forward occurred with the third edition, published in 1980. In place of contentious and distracting speculations about the causes of psychological problems (an issue experts rarely agree upon), the emphasis switched to a detailed enumeration of symptoms, designed to make the clinician's task of diagnosis much easier and more consistent. This was an effort that continued in the current edition, published in 1994.

As the *DSM* has evolved, efforts have been made to co-ordinate its approach with that of the *ICD*; consequently, mental-health professionals worldwide are increasingly able to sing from the same hymn sheet. If you see your GP about a psychological problem, or a psychologist or psychiatrist, it's the categories set out in the *DSM* and *ICD* that they'll be using to decide what exactly you're suffering from and how best to treat it. The fifth edition of the *DSM*, by the way, is due for publication in 2013. Planning began in 1999 – these things take time.

The *DSM* has altered considerably over its four editions. The first two, for example, were heavily influenced by psychoanalysis, which dominated US psychotherapy in the middle of the twentieth century. The number of disorders included has grown hugely. The first edition included 60, the second 145, and the third 230. The 2000 revision of the fourth edition includes over 400 diagnostic categories. New disorders continue to be added, while others are dropped. In 1980's third edition, for example, homosexuality was removed and post-traumatic stress disorder was added after extensive lobbying by Vietnam War veterans' organizations, many of whose members could provide first-hand accounts of the illness's authenticity.

As the quotation at the beginning of this chapter makes clear, experts still can't agree on a definition of mental illness. All one can do, it seems, is recognize the elusiveness of that aspiration and do the best one can. *DSM* acknowledges that many disorders are simply extreme examples of ordinary feelings (compare sadness and depression, for example). It's when those feelings become highly distressing, or interfere significantly with one's everyday life, that they cross the line separating normal feelings and clinical illness. Not that this has ended the argument among professionals: many continue to question the validity and reliability of the *DSM*'s diagnoses. Indeed, it may be that the *DSM*'s focus on the diagnosis of individual conditions – as though psychological problems were simply physical ailments – is inherently flawed. Instead of seeing a person's symptoms in the round, we may be squeezing them into reductive and relatively arbitrary diagnostic categories. This is not a debate that seems likely to end any time soon.

The *DSM* groups psychological disorders into ten broad categories. Over the next few pages we'll take a look at these categories and a small sample of the illnesses that they contain.

Neurological disorders. These include problems caused by head injuries and also various forms of dementia, such as those resulting from Alzheimer's and Parkinson's disease. This category is very much the exception among the ten, since the cause of the illnesses is very clearly and exclusively physical (both Alzheimer's and Parkinson's involve significant deterioration of areas of the brain).

Disorders usually first diagnosed in childhood. If that heading strikes you as a bit of a catch-all, you'd be right. This category includes a very wide range of problems, many of them united only by the age at which they typically develop. Among the most significant are:

- **Learning disorders**, in which the child is a very long way off the level of competence in reading, writing and mathematics deemed appropriate for their age group. These problems used to be known as 'academic skills disorders'.
- **Mental retardation**, of which the key feature – to use the clinical terminology – is 'significantly subaverage general intellectual functioning' (usually an IQ of 70 or less) that has a significant impact on the individual's ability to function normally.
- **Attention Deficit Hyperactivity Disorder (ADHD)** affects around 3–5 per cent of children. If a child is excessively poor at concentration, or constantly restless, fidgety and impulsive; if this behaviour has been going on for more than six months; and if it's causing real problems at home and at school, then they may be suffering from ADHD.
- **Conduct disorder** describes persistently antisocial behaviour – for example, fighting, bullying, cruelty to animals or people, destruction of property, lying and theft.
- **Autism** is a disorder in which individuals have real difficulties in communicating with others, find social interaction very difficult, and have extremely fixed and restrictive ideas about how to behave, what is interesting, and how their world should be organized. Asperger's disorder is very similar, though without the problems with language that characterize autism.

Anxiety disorders are among the most common psychological problems. We met some of these in Chapter 8, and they include:

- **Phobias.** Eleven per cent of people suffer from a phobia – an intense feeling of fright and anxiety that's out of all proportion to the reality of the threat – at some point in their life. Fear of animals, heights, blood, enclosed spaces, water and flying are the most common.

- **Panic disorder (PD)** is characterized by regular, sudden and very frightening panic attacks. Charles Darwin, it has been suggested, developed PD at the age of twenty-eight, which helps explain why he never made another research trip after his famous voyage on the *Beagle*. Contemporary doctors diagnosed 'dyspepsia with an aggravated character', 'catarrhal dyspepsia' and 'suppressed gout'.
- **Obsessive–compulsive disorder (OCD)** affects around 3 per cent of people. It's defined by frequent distressing thoughts ('I am going to catch an infection,' for instance), which the individual attempts to neutralize by specific, and often very time-consuming, rituals (for example, washing). Perhaps the most famous sufferer was the American billionaire Howard Hughes. Petrified by the threat of contamination, he insisted that objects he handled be covered by several layers of tissue paper and cellophane.
- **Social anxiety.** A fear that other people will notice your supposed inadequacies, making many social situations extremely distressing experiences. Social anxiety is essentially an extreme version of shyness.
- **Post-traumatic stress disorder (PTSD)** is triggered by particularly stressful and distressing events (for example, violent physical assault, a bad car accident, a terrorist incident, or physical and sexual abuse). The fear naturally caused by the event doesn't diminish with time, but instead causes nightmares, flashbacks and persistent feelings of anxiety.
- **Generalized anxiety disorder (GAD)** is an extreme form of worry.

Affective disorders include *depression* and *bipolar disorder* (a condition that used to be known as 'manic depression'). Public attitudes towards depression have undergone a rather dramatic transformation in recent years. Though formerly it was so stigmatizing that sufferers rarely spoke openly about their problems, nowadays people are often much more willing to admit to depression, aided no doubt by the number of celebrities – for example, J. K. Rowling, Alistair Campbell and Stephen Fry – who have admitted to battling the illness. The World Health Organization has identified depression as the single most significant cause of disability, with around 120 million people affected by it at any one time. So common is depression now considered that it's been dubbed the 'common cold of the mind'.

Bipolar disorder is characterized by severe mood swings – from profound depression to intense and exaggerated euphoria (or mania) and back again. It affects about one in a hundred people, usually first manifesting itself in the late teens or early twenties.

Eating disorders comprise anorexia nervosa, bulimia nervosa and binge eating disorder.

- **Anorexia** used to be trivialized as the 'slimmer's disease'. But of course there's nothing trivial about anorexia, which is defined by the failure to eat enough to maintain one's normal body weight. Usually this behaviour has its roots in an obsessional, and sometimes catastrophic, fear of becoming overweight.
- **Bulimia** was first identified in the mid-1970s, when doctors began to encounter a number of young women prone to bouts of frenzied eating, followed by attempts to undo any weight gain by vomiting, using laxatives, fasting or excessive exercise. This is the illness that Diana, Princess of Wales, described in an interview in 1995: 'I had bulimia for a number of years. And that's like a secret disease. You inflict it upon yourself because your self-esteem is at a low ebb, and you don't think you're worthy or valuable. When you have bulimia, you're very ashamed of yourself and you hate yourself ... so you don't discuss it with people.'

Like anorexia, bulimia seems to stem partly from the idea that one's self-worth depends on being slim and attractive. But it's also a response to difficulties in dealing with emotions. A person with bulimia may be uncomfortable with strong feelings of any type, or struggle to cope with unpleasant emotions such as unhappiness, worry or boredom.

Because many people keep their eating disorder secret, it's difficult to put a figure on the numbers affected. Anorexia and bulimia predominantly – although not exclusively – affect women. The best guess is that perhaps 0.3 per cent of women have anorexia, though the proportion is higher for young women. Perhaps 1 to 2 per cent of women suffer from bulimia, though that figure jumps to 4.5 per cent for the eighteen-to-twenty-four age group.

- People who regularly binge without trying to purge themselves afterwards may be suffering from *binge eating disorder*. Men are much more likely to develop binge eating disorder than either anorexia or bulimia.

Substance abuse and dependency. As you'll have gathered from the figures on page 242, a substantial proportion of the population either abuses or is addicted to substances ranging from alcohol and cigarettes to marijuana, cocaine and heroin.

The *DSM* defines abuse as behaviour that causes an individual to be regularly unable to meet their commitments at home and at work, to have relationship problems, to get into dangerous situations (for example, driving while drunk or high), or to end up in trouble with the police. Dependency (addiction) means increased tolerance for the substance (so that it takes more of it to produce the effect we're looking for), withdrawal problems when we stop consuming it, consuming more than we planned to, repeatedly trying and failing to give up, prioritizing the substance over other areas of life, and carrying on using the substance even though we know that it's doing us harm.

Sleep disorders. As mentioned in Chapter 7, by far the most common form of sleep disorder is *insomnia*, defined by the *DSM* as:

- taking longer than half an hour to fall asleep
- experiencing this problem several nights a week and for more than a month
- finding it very difficult to function during the day

It's estimated that around a third of adults suffer from insomnia. Women are twice as likely to be affected as men. Why this should be the case isn't clear, though it may be at least partly related to the fact that women are much more likely than men to suffer from anxiety and depression.

Other sleep disorders include:

- **Narcolepsy** – suddenly falling asleep regardless of where you are and what you may be doing.
- **Nightmare disorder.** As the name suggests, people with this disorder are plagued with regular and distressing nightmares. In order to meet the clinical criteria for a diagnosis, the individual's broken sleep must make it very difficult for them to perform normally in day-to-day life.
- **Sleepwalking disorder.** Much like nightmare disorder, for a diagnosis of this disorder the sleepwalking needs to be repeated, distressing, and interfering significantly with the person's ability to function properly during the day.

Psychotic disorders. The most well-known of these is *schizophrenia*. Some experts now question the validity of the term 'schizophrenia'. It's also plainly loaded with pejorative connotations: the media, for example, frequently portrays those with the illness as dangerous psychopaths, when in fact the chance of such a person harming anyone other than themselves is extremely remote. Moreover, in many cases it may be more helpful to focus on the precise symptoms affecting an individual, tackling them in their own right rather than seeing them through the lens of 'schizophrenia'.

Typical symptoms of psychotic disorders include hallucinations, technically defined as a perception (such as hearing voices) without an obvious cause, and delusions (unfounded and exaggerated beliefs). In former times, psychotic disorders would have been called 'madness'.

Personality disorders constitute one of the more contentious areas of psychiatric classification. After all, what is a 'normal' personality? When does oddness or eccentricity become a personality disorder? The answer, according to the *DSM*, is when it is 'inflexible or maladaptive, and cause[s] significant functional impairment or subjective distress'. As we saw in Chapter 1, personality disorders are categorized in three groups:

- **odd-eccentric**, including paranoid personality disorder (just what its name suggests) and schizotypal personality disorder, a schizophrenia-like collection of symptoms
- **dramatic-emotional**, including antisocial personality disorder, which is characterized by wildly rebellious, aggressive and deceitful behaviour, and borderline personality disorder, whose sufferers are emotionally fragile, very unsure of themselves and their identity, and fearful of abandonment
- **anxious/fearful**, including dependent personality disorder, in which the individual feels unable to cope without the constant help of another person, and avoidant personality disorder, in which self-esteem hits rock bottom and the person therefore avoids all social situations

Sexual and gender identity disorders. This category comprises two very different, and unrelated, sets of disorders. The sexual ones include:

- **hypoactive sexual desire disorder** – a prolonged lack of interest in sex that causes distress or relationship problems (these latter criteria apply to all the sexual disorders)
- **dyspareunia** – pain during sex, or even sometimes at the thought of sex
- **male erectile disorder** and **female sexual arousal disorder** – the inability to become fully aroused during sex

People with gender identity disorders are convinced that their biological sex is the 'wrong' one for them – that they are, for example, a woman locked in a man's body. As you might suspect, it's a very rare occurrence: only one in tens of thousands of people is affected, though it's more than twice as common in men as it is in women. Sex-reassignment surgery is the usual treatment.

*

The general pattern of drug therapy for mental illness has been one of initial enthusiasm followed by disappointment.
– F. G. Alexander and S. T. Selesnick,
The History of Psychiatry (1967)

So much for psychological disorders. What options are available for treating them?

Before we look at the alternatives – generally medication and/or psychotherapy – a word on the personnel who offer those treatments.

What's the most common question asked of psychologists? Answer: 'Are you reading my mind?' (We knew you wouldn't know the answer to that one.) And the second most common question? 'What's the difference between a psychologist and a psychiatrist?' Well, psychiatrists have trained as medical doctors and then specialized in the care of people with mental-health problems. Their first line of treatment is usually medication, though some psychiatrists are also trained in psychological therapies. There are several different types of psychologist, but the ones who specialize in psychological problems are called *clinical psychologists*. Clinical psychologists have studied psychology at university, followed by a three-year doctoral degree (meaning that, like psychiatrists, they can use the word 'Doctor' before their name). They are trained to apply psychological knowledge to reduce the distress caused by mental disorders (and are not licensed to prescribe medication). Besides psychologists and psychiatrists, counsellors and psychotherapists abound, though these titles are used by people with widely differing types and amounts of training.

Right, now we have that sorted out, let's look at the three main types of medication: antipsychotics, anxiolytics and antidepressants.

When *antipsychotics* (or 'major tranquillizers') arrived on the scene, in the early 1950s, they seemed like a miracle: the first pharmaceutical cure for serious mental illnesses such as schizophrenia. Like many medications, antipsychotics were discovered by accident: chlorpromazine, for example, was intended as a sedative for surgical patients.

Chlorpromazine, and the later antipsychotics that have followed, such as clozapine and riperidone, can undoubtedly bring about a huge improvement in some patients' symptoms, allowing many people to live independently rather than confined to a hospital. But they don't work for everyone, and they're not a cure: symptoms frequently remain, albeit at reduced levels, and recur when medication is stopped. They also often provoke some pretty nasty side effects, including restlessness, tremors, involuntary chewing and sucking movements, blurred vision, constipation and dry mouth. Some patients find these side effects worse than their illness and hence stop taking their medication. The situation isn't helped by the fact that antipsychotics are often prescribed in unhelpfully large doses. It's usually recommended that patients undertake psychological therapy alongside drug treatment.

Anxiolytics – sometimes known as 'minor tranquillizers' – are used to treat anxiety disorders. The most famous anxiolytic (indeed, one of the most famous drugs ever) is diazepam, a member of the benzodiazepine class of drugs and better known under its trade name Valium. Diazepam was the Prozac of its era: as mentioned in Chapter 8, a staggering 2.3 billion Valium tablets were sold in the US in 1978 alone. But these days anxiety is usually treated with SSRIs, one of the new class of antidepressants (see below). Benzodiapezines can be very effective when used in small doses and for short periods, but they often cause unwelcome side effects and pose a real risk of dependence. Whatever medication is used for anxiety, the evidence suggests that psychological therapies are typically more effective.

Antidepressants first appeared in the early 1950s, when monoamine oxidase inhibitors (MAOIs) were discovered (though the scientists developing them were actually looking for a tuberculosis drug). MAOIs could be moderately effective, but their potentially fatal side effects meant they were rapidly superseded by the arrival towards the end of the 1950s of the so-called *tricyclics*, such as imipramine, amitriptiline and trazedone. Tricyclics – which were originally developed as antipsychotic drugs – boost the amount of dopamine, noradrenaline and/or serotonin in the brain. (These are neurotransmitters: chemicals that allow brain cells to communicate with one another.) Tricyclics can cause side effects, but they're still sometimes considered the best treatment for severe depression and can be effective for milder cases too.

However, tricyclics have tended to be overshadowed by the enormous commercial success of the selective serotonin reuptake inhibitors (SSRIs), which first appeared on the scene in the late 1980s. SSRIs like paroxetine, citalopram and fluoxetine (Prozac) are some of the most widely prescribed drugs in the world. But do they work? Some doctors (and patients) argue that they can be very effective for mild to moderate depression. Yet a growing number of experts who have analysed the results of SSRI drug trials (and especially those run by the pharmaceutical companies themselves) have expressed scepticism about their efficacy. As the psychiatrist David Healy has written, 'There is no evidence that there is anything wrong in the serotonin systems of people who are depressed. Ideas of lowered serotonin or chemical imbalances are nothing more than marketing myths.' Far from demonstrating the efficacy of SSRIs, it's suggested that close scrutiny of the trial data indicates that the drugs perform little better than placebos for mild to moderate depression, though they may be more helpful for people suffering from more serious depression.

In fact many experts argue that none of the antidepressants – be they tricyclics, MAOIs or SSRIs – is a great deal more effective than a placebo. This isn't to say that the improvement in mood that many people experience while taking these drugs is illusory, but rather that it can be accounted for by the immense power of the placebo effect, whereby simply taking a pill prescribed by one's immensely knowledgeable and experienced doctor is sufficient to trigger genuine progress. However, antidepressants often come with unpleasant side effects, they take a few weeks to kick in, and the gains often don't last long once medication is stopped (unlike the improvement brought about through psychological therapy).

*

I feel like a snake-oil salesman sometimes when people say,
'What can it cure?' and I reply, 'What can't it help?'
  – **Aaron T. Beck** (inventor of cognitive behavioural therapy)

Surveys in the 1980s put the number of psychological therapies at more than 130. You will doubtless be relieved to know that we do not plan to talk you through all of them here. Instead, here's a brief look at the five main types. Which one is best? To some extent, that depends on the personal circumstances of the individual undergoing therapy and the nature of the problem: different approaches suit different people. However, clinical trials have provided convincing evidence that cognitive behavioural therapy (CBT) is particularly effective for a wide range of problems. It's also clear that, whichever therapy is used, people often benefit simply from the opportunity to discuss their problems openly with a sympathetic and knowledgeable ally.

Psychodynamic therapies are inspired by psychoanalysis, and specifically its assertion that psychological problems are the result of unconscious conflicts developed in childhood. To unravel and resolve these conflicts, the client's relationship with the therapist is seen as crucial. The type of 'classical' psycho-analysis pioneered by Freud is rarely practised these days, not least because the cost of the required two or three sessions a week for several years is well beyond the financial reach of most people (or state health care systems). Instead, psychodynamic approaches tend to be briefer and less intensive than this, though still typically remain the longest therapies. The effectiveness of these approaches is hard to judge, since they're rarely studied.

Behavioural therapies emerged from behaviourism, an approach that dominated psychology (especially in the US) during much of the twentieth century. This form of therapy is based on the idea that all behaviour is learned, and that unhelpful behaviour can therefore be unlearned. In the 1950s, for example, Joseph Wolpe developed behavioural desensitization to tackle fears and phobias. This technique, which involves exposing individuals to the situation they fear so that they can see that there's actually nothing to be afraid of, is still the standard – and extremely effective – treatment for such problems today.

Humanistic therapies were pioneered by the American psychologist Carl Rogers in the 1940s and '50s. In these the focus is less on tackling individual symptoms than on helping the individual to develop to their fullest potential. (Rogers had no interest in making diagnoses.) Rogers emphasized the responsibilities of the therapist, arguing that progress was impossible unless they could win the client's trust, demonstrate genuine respect and affection, and work with the client as an equal.

Family and systemic therapies attempt to understand an individual's psychological problems by looking at them in the context of the overall family dynamic. The therapist will work with all the members of the family, not just the person with the issue, often in group sessions. The idea is to identify the kind of behaviour that's causing problems and replace it with better alternatives.

Cognitive behavioural therapies (CBT) have the strongest links with mainstream psychological research of any psychological therapy. Treatment is based on the construction of detailed models showing how a disorder is caused, maintained and overcome. As more is discovered, the model is updated and the techniques evolve accordingly. Nevertheless, often at the heart of cognitive therapies is the insight that the way we think can have a profound effect on the way we behave and feel. Thus, if one can change the way one thinks, one can also alter one's feelings and behaviour.

In the UK and mainland Europe, CBT is now the officially recommended treatment for a wide range of psychological conditions. Indeed, it forms the core of the UK's Improving Access to Psychological Therapies scheme, which was launched in 2007 with the aim of training 3,600 new therapists to help more of the 6 million people currently battling anxiety and depression. In the US, a quarter of a billion dollars are being spent each year training therapists in CBT and related therapies to help military personnel cope with the psychological legacy of service in Iraq and Afghanistan.

So what is CBT, and why has it become such a dominant approach in mental-health care? Its inventor, the American psychiatrist Aaron T. Beck, began practising as a psychoanalyst in the 1950s. 'The psychoanalytic mystique was overwhelming,' Beck recalled in 2009. 'It was a little bit like the evangelical movement.' But the evidence presented to Beck when talking to his depressed patients didn't seem to fit with the principles of psychoanalysis. What struck Beck most forcefully was that these people typically held very distinctive – and distinctly unhelpful – views about themselves, other people and the world in general: for example, 'I am worthless and incompetent', 'No one likes me', 'Everyone else is happier, more successful and better adjusted than I am', 'Life is precarious and fragile: trouble is always just around the corner' ...

If this is the way you typically see things, it's hardly surprising that you're likely to be vulnerable to depression, especially at stressful times of your life. As the psychologist Gillian Butler has written, CBT is 'based on the recognition that thoughts and feelings are closely related. If you *think* something is going to go wrong, you will *feel* anxious; if you *think* everything will go fine, you will *feel* more confident.' So CBT therapists work with their clients to identify and challenge negative thoughts.

One of the undoubted attractions of CBT, both for many clients and for the government footing the bill, is the speed with which improvements are often seen. CBT treatment generally runs to around ten one-hour weekly sessions, with the focus on practical steps to help individuals overcome their problems. It doesn't work for everyone, but when you consider its performance in randomized controlled trials (the most rigorous form of scientific testing) it's no surprise that CBT is so prevalent today.

*

Whatever one might think of contemporary treatments for psychological disorders, we should be grateful that none (or almost none) of the following 'cures' is still practised:

- **Removal of all teeth** – a 1920s fad, based on the rather bizarre belief that psychosis was fuelled by dental infection.
- **Vomiting.** This was regarded as an effective way of restoring balance to the body's four humours. In his monumental *The Anatomy of Melancholy*, the seventeenth-century scholar Robert Burton recommends eating tobacco and partially boiled cabbage as a way of inducing vomiting and thereby curing depression.
- **Cutting the head** – a technique recommended by the monks called in to cure King Charles VI of France (1368–1422). From his twenties onward Charles had suffered from spells of acute mental illness: he would forget who he was, rampage around his castle baying like a wolf, and fear that he was made of glass. One small consolation for the unfortunate king was that the monks' suggestion was refused by his courtiers.
- **Bleeding** – a favourite technique of the American doctor and psychiatric pioneer Benjamin Rush, whom we met earlier in this chapter. He thought many psychological problems were caused by problems in the circulation of the blood.
- **Mesmerism.** Developed by the German doctor Franz Anton Mesmer (1734–1815), mesmerism was based on the idea that illness could be cured by the clinician transmitting magnetic waves to the patient in order to replenish the 'animal magnetism' that Mesmer believed constituted the life force of every creature. Mesmerism remained influential long after having been comprehensively dismissed by the scientific authorities of the day.
- **Phrenology** – the belief that one's personality and psychological health were determined by the size of the

various regions of the brain, which could in turn be divined by observing the various bumps and indentations of the skull (a bump indicating that the area of the brain directly beneath was enlarged; an indentation that it was abnormally small). Invented by Franz Joseph Gall (1759–1828), phrenology lacks any scientific basis. But, like mesmerism, it enjoyed a prolonged half-life as a pseudoscience, despised by the academy but widely – and lucratively – practised outside it right up to the early decades of the twentieth century.

- **Bromides.** These are drugs containing the chemical element bromine. Potassium bromide was widely used as a sedative in the nineteenth and early twentieth centuries – a practice initiated by Charles Locock, a London doctor, who first tried it with a patient suffering from 'hysterical epilepsy'. Bromides accounted for 20 per cent of prescriptions issued in the US in 1928, but they did nothing to tackle the causes of psychological illness and could also have some pretty unpleasant side effects.

- **Insulin shock therapy.** In vogue in the 1930s, this 'treatment' was inspired by the belief that high doses of insulin – enough to produce convulsions and coma – could cure psychosis. It was abandoned because of the very real danger of killing the patient, though the idea that mental illness could be overcome by inducing convulsions subsequently found its outlet in electroconvulsive therapy (ECT), a technique invented in 1938 and still used today to treat severe depression, albeit rarely and only as a last resort.

- **Prefrontal lobotomy.** A technique devised in the 1930s by the Portuguese neurologist António Egas Moniz (1874–1955), this involving severing links between areas of the brain. The procedure was widely used to treat schizophrenia and, although much less common nowadays (only around twenty lobotomies are performed annually in the UK), it hasn't disappeared entirely, particularly in the US and Australia. Moniz, who was awarded the Nobel Prize in 1949 for his work, spent his last sixteen years in a wheelchair after being shot by a former patient.

15. THE BRAIN

If the human brain were so simple that we could understand it,
we would be so simple that we couldn't.
  – Emerson M. Pugh

Professor Pugh may have had a point. The human brain is a bewilderingly complex organ: no computer, for example, can even approach its level of sophistication and power. It's hardly surprising, then, that much about the brain remains a mystery. That said, the last hundred years or so have seen many of the most baffling questions about the brain answered, at least partially. As we'll see in the next few pages, the basic structure of the brain has been identified, we know much about how the various regions of the brain communicate with one another, and we have a broad understanding of the specialist roles performed by many of these regions.

Our brain, together with the spinal cord, constitutes the *central nervous system* (CNS). Radiating out from the brain and spinal cord are thirty-one nerves; throughout the rest of the body, these nerves constitute the peripheral nervous system. So critical is the CNS to our survival that it is exceptionally well defended. The bones of the spine protect the spinal cord, and the brain is shielded by the skull. The brain – comprising the *hindbrain*, *midbrain* and *forebrain* – is sheathed in layers of strong membrane, known as the meninges, and is cushioned by a covering of fluid against possible damage caused by sudden or dramatic movements. Moreover, the so-called *blood–brain barrier* prevents unwanted matter from the bloodstream reaching the brain.

Now for some mind-boggling numbers. The human brain contains approximately 80 billion neurons. (Neurons are nerve cells: that's to say, cells dedicated to the processing of sensory data.) Each neuron may communicate directly with up to 10,000 other neurons. This means literally trillions of neural connections, or *synapses* – in fact some have argued that the human brain contains more connections than there are atoms in the universe. At the risk of complicating matters even further, we should mention that neurons aren't the only cells in the brain: there are almost ten times as many *glial* cells. These used to be seen as so much glue linking the brain's neurons together – the word glial is derived from the Greek for 'glue' – though it's since been discovered that they play a vital role in helping to determine the network of communication between neurons. The brain is so powerful that, even though it accounts for just 2.5 per cent of body weight, it devours 20 per cent of the body's energy. (This is why it's hard to think straight when you're hungry.)

The average human brain weighs approximately 1.4 kilograms. It isn't the heaviest in the animal world – an elephant's brain weighs in at around 4.7 kilograms, for example, and a sperm whale's at about 7.8 kilograms – but no animal has a larger brain-to-body-weight ratio than humans.

Incidentally, pet lovers may be interested to know that the average rabbit possesses a brain weighing around 10 grams – not much, but ten times heavier than a hamster's brain and positively colossal when compared to the humble goldfish, whose brain weighs less than a single gram. Cats' brains typically weigh about 30 grams, and the average dog's more than twice that – though you'd need to produce more evidence than this to convince us that it's dogs who are the more intelligent of the two species. After all, cats' brains may be lighter, but the cerebral cortex – the most advanced part – contains more neurons.

At this point, you may be wondering whether all this talk about brains and neurons and synapses – fascinating though it is – might not be out of place in a book about thoughts, feelings and behaviour. But to understand human psychology fully we must analyse it from a variety of viewpoints. Imagine, for example, a middle-aged man crippled by anxiety at the thought of meeting new people. How should we explain his behaviour? Is it a result of his upbringing? Is the bullying he suffered at school to blame? Might his fear be genetically determined? Does it spring from the negative beliefs he holds about himself and the world in general? Or might he possess a brain that is simply exceptionally sensitive to potential danger? Quite possibly his anxiety is the product of all these factors and more. Unless we look at things from the full range of perspectives – including the biological – any conclusions we reach can only be incomplete.

The earliest brains, found in the microscopic organisms that floated in the Earth's oceans around a billion years ago, consisted simply of a few nerve cells bundled together. Fast-forward around 650 million years, however, and evolution had produced the first reptiles, from which mammals would later evolve. The brains of reptiles have much in common with the most ancient parts of the human brain: the *hindbrain* (or rhombencephalon) and the *midbrain* (mesencepahlon), which together comprise the *brainstem*. Indeed, these regions are sometimes referred to as the 'reptilian brain'. As well as being the oldest parts of the human brain in evolutionary terms, they are also the first to develop in a foetus. (No organ in the body is as fully developed in a newborn as the brain. By the time a child is just six months old, its brain is already halfway to its adult weight.)

The hindbrain is positioned at the top of the spinal cord, with the rest of the brain sitting above. It includes three structures: the *medulla oblongata*, the *pons* and the *cerebellum*. The medulla (its full name meaning 'rather long marrow' in Latin) emerges from the spinal cord and is the most ancient region of the brain. It oversees many of the most basic and essential mechanisms of life, including breathing, digestion, swallowing and circulation of the blood. Located on top of the medulla is the pons (Latin for 'bridge'), which helps determine how alert we are at any given moment and plays an important role in regulating when we sleep and dream. It also ensures that the two sides of the body move in tandem.

Nestling behind the pons and medulla at the back of the head is the cerebellum. The name is Latin for 'little brain', and indeed the cerebellum looks rather like the roughly spherical, corrugated cerebral cortex (of which more in a moment) that it sits beneath. The cerebellum is responsible for motor co-ordination – that is, ensuring we're able to move our bodies in the way that we intend – and helps us maintain our balance. Around half of the brain's neurons are located in the cerebellum, even though it accounts for just 10 per cent of the brain's total weight.

The midbrain comprises the *superior colliculus*, the *inferior colliculus* and the *substantia nigra*. As its name suggests, the midbrain is sandwiched between the hindbrain and the forebrain, and its main job is to ferry information from one to the other.

The story of life on Earth very nearly ground to an abrupt halt around 250 million years ago. Scientists don't know exactly what triggered the 'Permian–Triassic extinction event', though it's believed it may have been the result of intense volcanic activity and the impact of a vast meteorite in Antarctica. Whatever the cause, 95 per cent of marine life and 75 per cent of all land-dwelling organisms were extinguished. Among the few creatures to survive this catastrophe were the cynodonts, a reptilian species named for their dog-like teeth and equipped with relatively large brains, which developed into the first mammals. By 200 million years ago, eucynodonts had evolved. These animals, which could be as big as a dog, benefited from superb hearing and savagely efficient teeth. Crucially, however, eucynodonts were also the first creatures to possess a *cerebral cortex*, giving them a brain of such power that they were peerless hunters. Even today, only mammals boast a cerebral cortex.

The cerebral cortex is part of the human *forebrain* (or

prosencephalon), and for most of us it's what we picture when we think of the brain. This is hardly surprising, since the cerebral cortex is by far the most visible portion. The word 'cortex' derives from the Latin word for 'bark'; however, what the cerebral cortex most resembles is not the outermost covering of a tree, but a wrinkled grey blanket enveloping the other regions of the brain. The cortex is around two to three millimetres thick, and is wrinkled in order to fit into the relatively limited space offered by the skull; indeed, it's so densely packed that it amounts to as much as 80 per cent of the brain.

Look at the brains of animals and you'll see that the smaller the cerebral cortex, the smoother it is. Were you to spread out the human cortex on the ground, it would be large enough to sit on comfortably (not an appealing image, perhaps). Attempt the same procedure with a chimpanzee's cortex and you'd be trying to squeeze on to something roughly the size of a sheet of A4 paper; as for a rat, its cortex would amount to no more than a postage stamp.

There are around 16 billion neurons in a human cerebral cortex. By way of comparison, the cerebral cortex of the average chimpanzee – considered the most intelligent primate – contains around 6.2 billion neurons. A cat's cerebral cortex holds 300 million neurons (the same as that of an octopus) while that of a rat contains 15 million.

The forebrain is split into two hemispheres, each of which is a mirror image of the other. The hemispheres are attached via the *corpus callosum*, the largest bundle of nerve fibres in the body (it contains around 250 million). Each of the hemispheres has four main sections, or *lobes*. Although they aren't completely separate from one another, the lobes are divided by deep fissures. Each of the lobes has a specific function:

- The **frontal** lobe, which lies directly behind the eyes, handles many of the tasks we tend to regard as quintessentially human, such as planning, decision-making, language and conscious thought. It's really our control centre, analysing the stream of information generated by all the other parts of the brain and deciding how best to respond. The frontal lobe plays a big part in determining the kind of person we are – as we'll see on p. 276, an injury to this part of the brain can radically alter someone's personality.

- The **occipital** lobe, situated at the very back of the head, handles visual data.
- The **parietal** lobe, located at the top of the brain towards the back of the head, makes sense of information received from the body's internal organs.
- The **temporal** lobe lies close to the ears and, appropriately enough, specializes in processing auditory data.

Incidentally, if you're wondering why the lobes have the names they do, there's a simple answer: they're named after the bones of the skull that they lie closest to.

*

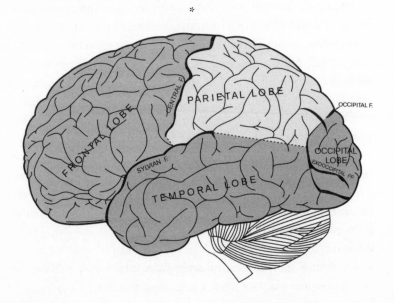

The cerebral cortex is clearly a critically important area of our brain – indeed, many experts have argued that its size and complexity are what distinguish human beings from all other species. (The vast majority of creatures don't possess a cerebral cortex, and it's much smaller in those that do – that is, other mammals – than in humans.) Yet the cerebral cortex is not the only part of the forebrain. Hidden beneath it, and positioned at the top of the brainstem, lies the *subcortex*, which itself contains several highly evolved regions of the brain.

The *basal ganglia* ('lower nerve knots'), situated deep within the forebrain towards the forehead, control voluntary movement, and particularly the very precise and co-ordinated 'fine motor skills'. The shakes and tremors characteristic of Parkinson's disease are partly caused by problems in the basal ganglia. This area of the brain also stores our procedural memories – that is, our automatic memory for how to perform particular tasks, such as playing the piano or putting on a shirt.

Virtually all sensory information reaching the brain passes through the *thalamus* ('deep chamber' in Greek), which then passes it on to the cerebral cortex. Just below the thalamus lies the *hypothalamus* (literally 'under the deep chamber'). As we saw in Chapter 6, this functions as the 'homeostat' of the body, keeping track of such crucial indicators as our temperature, blood pressure, water content, sleepiness and nutritional stores, and prompting the body to take corrective action when these reach a potentially problematic level. All this in a structure no bigger than a fingertip!

Arranged in an approximate circle around the brainstem is the *limbic system* ('limbic' is derived from the Latin for 'border'), whose primary purpose is to help regulate our behaviour and emotions. The limbic system in humans closely resembles that found in the first mammals around 200 million years ago, hence it's sometimes known as the 'old mammalian brain'. As we saw in Chapter 8, it includes the *amygdala*, which helps determine our emotional reaction to a given situation and is particularly important in alerting us to possible threats. Individuals who've sustained damage to their amygdala find it very difficult to read other people's emotions. On the other hand, a hyperactive amygdala, constantly detecting danger where there is none, is thought to lie behind some anxiety disorders.

Also located in the limbic system is the *hippocampus,* which plays a crucial role in the formation of memories. As we saw in Chapter 4, unlike most other regions of the brain the hippocampus can actually increase in size. London taxi drivers, for instance, typically have a much larger hippocampus than other people, presumably because they need to store so many locations in their memory. On the other hand, the hippocampus is one of the regions of the brain most affected by Alzheimer's disease. For another perspective on what can happen if the hippocampus is damaged, take a look at the story of H.M. on p. 63.

Few neurological problems are as distressing and debilitating as severe epilepsy. Epilepsy is believed to be caused by a problem in the electrical wiring of the brain. A signal designed to arouse one area of the brain somehow triggers frenzied activity right across the neural networks, leading to epileptic fits. (This theory was first proposed by the 'father of British neurology', John Hughlings Jackson (1835–1911), whose insights were sparked by observing his wife's epilepsy.)

One technique formerly employed by doctors in order to treat the most intractable forms of epilepsy was to sever the corpus callosum, the bridge between the right and left hemispheres of the cerebral cortex, in the hope that this would prevent the electrical storm from spreading from one side of the brain to the other. This 'split-brain' procedure sometimes diminished the patient's fits, but at the cost of some very dramatic side effects.

In a classic demonstration of these side effects, a split-brain patient sits in front of a screen. On the left-hand side of the screen appears the image of a horse. When asked what one would put on the horse's back, the patient is unable to say: they simply don't know. But if they're then asked to *draw* the answer to the question, they'll easily produce a picture of a saddle.

Why is someone with a split brain so befuddled by such an apparently simple assignment? Part of the explanation lies in the fact that signals from sensory organs on one side of our body are processed by the opposite hemisphere of the brain. So the image of the horse, positioned on the left of the screen, duly appears in the left-hand visual field and thus this information should be conveyed to the *right-hand* side of the brain. Now, it just so happens that the left hemisphere specializes in language and the right in spatial skills. The split-brain patient can't tell you that a saddle goes on a horse, because, now that their corpus callosum has been cut, the left side of their brain hasn't received the necessary visual information. And the right side, which did see the horse, doesn't have the language skills necessary to produce a verbal response, though it can offer a non-linguistic version.

So, although the two hemispheres appear as virtual carbon copies of one another, they clearly don't function in exactly the same way. The left specializes in detailed, analytical tasks, including language and mathematical calculation; the right is better at seeing the metaphorical 'bigger picture', and excels at spatial awareness and imaginative thought. However, the differences between the two hemispheres are often grossly exaggerated, leading to stereotypes of 'right-sided' people as sensitive and artistic mavericks and 'left-sided' folk as pedantic, rational systematizers. In fact the hemispheres aren't independent structures, but are designed to work together. And it's not simply a question of one hemisphere complementing the other. The vast majority of tasks rely on activity in multiple areas of the brain, distributed across both hemispheres. If one area of the brain is damaged, other regions are usually able to step in and cover for it. It seems that the difference between the hemispheres really amounts to nothing more dramatic than preferences in the sort of information processed.

Theories about the nature of the brain extend right back to the ancient civilizations of Egypt and Greece, during which the principal topic of debate was whether intelligence and emotion resided in the heart (as Aristotle, for example, believed to be the case) or in the brain. But modern brain science really took off only with the work of Thomas Willis, whose *Cerebri Anatome*, published in 1664 and illustrated by his friend Sir Christopher Wren, set out the basic structure of the brain for the first time and also introduced terms such as 'lobe', 'reflex' and 'hemisphere' that continue to be used today. Willis has the distinction of being the first neurologist – and not simply because this was another of the words he coined.

Progress continued steadily during the eighteenth and nine-teenth centuries, but brain science took a dramatic leap forwards around the start of the twentieth century, a development recog-nized by the award in 1906 of the Nobel Prize in Physiology or Medicine to Camillo Golgi (1843–1926) and Santiago Ramón y Cajal (1852–1934). Golgi, who was born in Brescia in northern Italy, devised a method of staining tissue so that individual cells could be distinguished. The Spaniard Cajal – often described as the 'father of neuroscience' – employed Golgi's invention to identify for the first time the neurons that compose the essen-tial elements of the brain. (Cajal was apparently something of a rebel in his youth, and at the age of eleven reportedly blew up the gates of his home town using a cannon he'd built himself.) A prodigiously gifted artist as well as scientist, Cajal was able to illustrate his monumental *Manual of Histology and Micro-graphic Technique* (1889) with beautifully drawn and stunningly accurate representations of what he had observed in the brain.

What Cajal saw using Golgi's staining technique was a cell body (a *soma*), containing a nucleus imprinted with genetic code. From the top of the cell body emerges a set of spiky branches known as *dendrites* (the name taken from the Greek word for 'tree'), and from the bottom extends a long, thin *axon*. Some axons are incredibly long: the sciatic nerve, for example, stretches all the way from the spine to the big toe. Others are tiny, measuring no more than a small fraction of an inch. (When we talk about nerves, what we mean is a cable often comprising hundreds or even thousands of axons.) The dendrites collect information transmitted by other neurons and pass this down to the cell body. If the conditions are right, the cell will send a message via its axon to neighbouring neurons (how exactly this happens we'll see shortly.)

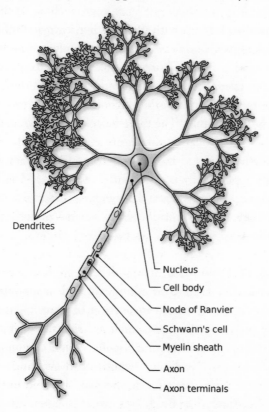

Dendrites

Nucleus

Cell body

Node of Ranvier

Schwann's cell

Myelin sheath

Axon

Axon terminals

Source: Nicolas Rougier, Wikimedia Commons

The cell body is grey in colour. Axons, on the other hand, are white, because they're covered in a layer of myelin, a fatty substance that helps protect the axons from damage. Why do we refer to the brain as 'grey matter' rather than white? Well, it's because the most visible part of the brain is the cerebral cortex, which is largely composed of cell bodies rather than axons.

There are three main types of neuron. Data from the senses is brought to the central nervous system by *sensory* (also known as afferent) neurons. *Motor* (or efferent) neurons convey messages from the CNS to the rest of the body. The vast majority of neurons – approximately 97 per cent of those in the CNS – are designed to link up with one another, carrying information across numerous neural networks, and are known as *interneurons*.

By the time a child is born, most of its neurons are already formed. But over the following months and years these neurons both increase in size and, perhaps most crucially, develop connections with one another. The experiences a child amasses during this period are critical: connections are more likely to form if they are called for, and more likely to endure if they are used. This helps explain why certain skills – reading and writing, for instance, or speaking a second language – are easily learned in childhood (and deeply entrenched in our memories), and much more difficult to pick up in later life.

Possessing 80 billion neurons is all very well, but in order to be much use they need to communicate with one another. How does this happen? A small proportion of neurons are directly adjoining but, as we've seen, most are separated by a gap, or synapse. Neurons talk to one another using chemicals called *neurotransmitters*. Nothing happens until the level of stimulation that a given neuron experiences from other neurons reaches a critical threshold, but when it does the electrical balance of the neuron shifts dramatically and a charge (known as an action potential) is transmitted along its axon. A neuron can't partially fire in this way: either it does or it doesn't – it's all or nothing.

At the tip of the axon are dozens of *vesicles* containing liquid neurotransmitter; the vesicles empty their stock of neurotransmitter into the gaps (or *synaptic clefts*) between this neuron and those next to it. If a receiving neuron has reached its own critical threshold of stimulation, it will absorb the chemical via its dendrites.

There are thought to be at least thirty types of neurotransmitter. Most will be unknown to anyone who has not devoted at least a few happy hours to a neurological textbook, but one or two have become more generally familiar.

It's easy to oversimplify the role of individual neurotransmitters. How they function largely depends on which regions of the brain they're operating in, and how they combine with each other. That said, *dopamine* seems to plays a crucial role in our experience of pleasure. As we saw earlier, we seem to be hard-wired to pursue any activity or substance that can increase the quantity of dopamine, which is produced by the brain's 'pleasure centre', the nucleus accumbens (part of the subcortex). Much of the time, this makes perfect evolutionary sense – without the urge to eat, we will not survive for long; without the desire for sex, nor will our genes. But our liking for dopamine can have more undesirable consequences. A wide range of drugs, from alcohol and nicotine to marijuana and cocaine, trigger a dramatic upsurge in dopamine activity in the nucleus accumbens, which helps explain why they can be so powerfully addictive.

In the mid-1980s a new class of antidepressant drugs began making their way on to the market. Their development was prompted by the idea that depression is caused by a lack of the neurotransmitter *serotonin*. Increase the amount of serotonin in your brain, so the theory goes, and your mood will inevitably improve. This is just what the selective serotonin reuptake inhibitors (or SSRIs) – Prozac being the most famous – are designed to do. As we commented in the last chapter, just how valid the theory is and how effective the drugs are is a hugely controversial issue (and one that we don't have the space to get into here). But there's no doubting the commercial success of SSRIs. Between 1998 and 2008, the number of prescriptions written for SSRIs in the UK increased by more than a third, to close to 20 million. In 2004, three times as many prescriptions for antidepressants (including SSRIs) were issued in the US compared with just ten years earlier. Serotonin may or may not help alleviate depression, but it's certainly done wonders for the fortunes of pharmaceutical companies.

On 13 September 1848 a twenty-five-year-old railway worker named Phineas Gage was helping to prepare the ground for the laying of track near the town of Cavendish in Vermont. His task was to insert explosives into holes drilled into the rock, cover them with sand, and tamp down the mixture using a metre-long iron bar. Late in the afternoon, a charge exploded without warning (it seems that Gage had forgotten to include the sand). The tamping iron hurtled upwards, its tapered end smashing through Gage's left cheek and exiting from the top of his head. Remarkably, Gage survived; indeed, he remained conscious throughout, picking himself up and riding on the back of a wagon into town. Shortly afterwards he lapsed into a coma, but he eventually recovered and within a few months was able to lead a relatively normal life.

Gage's accident did kill him eventually, but only more than a decade later, when he became prone to violent epileptic fits. Until then, he seemed to have escaped with virtually no permanent damage – save, that is, for the loss of his left eye and, most dramatically, a radical transformation in his personality. Once a polite, conscientious and friendly fellow, Gage became argumentative, abusive and unreliable. For many years after

Gage's death, scientists looked to his case to help develop theories about the functions performed by particular regions of the brain. In 1994, researchers at Harvard Medical School used brain-imaging technology on Gage's skull to reveal the true nature of the the damage caused to his brain by the accident. The tamping iron had obliterated large portions of Gage's frontal lobes, on both sides of the brain: the very areas that determine personality, rational thought and appropriate behaviour.

For centuries, scientists had three principal ways of learning about the brain. They could inspect it during a post-mortem examination, though by then of course the brain had ceased to function (moreover, this method was unavailable to European scholars during the Middle Ages, since the Christian Church forbade dissection). They could carry out experiments on animals, though any conclusions about the nature of the human brain could only be provisional. And, as in the case of Phineas Gage, they could observe what happened when parts of the brain were damaged by accidents, disease or illness.

Over the last few decades, however, the study of the brain has been transformed by the availability of various forms of scanner that enable scientists directly to observe a living brain in operation. The electroencephalogram (better known as the EEG) detects electrical activity in the brain via electrodes placed on the head; CAT (computerized axial tomography) scanning employs X-rays; PET (positron emission tomography) uses radiation; and MRI (magnetic resonance imaging) bombards the head with exceptionally strong magnetic waves in order to build up an image of the brain.

These technologies provide a fantastically detailed picture of the structure of the brain, but they don't reveal much about how it *functions*. The situation changed, however, with the advent of functional magnetic resonance imaging (fMRI for short) – a development so revolutionary that the British physicist Peter Mansfield and US chemist Paul Lauterbur were awarded a Nobel

Prize in 2003 for their work on the technology. The brilliantly simple insight behind fMRI scanning is that those parts of the brain that are most active at any one time are also those that use the most oxygen. The changing patterns of oxygen consumption can be detected by the way the blood responds to the magnetic field generated by the fMRI scanner. So wire someone up to a scanner, set them a task, and within a few seconds you can see exactly which areas of the brain are being used to complete that assignment.

Stop reading for a moment. Instead, try to recall the thoughts you've had over the last ten minutes. Perhaps you've been fully focused on this chapter. Maybe you've been reflecting on the ways in which the information you've read relates to your own experiences. Perhaps your mind has wandered back to the film you watched last night, or forward to the evening out you have planned for the weekend. Or you may have decided that you're so hungry/thirsty/tired/bored that it's time to put down this book in favour of something more immediately rewarding.

Thanks for staying with (or rejoining) us. Now, almost regardless of the content of your thoughts, their sophistication – for example, decoding language, recalling the past and speculating about the future, making decisions in response to signals from the body – is probably unparalleled in any other species. These mental phenomena are often seen as examples of *consciousness*: the property that distinguishes humans from the rest of the animal world. But what exactly *is* consciousness? This is a topic of much feverish debate among scientists and philosophers, for whom an answer to this question has become something of a Holy Grail, but five characteristics have been suggested:

- knowing you're alive and in the world
- thinking, reflecting and making decisions
- perceiving the world around you via your senses

- using this information about the environment to guide your behaviour
- seeing oneself and the world from a personal perspective

Such characteristics are useful, of course, but they are more of a description than an explanation. Do we know which parts of the brain are responsible for consciousness? Not exactly, though it seems inevitable that the forebrain is prominently involved. (Descartes, by the way, thought that consciousness was located in the pineal gland – which in fact represented a major advance on previous theories, since this gland is at least located within the brain. The pineal gland, however, actually helps regulate our body clock.) Perhaps the most that can be said is that consciousness is an *emergent property* of the human brain – that's to say, a product of the totality rather of than specific areas.

Do we know what the purpose of consciousness may be? No, we don't. Perhaps consciousness doesn't *have* a purpose: some experts contend that it's simply an inessential by-product of our brain's exceptional complexity. Put all those incredibly sophisticated neural networks together and consciousness results – but don't let that fool you into thinking that the purpose of those networks is consciousness. Others have suggested that consciousness is the 'workplace' where the multitude of neural systems involved in almost any brain activity are integrated and a single outcome is generated. Rather than relying on automatic processing of sensory information, consciousness allows us to think creatively, to draw upon our store of memories, and thus to choose the best option in a given situation.

Yet if consciousness implies the capacity for personal, reflective thought and carefully chosen action, what should we make of the work of the Chicago-born neuroscientist Benjamin Libet (1916–2007)? Libet demonstrated that by the time we take a conscious decision to act, the outcome is already visible in our brain activity, pre-dating our 'decision' by anything from a few hundred milliseconds right up to several full seconds. We may believe that our behaviour is the result of conscious thought, but it appears that the unconscious mechanisms of the brain are really calling the shots.

You can see this process at work in a recent study inspired by Libet's research and carried out by scientists in Germany and Belgium. While in an fMRI scanner, a number of volunteers were asked to look at a computer screen on which appeared a sequence of letters. Whenever they felt like it, the volunteers pressed either a button with their left hand or a different button with their right hand. As they did so, the stream of letters was interrupted; the participants then saw a screen showing four letters and were invited to select the one that they'd been looking at when they'd made the conscious decision to press the button. The researchers discovered that the volunteers' brains – and specifically the prefrontal and parietal lobes of their cerebral cortex – registered the 'decision' to press either the left- or the right-hand button up to *ten seconds* before the volunteer was aware of it. And thus the riddle of consciousness acquires yet another layer of mystery.

16. THEORIES, THEORIES, THEORIES: A BRIEF HISTORY OF PSYCHOLOGY

Today, anyone curious about the nature of the human mind, and its relation to the way we behave, is spoilt for choice. Those keen to find out more about how the mind processes information from the senses, for example, can turn to the findings of cognitive psychology. If you're interested in how individuals interact with other people, you'll find much to ponder in the works of social psychologists. People struggling with mental illness may well find it helpful to consult a clinical psychologist. Coaches attempting to draw the best possible performances from their athletes will look to the principles of sports psychology. Those keen to understand what's going on in our brains when we think and feel and act can delve into the branch of psychology termed cognitive neuroscience. And so on: psychology has never been so diverse in its areas of interest (one current textbook lists twenty-six separate specialisms). Few if any are the corners of the mind that psychology is not currently seeking to illuminate.

Of course, psychology is by no means the only discipline with things to say about the mind – medicine, philosophy, sociology and the arts, for example, all have much to contribute. But psychology is the only one to make the mind its primary focus – its *raison d'être*, indeed. As such, it's the discipline that has most informed this book.

*

In 1879, at the ancient University of Leipzig in Germany, a new scientific laboratory was set up. This laboratory was the brainchild of the university's professor of physiology, Wilhelm Wundt (1832–1920), and it was quite unlike any other facility anywhere in the world, for the new lab was to be dedicated to psychological research. (Indeed, in 1886 it was formally named the Institute for Experimental Psychology.) Its opening marks the commonly accepted beginning of psychology as a discrete, scientific enterprise.

What kind of psychology was Wundt doing in his ground-breaking laboratory? Much of it was concerned with identifying the basic building blocks of experience. For Wundt, that meant focusing on how we perceive the world around us – for example, its colours, smells and tastes. What Wundt was trying to get at was our raw, unmediated perceptual experience, before our rational, judgemental, analytic mind kicks in. His method was to present his students with sensory stimuli – an image perhaps, or a sound – and then have them use a technique called intro-spection to home in on the essential characteristics of their experience.

Wundt was a tireless advocate for the fledgling science. The inaccurately named historian of psychology Edwin G. Boring calculated that Wundt wrote 54,000 pages between 1853 and 1920, or 720 words every day for sixty-eight years. (He completed his autobiography just eight days before his death.) Wundt edited the first journal of experimental psychology, supervised dozens of doctoral students, and hugely influenced psychologists both in mainland Europe and in the US. (The UK was slower to be impressed. Indeed, Cambridge University might have scooped Wundt and Leipzig, but a request to open a psychology labora-tory was declined on the grounds that to do so would 'insult religion by putting the human soul in a pair of scales'. The university changed its mind in 1912; Oxford University began to offer courses in psychology only in 1936.)

Wundt's interest in identifying the basic elements of conscious experience led to his identification with a school of psychology named *structuralism*, which was concerned, as its name suggests, with setting out the essential structure of our mental processes. Across the Atlantic, however, a rather different approach to these issues was being taken by arguably the first great American psychologist, William James.

For some, William James (1842–1910) is most famous as the elder brother of the novelist Henry James. This rather obscures the fact that William was himself a colossal figure in nineteenth-century American intellectual life. In 1890 he published the hugely influential *Principles of Psychology*, which contained the famous definition of psychology as 'the Science of Mental Life'. Taking issue with the notion that consciousness could be broken down into constituent parts (James saw it as an indivisible stream), he argued that psychology's primary task was to identify how our mental processes help us to survive and thrive in the world (a viewpoint known as *functionalism*). Wundt, perhaps unsurprisingly, was unconvinced: 'It [James's *Principles*] is literature, it is beautiful, but it is not psychology.'

At a conference held in 1909 at Clark University in Worcester, Massachusetts, America's leading psychologists played host to a celebrated – perhaps even notorious – visitor from Europe. The guest was Sigmund Freud (1856–1939), making his first and only trip to the US from his home in Vienna. William James was among the distinguished attendees at the conference, convened to mark the twentieth anniversary of the foundation of the university. Freud's colleague Carl Gustav Jung (1875–1961) had travelled with him. The founder of psychology, Wilhelm Wundt, declined the invitation, explaining that his presence was required at the celebrations of his own university, Leipzig, for its five-hundredth anniversary, no less.

At the risk of understatement, the Clark University conference must have been a fascinating event. Freud's psychoanalytic theories of the human mind and behaviour were light years away from the experimental psychology being practised in the US (or anywhere else). Psychology was – and indeed to a large extent it still is – regarded as the experimental, scientific study of observable, measurable mental processes and behaviour. Psychoanalysis, however, took as its subject invisible, *immeasurable* psychological forces, which it saw as predominantly sexual in character. One couldn't hope to identify such forces in a laboratory; instead, their presence could be detected only through the interaction of patient and psychoanalyst.

Freud was not a man to tolerate dissent from his colleagues in the psychoanalytic movement. Disciples came and, usually after taking issue with some aspect of Freud's theories, left. Frequently the leave-taking was acrimonious. In one of his last letters to Jung, Freud wrote, 'I propose that we abandon our personal relations entirely. I shall lose nothing by it, for my only emotional tie with you has long been a thin thread – the lingering effects of past disappointments.'

The break with Freud was traumatic for Jung, triggering a prolonged depression. But it also coincided with Jung's most ground-breaking and productive work. Freud had proposed that we are each the product of a five-stage process of unconscious psychosexual development that begins when we are babies. Jung downplayed the importance of these personal, sexual factors and argued instead for the existence of a *collective* unconsciousness, with which we are all born and which refers back to the experiences of our most ancient ancestors. The collective unconsciousness, Jung argued, contains a number of archetypes, habitual ways in which humans have conceptualized the world around them (for example, God, birth, death, the mother and – most powerfully of all – the self). Jung suggested that these archetypes could be traced in the myths, literature and art of human civilizations across the ages. Jung was also first to intro-duce the personality categories of introversion and extroversion, though his use of the terms was very particular, introversion signifying a preoccupation with the self, and extroversion a focus on the outside world.

Freud died in London in 1939, little more than a year after he had finally fled Nazism. Psychoanalysis's influence on main-stream psychology was limited; many of its claims about how the human mind works have been discredited, or at least vigor-ously disputed. Yet its impact on wider literary, artistic and intellectual culture has been immense. Moreover, psychoanalysis, and the related 'psychodynamic' approaches developed from the work of Freud's followers such as Jung, Karen Horney (1885–1952) and Melanie Klein (1882–1960), are still used to treat psychological and emotional problems today.

'Give me a dozen healthy infants, well-formed, and my own specified world to bring them up and I'll guarantee to take any one at random and train him to become any type of specialist I might select – doctor, lawyer, merchant-chief and yes, even beggarman and thief, regardless of his talents, penchants, tendencies, abilities, vocation, and race of his ancestors.'

This bold claim was made by the American psychologist John Broadus Watson (1878–1958). Watson was the leader of *behaviourism*, which dominated US psychology for much of the twentieth century. As its name suggests, behaviourism focused on understanding the way in which people behave. And, more than this, it held that behaviour was the *only* appro-priate subject for a genuinely scientific psychology to study. Thoughts, emotions, dreams – all were so much superficial flimflam. In his so-called 'behaviourist manifesto' of 1913, Watson wrote, 'Psychology … is a purely objective experimental branch of natural science … Its theoretical goal is the prediction and control of behaviour.'

For Watson and his followers, all behaviour had a simple explanation: we *learn* it. Nothing about us is innate: behaviourists saw human beings as *tabulae rasae*, blank slates on which experience does all the writing. This is why behaviourism is also known as 'learning theory', and why Watson was so confident in his ability to teach anyone to be, say, a doctor. Get the input right, and the desired output will surely follow.

This learning, according to Watson, occurs through a process called *conditioning*. Inspired by the work of the Russian scientist Ivan Pavlov, Watson asserted that behaviour consists of learned responses to particular stimuli (or conditions). Thus Pavlov's dogs learned that they were about to be fed when they heard a particular bell ring; a child may learn to fear spiders from observing the way in which their parent behaves when confronted with the creatures. It's quite possible to teach someone to react to a stimulus in a particular way, as Watson demonstrated in his most famous experiment, involving a toddler known as Little Albert. (You can read about this remarkable experiment on p. 137.)

Incidentally, and notwithstanding his work with Little Albert, Watson was a rat man: that's to say, he had done his early research on rodents, and he continued to conduct experiments using animals. For the behaviourists, there was nothing contradictory about trying to understand humans by studying other species – a position partly inspired by the theories of Charles Darwin. Watson expressed the matter thus: 'The behaviourist ... recognizes no dividing line between man and brute.' Behaviour, whether human or rodent, is behaviour.

Watson's theories took psychology by storm and made him a major star in the academic world. His own behaviour, however, was to trigger a precipitous fall from grace. A messy divorce in 1920 – played out in gory detail in the national newspapers – saw him dismissed from his post at Johns Hopkins University. Much to his amazement, no other academic institution was prepared to take him on, and he spent the rest of his working life – albeit very lucratively – in advertising.

By all accounts, Watson could be a cold and difficult character: his relationship with his children was often fraught, and, like his father, he was prone to alcoholism and womanizing. When the American Psychological Association decided to honour him at its annual meeting in 1957, the year before he died, Watson could not bring himself to attend, changing his mind at the last moment. Fearing that he would be unable to contain his emotions, he sat alone in his car while his son accepted the award on his behalf.

Watson's career ran into the sand, but behaviourism went from strength to strength – particularly in the US, where the Harvard psychologist Burrhus Skinner (1904–1990) pioneered so-called 'radical behaviourism'. Skinner placed an even greater emphasis on the primacy of behaviour than Watson had done. Indeed, there was nothing about humans – including thoughts, emotions, dreams and language – that, in Skinner's view, could not be understood as learned behaviour.

Skinner's notion of how this learning happens was more nuanced than Watson's 'classical' conditioning, in which we simply develop habitual responses to particular stimuli. For Skinner, what is crucial is the effect our behaviour has on the world around us. If the effect is positive, we're likely to repeat the behaviour (this is called reinforcement); a negative effect, on the other hand, teaches us to try something different next time. This kind of learning is known as *operant conditioning*, because it refers to the way in which we 'operate' on our environment. The theory of operant conditioning informed many initiatives in the 1950s and '60s aiming – to cite just three examples – to improve the behaviour of schoolchildren, to help people learn more efficiently, and to treat emotional and psychological problems.

Skinner himself was a tireless inventor and innovator, always looking for ways in which his theories could be practically applied for the greater good. He even published a novel, *Walden Two*, in 1948, setting out his utopian vision of a world based on the principles of radical behaviourism. (As a young man, Skinner had hoped to make a career as a writer, and his early short stories were praised by the poet Robert Frost.)

Like Watson, Skinner derived his conclusions about human behaviour principally from tightly controlled and narrowly focused laboratory experiments, which usually involved animals. Perhaps the most famous of these experiments utilized 'Skinner's box', in which rats or pigeons were observed as they learned to press a lever in order to be fed. To use radical behaviourist terminology, the food reinforced the animals' lever-pressing behaviour, thus ensuring that it would be repeated.

Today, behaviourism can seem a rather reductive theory. Yet, because it's been supported by so many experimental tests, it's exerted a huge influence on mainstream psychology for more than half a century. The concepts of classical and operant conditioning are now widely accepted as very powerful explanations of human behaviour. And let's not forget how liberating an idea behaviourism can be, because behaviour that has been learned is behaviour that can be *changed*. Indeed, it was only with the development of behaviourism that psychologists began to think of themselves as therapists, rather than purely experimental scientists.

One of the most famous therapeutic behavioural techniques is *behavioural desensitization*, which Joseph Wolpe developed to treat fears and phobias, as we saw in Chapter 14. It involves controlled exposure to the situation or object you dread – for example, heights or snakes – during which gradually your anxiety subsides and you learn that there is nothing to be afraid of. Such techniques represented a major challenge to psychoanalysis's grip on therapy.

No one was more forceful in leading this challenge than Hans Eysenck, head of the Psychology Department at London's Institute of Psychiatry, and the person generally regarded as having done most to establish the profession of clinical psychology in the UK. Writing in 1959, Eysenck noted that 'In practically all its manifestations, psychotherapy is based on Freudian theories.' But, by arguing that mental illness was caused by unconscious drives, these theories were fundamentally mistaken: 'Neurotic symptoms ... [are] simply learned habits; there is no neurosis underlying the symptom, but merely the symptom itself. *Get rid of the symptom and you have eliminated the neurosis.*'

How do you get rid of the symptom? Well, because it has been learned, it can be unlearned. The therapist must teach the person to behave differently. It's an idea that continues to inform psychotherapy today, most notably in the shape of cognitive behavioural therapy (CBT).

Third ways may have fallen into disrepute in recent years, but by the 1950s some of those trying to fathom the mysteries of the human mind had become convinced of the need to find an alternative to the two great theories that were then dominant. On the one hand was behaviourism, which appeared to propose that in order to understand human beings all one required was a laboratory, a carefully designed experiment, and some rats (or pigeons, if you preferred). At the opposite end of the intellectual spectrum was psychoanalysis, which saw human life as a desperate battle to control wild, unconscious mental forces. The picture perhaps being distorted by Freud's focus on psychological illness (or psychopathology), it could seem as though this was a battle that many – if not most – people were losing.

The self-proclaimed 'third force' in the study of the human mind became known as *humanism*. It was an approach pioneered by two American psychologists, Abraham Maslow (1908–70) and Carl Rogers (1902–87), both of whom we have met earlier. Maslow and Rogers differed on the details, but both agreed that what was truly essential to human experience was the drive to be oneself and to develop to one's full potential (Maslow called this process *self-actualization*). Unlike behaviourism and psychoanalysis, which saw individuals as at the mercy of the environment or their unconscious desires, humanism argued – with characteristic optimism – that we are free to make our own choices.

One can only imagine the disdain with which the behaviourists would have greeted humanism's insistence on concepts such as the self and free will. Even worse, humanism argued that, far from aspiring to scientific objectivity, psychology could progress only by recognizing that what mattered was how the *individual* perceived their behaviour and the world around them. (This was not an idea to gladden the hearts of those psychologists working with rats.)

Humanism failed to make much of an impression on academic psychology. It had more of an effect on the world of psychotherapy, primarily through Carl Rogers's work between 1945 and 1957 at the University of Chicago Counseling Center. There he developed what was initially known as client-centred therapy and is now termed person-centred therapy. It's an approach that prioritizes the relationship between therapist and client – and places the responsibility for the success of that relationship firmly on the therapist. You can't hope to assist your client unless you demonstrate your trust in them, and your respect and friendship, and unless you communicate with them openly and as an equal. Thus Rogers gave us not only person-centred therapy (still influential today), but also counselling in general.

Which events do you associate with the year 1956? The failed Hungarian uprising against Soviet rule? The outbreak of the Suez crisis? Elvis Presley's first hit ('Heartbreak Hotel')? Or perhaps the inaugural Eurovision Song Contest (won for Switzerland by Lys Assia)? As it happens, 1956 also saw the beginnings of a dramatic shift in the way in which scientists think about the human mind: it was the year of the *cognitive revolution*.

'Revolution' is a rather sensational term, of course. But remember that in 1956 behaviourism dominated psychological thinking: if you couldn't observe something directly, it wasn't worth studying (indeed, it *couldn't* be studied, at least not in a properly scientific fashion). Cognitivism took a radically different view: it was dedicated to identifying and understanding the nuts-and-bolts processes underlying how human beings think. In some ways this was a return to the concerns of early psychology. The radical behaviourist Burrhus Skinner certainly thought so, accusing cognitivism of reviving a set of internal, unverifiable and probably mystical concepts (such as thought) that he and John Watson had attempted to excise from psychology.

The new approach was summarized in the ground-breaking *Cognitive Psychology*, published by Ulric Neisser (1928–) in 1967. Its subject was cognition, defined as 'all the processes by which the sensory input is transformed, reduced, elaborated, storied, recovered, and used ... Such terms as sensation, perception, imagery, retention, recall, problem-solving, and thinking, among many others, refer to hypothetical stages or aspects of cognition.'

To clarify these processes, cognitive psychologists represented them graphically using a metaphor drawn from another boom area of the time: computing. According to this kind of model, sensory information is received by the brain and then processed via a series of binary yes/no steps, just as signals are processed in the flow diagrams on which many computer programs are based. (Indeed, some cognitive psychologists actually wrote programs to simulate human thought.) This 'information-processing' approach was pioneered by the British psychologist

Donald Broadbent (1926–93), who for many years headed the Medical Research Council's Applied Psychology Unit at Cambridge University. Today the models are more sophisticated: rather than a linear flow chart, in which a specified part of the brain deals with inputs one at a time, multiple mental processes occur simultaneously and in tandem across a complex, multi-layered 'neural network'. Aptly, this approach is known as *connectionism*.

Fifty years after the revolution, cognitivism is still alive and kicking – and more vigorously than ever. In fact, as we've seen in this book, cognitivist ideas have been applied to virtually all the big topics in psychological research. Moreover, cognitivism's influence isn't confined to the laboratory-based experimental psychology that attempts to piece together the ways in which the mind functions. In its focus on how we think, cognitivism has also pointed the way for therapeutic clinical psychology (the branch of psychology that aims to treat mental illness). As we saw earlier, cognitive behavioural therapy (CBT), pioneered in the late 1960s by the US psychiatrist Aaron T. Beck, is now the treatment of choice for a wide range of emotional and psychological problems (leading to Beck being cited as one of the five most important psychotherapists of all time).

At the core of CBT – and its precursor, rational emotive behaviour therapy (REBT), developed by Albert Ellis (1913–2007) – is the idea that how we think about ourselves and the world around us has a huge impact on the way that we feel and behave. This is why so much of CBT is devoted to teaching people how to change the way they think, replacing problematic habits with new positive strategies – because if you can do that, the chances are that you'll also find that you'll *feel* better too. In true cognitivist style, thought is (almost) everything.

By now you may have spotted the biological elephant in the psychological corner. This elephant is the brain. After all, psychologists have spent the last 130 or so years trying to understand the ways in which we think and behave – aspects of human experience in which the brain is intimately involved. How then has psychology attempted to integrate the brain into its theories of the mind?

The short answer to this very big question is that, until the last couple of decades, it hadn't – at least not to any great degree. This isn't to say that psychology was uninterested in the brain. Psychologists certainly used findings from medical and biological science to speculate about the brain events underlying a particular mental process or aspect of human behaviour. But they weren't able to get beyond such speculation, for the simple reason that it was impossible to study – directly rather than by inference – what was going on in a living brain. (Most of what scientists knew about the brain was, until recently, derived by inference from psychological tests and from research into the thought processes and behaviour of individuals who had suffered brain damage.) This is why cognitive psychologists, when they tried to depict human thought processes, had to use analogies such as the computer: obtaining a picture of the 'real thing' – the brain in action – wasn't yet possible.

That changed with the advent in the 1980s and '90s of neuro-imaging technology, and particularly functional magnetic resonance imaging, or fMRI. These technologies allow scientists to observe a living brain as it processes information and to pinpoint which parts are involved in specific mental functions, and when. Neuro-imaging has facilitated the development of a new branch of psychological research, albeit one closely allied to cognitive psychology (both, after all, are concerned with the mechanisms of human thought). This new approach is called *cognitive neuroscience* (a term apparently coined by the psychologists George Miller and Michael Gazzaniga in the late 1970s while travelling in a New York City taxi cab). It's thanks to cognitive neuroscience that we now understand, for example, the central role played by the part of the brain known as the amygdala in our experience of anxiety and fear. (You'll find more on this on p. 132.)

As it happens, the increasing influence of biological science on psychology isn't simply a consequence of our new-found ability to observe a living brain in action. It's also driven by the recent explosion of research into the structure and function of human genes. Thus over the past few years psychologists have explored the role of our genetic inheritance in such fundamental aspects of human experience as personality, intelligence and mental illness. For each of these, the evidence suggests that our genes are often a key influence – though always in combination with environmental factors (that's to say, the events that we experience in our lives). But, with the possible exception of a few rather fanatical neuroscientists and geneticists, no one believes that a biological account alone is sufficient. There is much more to explaining anxiety, for example, than simply detecting activation of the amygdala: a fuller explanation will describe the psychological functions of the amygdala and how that leads to feelings of fear. Biology illuminates only part of the picture: to truly understand what's going on in these experiences, we need to look from as many angles as possible.

'When I was a child, I spoke like a child, I thought like a child, I reasoned like a child. When I became a man, I gave up childish ways' (1 Corinthians 13:11).

How does this happen? How does a child develop – intellectually, emotionally and psychologically – into an adult? This is the question at the heart of *developmental psychology*.

Towering like a proverbial colossus above the field, even thirty years after his death, is Jean Piaget (1896–1980). As a child in Switzerland, Piaget had been fascinated by natural history, and particularly that of molluscs. Precociously talented, he was offered a position at the Natural History Museum of Geneva while still at school (the institution presumably not guessing that he was only fifteen years old). But, after doing a doctorate in natural sciences at the University of Neuchâtel, Piaget gravitated towards psychology.

His focus was on children's intellectual – or cognitive – development. (Piaget did not call himself a psychologist: in reference to the fact that his subject was the acquisition of knowledge, he coined the title 'genetic epistemologist'.) Piaget argued that, right from birth, children actively seek to understand the world around them, constantly adapting their ways of thinking to make sense of new experiences. But, though the developmental process is a continual one, Piaget identified a number of key, age-related stages. The way we think changes as we grow older: for example, young children aren't capable of the logical, abstract reasoning of older children and adults.

Here is one of Piaget's most well-known illustrations of his principal theory. Imagine that you were to show a child two identical glasses holding equal amounts of water. When you ask the child which glass contains more water, they will correctly answer, 'They're the same.' Now, in front of the child, you empty one glass into a tall, narrow beaker. Taking away the empty glass, you now ask the child whether the beaker or the remaining glass has more water in it. If the child is older than, say, seven, they will realize that both the glass and the beaker contain the same amount of liquid. A younger child, however, will probably tell you that the taller glass has more water in it: this is because they lack the intellectual skills necessary to understand that, though the dimensions of the containers have changed, the volume of water has not.

As we saw in Chapter 12, a rather different, but equally influential, take on human development was offered by the British psychiatrist John Bowlby (1907–90). In contrast to

Piaget's focus on the intellect, Bowlby's interest was in our *emotional* make-up, which he regarded as being determined principally by the closeness of our relationship with our parents and particularly with the primary caregiver, generally the mother. This first relationship, according to Bowlby's *attachment theory*, sets the tone for our future relationships. (The period from when the child is three months old to around three is especially critical.) If the relationship is warm, loving and supportive, this is the model we'll use – more or less unconsciously – for our own relationships in later life. If, on the other hand, the child is unable to bond with a parent – perhaps because of emotional or psychological issues on the part of the adult, or due to bereavement – the consequences can be significant.

Was Bowlby right? Well, his views were certainly controversial. Some feminists, for example, saw his work as an attack on mothers. After all, wasn't Bowlby attributing to them responsibility for much of the misery of human existence? From a scientific perspective, there is some evidence to support Bowlby's claims (see p. 209), and the notion that our relationship with our parents can have a profound and lasting effect on us has proved persuasive. Bowlby undoubtedly provided some important insights into our emotional development; however, a detailed understanding of this most complex of processes continues to elude us.

Would you administer a potentially fatal electric shock to someone just because you were asked to? Of course you wouldn't. Would you, on the other hand, call the police if you suspected that someone was being attacked in the street? Naturally you would.

If, however, you've read Chapter 13 you'll know that people don't always behave in the ways that one would expect. For example, when Stanley Milgram (1933–84) asked participants in his 1963 experiment at Yale University to punish mistakes made in a memory test by a fifty-year-old man with a heart condition by giving him progressively stronger electric shocks, fully two-thirds of them carried right on to the maximum level, flicking the switch labelled '450 volts: XXX – danger severe shock'. And when Kitty Genovese was murdered in New York City in 1964, not one of the thirty-eight neighbours who saw the assault and heard Genovese's cries did anything at all about it.

Milgram's experiments highlighted the extent to which people are prepared to obey authority figures. He himself was shocked by his findings, while the project caused such a furore that his application to join the American Psychological Association was held up while the ethics of his experiment were debated. (Certainly it's not a study that, without modification, would receive the green light today.)

When the psychologists Bibb Latané and John Darley investigated the behaviour of Kitty Genovese's neighbours, they discovered that the reason they hadn't intervened was not that they were too afraid, or that they didn't care: it was simply that they assumed someone else was going to make that crucial phone call to 911. Latané and Darley called this the 'bystander effect'.

What do these research studies have in common? Well, both make crystal clear the extent to which our behaviour is often determined not by our personality or morality or mood – that's to say, by internal factors – but by the particular situation in which we find ourselves. As such, they are famous examples of *social* psychology: the effort to understand the ways in which our thoughts, feelings and behaviour are influenced by the people around us. Social psychology's focus has been extraordinarily broad, taking in issues as diverse as the effect upon us of religion, class, family and work environment. Social psychologists have analysed the power of advertising, the ways in which groups function, and why people are attracted to one another. And, as we've seen, they have even probed the conditions under which we are prepared to kill, and to allow others to be killed.

SOURCES

1. PERSONALITY

Boswell, W. R., Roehling, M. V., and Boudreau, J. W., 'The role of personality, situational, and demographic variables in predicting job search among European managers', *Personality and Individual Differences*, 40 (2006): 783–94

Boudreau, J. W., and Boswell, W. R., 'Effects of personality on executive career success in the United States and Europe', *Journal of Vocational Behavior*, 58 (2001): 53–81

Burke, R. J., Matthiesen, S. B., and Pallesen, S., 'Personality correlates of workaholism', *Personality and Individual Differences*, 40 (2006): 1223–33

Chotai, J., Lundberg, M., and Adolfsson, R., 'Variations in personality traits among adolescents and adults according to their season of birth in the general population: further evidence', *Personality and Individual Differences*, 35 (2003): 897–908

Davey, G., *Psychopathology: Research, Assessment and Treatment in Clinical Psychology* (Chichester: Wiley–Blackwell, 2008)

Dixon, M. M., Reyes, C. J., Leppert, M. F., and Pappas, L. M., 'Personality and birth order in large families', *Personality and Individual Differences*, 44 (2008): 119–28

Egan, S., and Stelmack, R. M., 'A personality profile of Mount Everest climbers', *Personality and Individual Differences*, 34 (2003): 1491–4

Gleitman, H., Reisberg, D., and Gross, J., *Psychology*, 7th edn (New York and London: W. W. Norton, 2007)

Gosling, S. D., and John, O. P., 'Personality dimensions in nonhuman animals: a cross-species review', *Current Directions in Psychological Science,* 8 (1999): 69–74

Hartmann, P., Reuter, M., and Nyborg, H., 'The relationship between date of birth and individual differences in personality and general intelligence: a large-scale study', *Personality and Individual Differences*, 40 (2006): 1349–62

Hewstone, M., Fincham, F. D., and Foster, J. (eds.), *Psychology* (Oxford: BPS Blackwell, 2005)

Michalski, R. L., and Shackelford, T. K., 'An attempted replication of the relationships between birth order and personality', *Journal of Research in Personality*, 36 (2002): 182–8

Morris, P. H., Gale, A., and Duffy, K., 'Can judges agree on the personality of horses?', *Personality and Individual Differences*, 33 (2002): 67–81

Nettle, D., *Personality: What Makes You the Way You Are* (Oxford: Oxford University Press, 2007)

—— 'Psychological profiles of professional actors', *Personality and Individual Differences*, 40 (2006): 375–83

Pervin, L. A., Cervone, D., and John, O. P., *Personality: Theory and Research*, 9th edn (Hoboken, NJ: John Wiley, 2005)

Plomin, R., DeFries, J. C., McClearn, G. E., and McGuffin, P., *Behavioral Genetics*, 5th edn (New York: Worth Publishers, 2008)

Roets, A., and Van Hiel, A., 'The ideal politician: impact of voters' ideology', *Personality and Individual Differences*, 46 (2009): 60–65

Saulsman, L. M., and Page, A. C., 'The five-factor model and personality disorder empirical literature: a meta-analytic review', *Clinical Psychology Review*, 23 (2004): 1055–85

Silverthorne, C., 'Leadership effectiveness and personality: a cross cultural evaluation', *Personality and Individual Differences*, 30 (2001): 303–9

2. INTELLIGENCE

American Psychological Association., 'Intelligence: knowns and unknowns' (1995), available at http://www.lrainc.com/swtaboo/taboos/apa_01.html

Arden, R., Gottfredson, L. S., and Miller, G., 'Does a fitness factor contribute to the association between intelligence and health outcomes? Evidence from medical abnormality counts among 3654 US veterans', *Intelligence*, 37 (2009): 581–91

Arvey, R. D., et al., 'Mainstream science on intelligence', *Wall Street Journal*, 13 December 1994, available at http://www.psychpage.com/learning/library/intell/mainstream.html

Batty, G. D., Deary, I. J., and Gottfredson, L. S., 'Premorbid (early life) IQ and later mortality risk: systematic review', *Annals of Epidemiology*, 17 (2007): 278–88

Deary, I. J., *Intelligence: A Very Short Introduction* (Oxford: Oxford University Press, 2001)

—— Batty, G. D., and Gale, C. R., 'Bright children become enlightened adults', *Psychological Science*, 19 (2008): 1–5

Fagan, J. F., and Holland, C. R., 'Racial equality in intelligence: predictions from a theory of intelligence as processing', *Intelligence*, 35 (2007): 319–34

—— Holland, C. R., and Wheeler, K., 'The prediction, from infancy, of adult IQ and achievement', *Intelligence*, 35 (2007): 225–31

Gale, C. R., Deary, I. J., Schoon, I., and Batty, G. D., 'IQ in childhood and vegetarianism in adulthood: 1970 British cohort study', *British Medical Journal*, 334 (2007): 245

Hewstone, M., Fincham, F. D., and Foster, J. (eds.), *Psychology* (Oxford: BPS Blackwell, 2005)

Judge, T. A., Hurst, C., and Simon, L. S., 'Does it pay to be smart, attractive, or confident (or all three)? Relationships among general mental ability, physical attractiveness, core self-evaluations, and income', *Journal of Applied Psychology*, 94 (2009): 742–55

Lubinski, D., Webb, R. M., Morelock, M. J., and Benbow, C. P., 'Top

1 in 10,000: a 10-year follow-up of the profoundly gifted', *Journal of Applied Psychology*, 86 (2001): 718–29

Nettle, D., 'Intelligence and class mobility in the British population', *British Journal of Psychology*, 94 (2003): 554–61

Plomin, R., 'Genetics and general cognitive ability', *Nature*, 402 (1999): C25–9

—— DeFries, J. C., McClearn, G. E., and McGuffin, P., *Behavioral Genetics*, 5th edn (New York: Worth Publishers, 2008)

Schmidt, F. L., and Hunter, J. E., 'The validity and utility of selection methods in personnel psychology: practical and theoretical implications of 85 years of research findings', *Psychological Bulletin*, 124 (1998): 262–74

Sheehy, N., *Fifty Key Thinkers in Psychology* (London and New York: Routledge, 2004)

Sternberg, R. J., Grigorenko, E. L., and Kidd, K. K., 'Intelligence, race, and genetics', *American Psychologist*, 60 (2005): 46–59

Sternberg, R. J., and Kaufman, J. C., 'Human abilities', *Annual Review of Psychology*, 49 (1998): 479–502

Welling, H., 'Prime number identification in idiots savants: can they calculate them?', *Journal of Autism and Developmental Disorders*, 24 (1994): 199–206

Yang, S. -Y., and Sternberg, R. J., 'Taiwanese Chinese people's conceptions of intelligence', *Intelligence*, 25 (1997): 21–36

Zagorsky, J. L., 'Do you have to be smart to be rich? The impact of IQ on wealth, income and financial distress', *Intelligence*, 35 (2007): 489–501

3. REASONING AND DECISION-MAKING

Edwards, K., and Smith, E. E., 'A disconfirmation bias in the evaluation of arguments', *Journal of Personality and Social Psychology*, 71 (1996): 5–24

Evans, J. St. B. T., and Over, D. E., *Rationality and Reasoning* (Hove: Psychology Press, 1996)

Eysenck, M. W., *Psychology: An International Perspective* (Hove and New York: Psychology Press, 2004)

Freeman, D., and Freeman, J., *Paranoia: The Twenty-first Century Fear* (Oxford: Oxford University Press, 2008)

Galinksy, A. D., and Mussweiler, T., 'First offers as anchors: the role of perspective-taking and negotiator focus', *Journal of Personality and Social Psychology*, 81 (2001): 657–69

Gilovich, T., Griffin, D., and Kahneman, D., *Heuristics and Biases: The Psychology of Intuitive Judgement* (New York: Cambridge University Press, 2002)

Gladwell, M., *The Tipping Point* (New York: Little, Brown, 2000)

Hardman, D., *Judgment and Decision Making: Psychological Perspectives* (Oxford and Malden, Mass.: BPS Blackwell, 2009)

Hewstone, M., Fincham, F. D., and Foster, J. (eds.), *Psychology* (Oxford: BPS Blackwell, 2005)

Iyengar, S. S., and Lepper, M. R., 'When choice is demotivating: can one desire too much of a good thing?', *Journal of Personality and Social Psychology*, 79 (2000): 995–1006

Manktelow, K., *Reasoning and Thinking* (Hove: Psychology Press, 1999)

—— and Chung, M. C., *Psychology of Reasoning: Theoretical and Historical Perspectives* (Hove: Psychology Press, 2004)

Nickerson, R. S., 'Confirmation bias: a ubiquitous phenomenon in many guises', *Review of General Psychology*, 2 (1998): 175–220

Slovic, P., Finucane, M., Peters, E., and MacGregor, D. G., 'The affect heuristic', in T. Gilovich, D. Griffin and D. Kahneman (eds.), *Heuristics and Biases: The Psychology of Intuitive Judgment* (New York: Cambridge University Press, 2002)

Tversky, A., and Shafir, E., 'The disjunction effect in choice under uncertainty', *Psychological Science*, 3 (1992): 305–9

http://news.nationalgeographic.com/news/2006/10/061012-shark-fin.html

http://www.flmnh. ufl.edu/fish/Sharks

http://www.timesonline.co.uk/tol/news/uk/article2167684.ece

4. MEMORY

Baddeley, A., *Your Memory: A User's Guide* (London: Carlton, 2004)

—— Eysenck, M. W., and Anderson, M. C., *Memory* (Hove: Psychology Press, 2009)

Carey, B., 'H. M., an unforgettable amnesiac, dies at 82', *New York Times*, 4 December 2008

Carnegie, D., *How to Win Friends and Influence People* (London: Vermilion, 1936)

Eysenck, M. W., *Psychology: An International Perspective* (Hove and New York: Psychology Press, 2004)

—— and Keane, M. T., *Cognitive Psychology*, 5th edn (Hove: Psychology Press, 2005)

Freeman, D., and Freeman, J., *Know Your Mind: Everyday Emotional and Psychological Problems and How to Overcome Them* (London: Rodale, 2009)

Miller, G. A., 'The magical number seven, plus or minus two: some limits on our capacity for processing information', *Psychological Review*, 63 (1956): 81–97

Mook. D., *Classic Experiments in Psychology* (Westport, Conn., and London: Greenwood Press, 2004)

Neisser, U., and Harsch, N., 'Phantom flashbulbs: false recollections of hearing the news about *Challenger*', in E. Winograd and U. Neisser (eds.), *Affect and Accuracy in Recall: Studies of 'Flashbulb' Memories* (New York: Cambridge University Press, 1992)

Nunn, K., Hanstock, T., and Lask, B., *Who's Who of the Brain* (London and Philadelphia: Jessica Kingsley, 2008)

Proust, M., *The Way by Swann's* (1913), tr. L. Davis (London: Penguin, 2002)

Sacks, O., *The Man Who Mistook His Wife for a Hat* (London: Picador, 1985)

Sheehy, N., *Fifty Key Thinkers in Psychology* (London and New York: Routledge, 2004)

Tulving, E., and Craik, F. I. M. (eds.), *The Oxford Handbook of Memory* (New York: Oxford University Press, 2000)

http://www.science.ca/scientists/scientistprofile.php?pID=20

5. SEEING AND HEARING

Gregory, R. L., *Eye and Brain: The Psychology of Seeing*, 5th edn (Oxford: Oxford University Press, 1998)

Grimby, A., 'Bereavement among elderly people: grief reactions, post-bereavement hallucinations and quality of life', *Acta Psychiatrica Scandinavica*, 87 (1993): 72–80

Gross, R., *Psychology: The Science of Mind and Behaviour*, 5th edn (London: Hodder Education, 2005)

Hewstone, M., Fincham, F. D., and Foster, J. (eds.), *Psychology* (Oxford: BPS Blackwell, 2005)

Mather, G., *Foundations of Sensation and Perception*, 2nd edn (Hove: Psychology Press, 2009)

Nunn, K., Hanstock, T., and Lask, B., *Who's Who of the Brain* (London and Philadelphia: Jessica Kingsley, 2008)

Wong, P. C. M., Warrier, C. M., et al., 'Volume of left Heschl's gyrus and linguistic pitch learning', *Cerebral Cortex*, 18 (2008): 828–36

http://www.nytimes.com/2008/12/23/health/23blin.html?_r=1

http://www.psychologie.tu-dresden.de/i1/kaw/diverses%20Material/

www.illusionworks.com/html/motion_aftereffect.html

6. MOTIVATION

Buss, D. M., 'Human mating strategies', *Samfundsøkonomen*, 4 (2002): 47–58

—— 'Sexual strategies: a journey into controversy', *Psychological Inquiry*, 14 (2003): 219–26

Elding, D. J., Tobias, A. M., and Walker, D. S., 'Towards a unified model of employee motivation', *Strategic Change*, 15 (2006): 295–304

Eysenck, M. W., *Psychology: An International Perspective* (Hove and New York: Psychology Press, 2004)

Ferguson, E. D., *Motivation: A Biosocial and Cognitive Integration of Motivation and Emotion* (New York: Oxford University Press, 2000)

Greiling, H., and Buss, D. M., 'Women's sexual strategies: the hidden dimension of extra-pair mating', *Personality and Individual Differences*, 28 (1999): 929–63

Gross, R., *Psychology: The Science of Mind and Behaviour*, 5th edn (London: Hodder Education, 2005)

Hewstone, M., Fincham, F. D., and Foster, J. (eds.), *Psychology* (Oxford: BPS Blackwell, 2005)

Heyman, G. D., 'Talking about success: implications for achievement motivation', *Journal of Applied Developmental Psychology*, 29 (2008): 361–70

Latham, G. P., and Ernst, C. T., 'Keys to motivating tomorrow's workforce', *Human Resource Management Review*, 16 (2006): 181–98

Mook, D., *Classic Experiments in Psychology* (Westport, Conn., and London: Greenwood Press, 2004)

Nunn, K., Hanstock, T., and Lask, B., *Who's Who of the Brain* (London and Philadelphia: Jessica Kingsley, 2008)

Reiss, S., 'Multifaceted nature of intrinsic motivation: the theory of 16 basic desires', *Review of General Psychology*, 8 (2004): 179–93

Rynes, S. L., Gerhart, B., and Minette, K. A., 'The importance of pay in employee motivation: discrepancies between what people say and what they do', *Human Resource Management*, 43 (2004): 381–94

Sheehy, N., *Fifty Key Thinkers in Psychology* (London and New York: Routledge, 2004)

7. SLEEP

Blagrove, M., 'Dreaming – motivated or meaningless?', *The Psychologist*, 22 (2009): 680–83

Espie, C. A., *Overcoming Insomnia and Sleep Problems* (London: Robinson, 2006)

Eysenck, M. W., *Psychology: An International Perspective* (Hove and New York: Psychology Press, 2004)

Freeman, D., and Freeman, J., *Know Your Mind: Everyday Emotional and Psychological Problems and How to Overcome Them* (London: Rodale, 2009)

Horne, J., 'Insomnia – Victorian style', *The Psychologist*, 21 (2008): 910–11

—— *Sleepfaring: A Journey Through the Science of Sleep* (Oxford: Oxford University Press, 2006)

—— 'State of the art: sleep', *The Psychologist*, 14 (2001): 302–6

Jacobs, G. D., *Say Good Night to Insomnia* (New York: Owl Books, 1998)

Kryger, M. H., *A Woman's Guide to Sleep Disorders* (New York: McGraw-Hill, 2004)

Stepansky, R., Holzinger, B., Schmeiser-Rieder, A., Saietu, B., Kunze, M., and Zeitlhofer, J., 'Austrian dream behavior: results of a representative population survey', *Dreaming*, 8 (1998): 23–30

http://www.cabinetmagazine.org/issues/30/foer.php

http://www.gelfmagazine.com/archives/sleeping_in.php

8. FEAR AND ANXIETY

American Psychiatric Association, *Diagnostic and Statistical Manual of Mental Disorders, DSM-IV-TR*, 4th edn, text revision (Washington, DC: American Psychiatric Association, 2000)

Barkham, P., 'Grounded', *The Guardian*, 12 February 2008

Barlow, D. H., *Anxiety and Its Disorders: The Nature and Treatment of Anxiety and Panic*, 2nd edn (New York: Guilford, 2002)

—— and Durand, V. M., *Abnormal Psychology: An Integrative Approach* (Belmont, Cal.: Thomson Wadsworth, 2005)

Beck, A. T., and Emery, G., *Anxiety Disorders and Phobias: A Cognitive Perspective* (Cambridge, Mass.: Basic Books, 2005)

Berrios, G., and Porter, R. (eds.), *A History of Clinical Psychiatry* (London: Athlone, 1995)

Clark, D. M., 'Anxiety disorders: why they persist and how to treat them', *Behaviour Research and Therapy*, 37 (1999): S5–27

Davey, G. C. L., and Wells, A. (eds.), *Worry and its Psychological Disorders* (Chichester: Wiley, 2006)

Edelmann, R. J., *Anxiety* (Chichester: Wiley, 1992)

Freud, S., 'Anxiety and instinctual life', in *New Introductory Lectures on Psychoanalysis,* vol. 2 (1933) (London: Penguin, 1991)

——— 'On the grounds for detaching a particular syndrome from neurasthenia under the description "anxiety neurosis"' (1895), in *On Psychopathology* (London: Penguin, 1979)

Gerull, F. C., and Rapee, R. M., 'Mother knows best: effects of maternal modelling on the acquisition of fear and avoidance behaviour in toddlers', *Behaviour Research and Therapy*, 40 (2002): 279–87

LeDoux, J., *The Emotional Brain* (London: Phoenix, 1998)

Lewis, A., 'The ambiguous word "anxiety"', *International Journal of Psychiatry*, 9 (1970): 62–79

McVeigh, Karen, 'Calypso band thrown off aircraft win damages', *The Guardian*, 6 February 2008

Mathews, A., Richards, A., and Eysenck, M., 'Interpretation of homophones related to threat in anxiety states', *Journal of Abnormal Psychology*, 98 (1989): 31–4

Mental Health Foundation, *In the Face of Fear: How Fear and Anxiety Affect our Health and Society, and What We Can Do about It* (London: Mental Health Foundation, 2009)

Nunn, K., Hanstock, T., and Lask, B., *Who's Who of the Brain* (London and Philadelphia: Jessica Kingsley, 2008)

Oatley, K., Keltner, D., and Jenkins, J. M., *Understanding Emotions*, 2nd edn (Oxford: Blackwell, 2006)

Rachman, S., *Anxiety*, 2nd edn (Hove: Psychology Press, 2004)

'Ryanair pays damages to "terrorist" calypso band thrown off plane at gunpoint', *Daily Mail*, 6 February 2008

Smoller, J. W., Gardner-Schuster, E., and Misiaszek, M., 'Genetics of anxiety', *Depression and Anxiety*, 25 (2008): 368–77

Vasey, M., and Borkovec, T. D., 'A catastrophising assessment of worrisome thoughts', *Cognitive Therapy and Research*, 16 (1992), 505–20

Watson, J., and Raynor, R., 'Conditioned emotional reactions', *Journal of Genetic Psychology*, 37 (1920): 394–419

Wegner, D. M., *White Bears and Other Unwanted Thoughts* (New York: Viking, 1989)

http://www.phobialist.com

9. HAPPINESS AND SADNESS

Bebbington, P. E., 'Sex and depression', *Psychological Medicine*, 28 (1998): 1–8

—— Dunn, G., Jenkins, R., Lewis, G., Brugha, T., Farrell, M., and Meltzer, H., 'The influence of age and sex on the prevalence of depressive conditions: report from the National Survey of Psychiatric Morbidity', *Psychological Medicine*, 28 (1998): 9–19

Beck, J. S., *Cognitive Therapy: Basics and Beyond* (New York: Guilford, 1995)

Bifulco, A., Brown, G. W., Moran, P., Ball, C., and Campbell, C., 'Predicting depression in women: the role of past and present vulnerability', *Psychological Medicine*, 28 (1998): 39–50

Biswas-Diener, R., and Diener, E., 'Making the best of a bad situation: satisfaction in the slums of Calcutta', *Social Indicators Research*, 55 (2001): 329–52

Blank, L., Grimsley, M., Goyder, E., Ellis, E., and Peters, J., 'Community-based lifestyle interventions: changing behaviour and improving health', *Journal of Public Health*, 29 (2007): 236–45

Christensen, K., Herskind, A. M., Vaupel, J. W., 'Why Danes are smug: comparative study of life satisfaction in the European Union', *British Medical Journal*, 333 (2006): 1289–91

Davies, J., Sandström, S., Shorrocks, A., Wolff, E., *The World Distribution of Household Wealth* (Helsinki: World Institute for Development Economics Research, 2006)

Diener, E., Horwitz, J., and Emmons, R. A., 'Happiness of the very wealthy', *Social Indicators Research*, 16 (1985): 263–74

Harker, L., and Keltner, D., 'Expressions of positive emotion in women's college yearbook pictures and their relationship to personality and life outcomes across adulthood', *Journal of Personality and Social Psychology*, 80 (2001): 112–24

Harris, T., 'Recent developments in understanding the psychosocial aspects of depression', *British Medical Bulletin*, 57 (2001): 17–32

Layard, R., *Happiness: Lessons from a New Science* (London: Penguin, 2005)

Linley, P. A., and Joseph, S., 'Trauma and personal growth', *The Psychologist*, 16 (2003): 135

Maruta, T., Colligan, R., Malinchoc, M., and Offord, K.P., 'Optimists vs pessimists: survival rate among medical patients over a 30-year period', *Mayo Clinic Proceedings*, 75 (2000): 140–43

Nolen-Hoeksema, S., 'The role of rumination in depressive disorders and mixed anxiety/depressive symptoms', *Journal of Abnormal Psychology*, 106 (2000): 504–11

Oatley, K., Keltner, D., and Jenkins, J. M., *Understanding Emotions*, 2nd edn (Oxford: Blackwell, 2006)

Peterson, C., and Park, N., 'Increasing happiness in lasting ways', *The Psychologist,* 22 (2009): 304–7

—— —— and Seligman, M. E. P., 'Orientations to happiness and life satisfaction: the full life versus the empty life', *Journal of Happiness Studies*, 6 (2005): 25–41

Peterson, C., Seligman, M. E., and Vaillant, G. E., 'Pessimistic explanatory style is a risk factor for physical illness: a thirty-five-year longitudinal study', *Journal of Personality and Social Psychology*, 55 (1988): 23–7

Power, M., and Dalgleish, T., *Cognition and Emotion: From Order to Disorder*, 2nd edn (Hove: Psychology Press, 2008)

Seligman, M. E. P., *Authentic Happiness* (London: Nicholas Brealey, 2002)

—— Steen, T. A., Park, N., and Peterson, C., 'Positive psychology progress', *American Psychologist*, 60 (2005): 410–21

Smith, D. B., 'The doctor is IN', *The American Scholar*, autumn 2009

Styron, W., *Darkness Visible: A Memoir of Madness* (London: Vintage, 1990)

Veenhoven, R., *World Database of Happiness, Distributional Findings in Nations* (Rotterdam: Erasmus University, 2009)

Watkins, E., 'Adaptive and maladaptive ruminative self-focus during emotional processing', *Behaviour Research and Therapy*, 42 (2004): 1037–52

Williams, J. M. G., 'Capture and rumination, functional avoidance, and executive control (CaRFAX): three processes that underlie overgeneral memory', *Cognition and Emotion*, 20 (2006): 548–68

—— *The Psychological Treatment of Depression: A Guide to the Theory and Practice of Cognitive Behaviour Therapy*, 2nd edn (London: Routledge, 1992)

—— Barnhofer, T., Crane, C., Hermans, D., Raes, F., Watkins, E., and Dalgleish, T., 'Autobiographical memory specificity and emotional disorder', *Psychological Bulletin*, 133 (2007): 122–48

Wolpert, L., *Malignant Sadness: The Anatomy of Depression* (London: Faber and Faber, 1999)

http://abcnews.go.com/2020/story?id=4086092&page=1

http://news.bbc. co.uk/1/hi/5224306. stm

http://www.foresight.gov.uk

10. MEN, WOMEN AND COMMUNICATION

Baron-Cohen, S., *The Essential Difference* (London: Penguin, 2003)

Carrère, S., and Gottman, J. M., 'Predicting divorce among newlyweds from the first three minutes of a marital conflict discussion', *Family Process*, 38 (1999): 293–301

Freeman, D., and Freeman, J., *Know Your Mind: Everyday Emotional and Psychological Problems and How to Overcome Them* (London: Rodale, 2009)

Golombok, S., and Hines, M., 'Sex differences in social behaviour', in P. K. Smith and C. H. Hart (eds.), *Blackwell Handbook of Childhood Social Development* (Oxford and Malden, Mass.: Blackwell, 2002)

Gross, R., *Psychology: The Science of Mind and Behaviour*, 5th edn (London: Hodder Education, 2005)

Hines, M., *Brain Gender* (New York: Oxford University Press, 2004)

Hyde, J. S., 'The gender similarities hypothesis', *American Psychologist*, 60 (2005): 581–92

—— 'New directions in the study of gender similarities and differences', *Current Directions in Psychological Science*, 16 (2007): 259–63

Miller, R., Perlman, D., and Brehm, S., *Intimate Relationships*, 4th edn (New York: McGraw-Hill, 2006)

Peplau, L. A., 'Human sexuality: how do men and women differ?', *Current Directions in Psychological Science*, 12 (2003): 37–40

Spelke, E. S., 'Sex differences in intrinsic aptitude for mathematics and science? A critical review', *American Psychologist*, 60 (2005): 950–58

11. FRIENDSHIP, ATTRACTION AND LOVE

Buss, D. M., 'Human mating strategies', *Samfundsøkonomen*, 4 (2002): 47–58

—— 'Sexual strategies: a journey into controversy', *Psychological Inquiry*, 14 (2003): 219–26

Crisp, R. J., and Turner, R. N., *Essential Social Psychology* (London: Sage, 2007)

Dutton, D. G., and Aron, A. P., 'Some evidence for heightened sexual attraction under conditions of high anxiety', *Journal of Personality and Social Psychology*, 30 (1974): 510–17

Dwyer, D., *Interpersonal Relationships* (Hove and New York: Routledge, 2000)

Freeman, D., and Freeman, J., *Know Your Mind: Everyday Emotional and Psychological Problems and How to Overcome Them* (London: Rodale, 2009)

Langlois, J. H., Kalakanis, L., Rubenstein, A. J., et al., 'Maxims or myths of beauty? A meta-analytic and theoretical review', *Psychological Bulletin*, 126 (2000): 390–414

Miller, R., Perlman, D., and Brehm, S., *Intimate Relationships*, 4th edn (New York: McGraw-Hill, 2006)

Sunnafrank, M., and Ramirez, A., Jr., 'At first sight: persistent relational effects of get-acquainted conversations', *Journal of Social and Personal Relationships*, 21 (2004): 361–79

12. BABIES, CHILDREN AND PARENTING

Bunting, M., 'Baby, this just isn't working for me', *The Guardian*, 1 March 2007

Department for Environment, Food and Rural Affairs, 'The structure of the United Kingdom poultry industry' (2006), available at http://www.defra.gov.uk/foodfarm/farmanimal/diseases/vetsurveillance/documents/non-commercial-poultry-sector.pdf

Eysenck, M. W., *Psychology: An International Perspective* (Hove and New York: Psychology Press, 2004)

Freeman, D., and Freeman, J., *Know Your Mind: Everyday Emotional and Psychological Problems and How to Overcome Them* (London: Rodale, 2009)

Gleitman, H., Reisberg, D., and Gross, J., *Psychology*, 7th edn (New York and London: W. W. Norton, 2007)

Gross, R., *Psychology: The Science of Mind and Behaviour*, 5th edn (London: Hodder Education, 2005)

Huston, A. C., and Aronson, S. R., 'Mothers' time with infant and time in employment as predictors of mother–child relationships and children's early development', *Child Development*, 76 (2005): 467–82

Premack, D. G., and Woodruff, G., 'Does the chimpanzee have a theory of mind?', *Behavioral and Brain Sciences*, 1 (1978): 515–26

Rutter, M., 'Out of a barren cradle', *Times Higher Education Supplement*, 24 April 1998

—— Kreppner, J. A., and O'Connor, T. G., 'Specificity and heterogeneity in children's responses to profound institutional privation', *British Journal of Psychiatry*, 179 (2001): 97–103

Scott, J., Dex, S., and Joshi, H. (eds.), *Women and Employment: Changing Lives and New Challenges* (Cheltenham: Edward Elgar Publishing, 2008)

Shaffer, D. R., and Kipp, K., *Developmental Psychology: Childhood and Adolescence*, 7th edn (Belmont, Cal.: Thomson Wadsworth, 2007)

Sheehy, N., *Fifty Key Thinkers in Psychology* (London and New York: Routledge, 2004)

Smith, P. K., Cowie, H., and Blades, M., *Understanding Children's Development*, 4th edn (Oxford and Malden, Mass.: Blackwell, 2003)
http://www.cdc.gov/nchs/fastats/divorce.htm

13. GROUPS

Crisp, R. J., and Turner, R. N., *Essential Social Psychology* (London: Sage, 2007)

Eysenck, M. W., *Psychology: An International Perspective* (Hove and New York: Psychology Press, 2004)

Hewstone, M., Fincham, F. D., and Foster, J. (eds.), *Psychology* (Oxford: BPS Blackwell, 2005)

Jackson, J. M., and Padgett, V. R., 'With a little help from my friends: social loafing and the Lennon–McCartney songs', *Personality and Social Psychology Bulletin*, 8 (1982): 672–7

Latané, B., and Darley, J. M., *The Unresponsive Bystander: Why Doesn't He Help?* (Englewood Cliffs, NJ: Prentice Hall, 1970)

Milgram, S., *Obedience to Authority: An Experimental View* (London: Tavistock, 1974)

Mook, D., *Classic Experiments in Psychology* (Westport, Conn., and London: Greenwood Press, 2004)

Sherif, M., Harvey, O. J., White, B. J., Hood, W. R., and Sherif, C. W., *Intergroup Conflict and Co-operation: The Robber's Cave Experiment* (Norman: University of Oklahoma, 1961)

Stroebe, W., and Diehl, M., 'Why groups are less effective than their members', *European Review of Social Psychology*, 5 (1994): 271–303

Tajfel, H., Billig, M., Bundy, R., and Flament, C., 'Social categorization and inter-group behaviour', *European Journal of Social Psychology*, 1 (1971): 149–78

http://www.prisonexp.org/

14. PSYCHOLOGICAL DISORDERS AND THEIR TREATMENT

American Psychiatric Association, *Diagnostic and Statistical Manual of Mental Disorders, DSM-IV-TR*, 4th edn, text revision (Washington, DC: American Psychiatric Association, 2000)

Barloon, T. J., and Noyes, R., Jr., 'Darwin and panic disorder', *Journal of the American Medical Association*, 277 (1997): 138–41

Barlow, D. H., and Durand, V. M., *Abnormal Psychology: An Integrative Approach* (Belmont, Cal.: Thomson Wadsworth, 2005)

Beck, A. T., *Cognitive Therapy and the Emotional Disorders* (London: Penguin, 1991)

Bentall, R., *Doctoring the Mind: Why Psychiatric Treatments Fail* (London: Allen Lane, 2009)

Butler, G., *Overcoming Social Anxiety and Shyness* (London: Constable & Robinson, 2008)

Davey, G., *Psychopathology: Research, Assessment and Treatment in Clinical Psychology* (Chichester: Wiley–Blackwell, 2008)

Frances, A., First, M. B., and Pincus, H. A., *DSM-IV Guidebook: The Essential Companion to the Diagnostic and Statistical Manual of Mental Disorders*, 4th edn (Washington, DC: American Psychiatric Press, 1995)

Freeman, D., and Freeman, J., *Know Your Mind: Everyday Emotional and Psychological Problems and How to Overcome Them* (London: Rodale, 2009)

—— —— *Paranoia: The Twenty-first Century Fear* (Oxford: Oxford University Press, 2008)

Gelder, M., Harrison, P., and Cowen, P., *Shorter Oxford Textbook of Psychiatry*, 5th edn (Oxford: Oxford University Press, 2006)

Gross, R., *Psychology: The Science of Mind and Behaviour*, 5th edn (London: Hodder Education, 2005)

Healy, D., *Psychiatric Drugs Explained* (Oxford: Churchill Livingstone Elsevier, 2009)

Kirsch, I., *The Emperor's New Drugs* (London: Bodley Head, 2009)

Routh, D. K., 'Hippocrates meets Democritus: a history of psychiatry and clinical psychology', in C. E. Walker (ed.), *Comprehensive Clinical Psychology*, vol. 1 (Oxford: Elsevier, 1998)

Singleton, N., Bumpstead, R., O'Brien, M., Lee, A., and Meltzer, H., *Psychiatric Morbidity among Adults Living in Private Households, 2000* (London: The Stationery Office, 2001)

Smith, D. B., 'The doctor is *IN*', *The American Scholar*, autumn 2009

Stein, D. J., Phillips, K. A., Bolton, D., Fulford, K. W. M., Sadler, J. Z., and Kendler, K. S., 'What is a mental/psychiatric disorder? From DSM-IV to DSM-V', *Psychological Medicine* (2010), doi:10.1017/S0033291709992261

US National Comorbidity Survey Replication, available at http://www.hcp.med.harvard.edu/ncs

World Health Organization, *The ICD-10 Classification of Mental and Behavioural Disorders: Clinical Descriptions and Diagnostic Guidelines* (Geneva: World Health Organization, 1992)

http://www.beckinstitute.org

http://www.iapt.nhs.uk

http://www.psych.org/

15. THE BRAIN

Barlow, D. H., and Durand, V. M., *Abnormal Psychology: An Integrative Approach* (Belmont, Cal.: Thomson Wadsworth, 2005)

Bentall, R., *Doctoring the Mind: Why Psychiatric Treatments Fail* (London: Allen Lane, 2009)

The Britannica Guide to the Brain (London: Robinson, 2008)

al-Chalabi, A., Turner, M. R., and Delamont, S. R., *The Brain* (Oxford: OneWorld, 2006)

Eysenck, M. W., *Psychology: An International Perspective* (Hove and New York: Psychology Press, 2004)

Gibb, B. J., *The Rough Guide to the Brain* (London: Rough Guides, 2007)

Gleitman, H., Reisberg, D., and Gross, J., *Psychology*, 7th edn (New York and London: W. W. Norton, 2007)

Gross, R., *Psychology: The Science of Mind and Behaviour*, 5th edn (London: Hodder Education, 2005)

Hewstone, M., Fincham, F. D., and Foster, J. (eds.), *Psychology* (Oxford: BPS Blackwell, 2005)

NHS Information Centre, 'Prescription cost analysis England 2008'

(2008), available at http://www.ic.nhs.uk/webfiles/publications/PCA%202008/PCA%202008v2.pdf

Nunn, K., Hanstock, T., and Lask, B., *Who's Who of the Brain* (London and Philadelphia: Jessica Kingsley, 2008)

Soon, C. S., Brass, M., Heinze, H.-J., and Haynes, J.-D., 'Unconscious determinants of free decisions in the human brain', *Nature Neuroscience*, 11 (2008): 543–5

http://faculty.washington.edu/chudler/facts.html

16. THEORIES, THEORIES, THEORIES

Barker, M., *Introductory Psychology: History, Themes and Perspectives* (Exeter: Crucial, 2003)

Benjamin, L. T., *A Brief History of Modern Psychology* (Oxford and Malden, Mass.: Blackwell, 2007)

Clark, D. A., Beck, A. T., and Alford, B., *Scientific Foundations of Cognitive Theory and Therapy of Depression* (New York: Wiley, 1999)

Crisp, R. J., and Turner, R. N., *Essential Social Psychology* (London: Sage, 2007)

Eysenck, H. J., 'Learning theory and behaviour therapy', *Journal of Mental Science*, 105 (1959): 61–75

Eysenck, M. W., and Keane, M. T., *Cognitive Psychology: A Student's Handbook*, 5th edn (Hove: Psychology Press, 2005)

Gross, R., *Psychology: The Science of Mind and Behaviour*, 5th edn (London: Hodder Education, 2005)

Hewstone, M., Fincham, F. D., and Foster, J. (eds.), *Psychology* (Oxford: BPS Blackwell, 2005)

Milgram, S., *Obedience to Authority: An Experimental View* (London: Tavistock, 1974)

Mook, D., *Classic Experiments in Psychology* (Westport, Conn., and London: Greenwood Press, 2004)

Neisser, U., *Cognitive Psychology* (Englewood Cliffs, NJ: Prentice Hall, 1967)

Schatzman, M., Obituary: 'Professor Hans Eysenck', *The Independent*, 8 September 1997

Sheehy, N., *Fifty Key Thinkers in Psychology* (London and New York: Routledge, 2004)

Watson, J. B., and Rayner, R., 'Conditioned emotional reactions', *Journal of Experimental Psychology*, 3 (1920): 1–14